W9-BFK-404

JWeintraub

Tenements of Clay

Tenements of Clay

An anthology of medical biographical essays

A fiery soul, which working out its way,
Fretted the pigmy-body to decay:
And o'er-informed the tenement of clay.

Absalom and Achitophel, I, 156
(John Dryden, 1631–1700)

Chosen and edited by

ARNOLD SORSBY

CHARLES SCRIBNER'S SONS · NEW YORK

Copyright © 1974 Arnold Sorsby

Copyright under the Berne Convention

All rights reserved. No part of this book
may be reproduced in any form without the
permission of Charles Scribner's Sons.

1 3 5 7 9 11 13 15 17 19 V/C 20 18 16 14 12 10 8 6 4 2

Printed in the United States of America
Library of Congress Catalog Card Number 74-14010
ISBN 0-684-14035-7

Contents

Illustrations

Preface

Dryden's designation of 'tenement of clay' for the mortal, corruptible human body not only recalls Shakespeare's 'muddy vestment of decay' but like it echoes the much older source which recorded man as 'formed of the dust of the ground' (or 'the slime of the earth' as the Douay version has it). The original Hebrew is still more emphatic—man and earth are linguistically related: *adam* and *adamah* respectively (Genesis ii, 7). Dryden's epithet thus reflected a theological tenet of his age.

To a physician such a denigration is unintelligible, for daily experience shows him man's body as an exquisitely balanced organism. To him decay is but an aspect of a complex series of events that ultimately ebb to extinction and the emphasis on tenements of clay merely stresses the incidental. For these reasons this anthology of medical biographical essays is not a discourse on Man but on the sick bodies of some of those whose works and deeds continue to be of interest to posterity.

Medical biography differs from a personal medical history in that, being retrospective, it is not constrained by the professional secrecy of the consulting room. This however, is of limited value, if only because professional secrecy, where practised, has ensured that no documentary evidence is available and where it has been ignored there is often a plethora of evidence, frequently contradictory. The greatest limitation arises from the fact that technical evidence from the past is not always adequate for a retrospective diagnosis. Medical biography, though a branch of history, is thus beset with difficulties well beyond those that face the general historian, and these are largely responsible for the unequal historical validity of the various essays produced here.

These essays have been culled from the medical literature over the past sixty years and with the exception of a professional historian's comment on one of the essays (that on George III), they have all come from physicians with knowledge of general medicine, otology, ophthalmology, anthropology and other relevant specialities. On the medical aspects these essays may therefore be taken as authoritative, though of course not incontrovertible.

The fifteen essays in this anthology fall readily into three groups: the two opening ones are historical only by courtesy; they deal with mythological figures: Noah and Job. Four essays concern rulers: Henry VIII, George III, Napoleon and Abraham Lincoln. The remaining essays are contributions to the history of civilisation: they deal with Shakespeare, Milton, Swift, Samuel Johnson, Beethoven, Jane Austen and Darwin.

The essays on rulers pose the question whether their illnesses influenced the course of events. It is almost certain that Henry VIII—England's Ivan the Terrible—suffered from syphilis and chronic alcoholism and it is a moot point whether in an age of absolute monarchy, Henry VIII without syphilis and inebriety would have used the axe and block less readily than his father used the sword to establish the Tudors. Whilst the age of George III was itself a great epoch, his rule was a disaster and it is clear that the King's illnesses contributed to the inadequacies of his reign. There is, however, nothing to suggest that Napoleon's fatal illness influenced his career and the course of events; his illness was a postscript to history rather than history in the making. As for Abraham Lincoln, his arachnodactily was clearly incidental, although it has contributed to the legend of the gaunt and rugged Yankee.

Genius has its own laws. Shakespeare remains inscrutable—and not only because the medical biographer is reduced to intelligent guesses when facts are needed. For others it is justifiable to ask whether their disabilities influenced their genius. In Milton a physical handicap inspired both the serenity of submission as in the sonnet on his blindness and the agonising protests of *Paradise Lost* and of *Samson Agonistes*. It is for the critic rather than the ophthalmologist to trace the effect of developing blindness on Milton as a poet, and it may well be asked whether his later writings show that calm of mind and all passion spent that he bestowed on Samson. With Beethoven there was no serenity, possibly because of the slower but relentless unfolding of the trouble, and it is a matter of opinion whether the numbing effect of increasing deafness is reflected in the Symphonies. As for Swift, how much of his misanthropy had its roots in his Ménière's disease? Did this misanthropy increase with increasing disappointments, or with the increasing severity of his dizziness and deafness? A different and rather confusing pattern of physical ailments was present in Samuel Johnson: was their diversity reflected in the diversity of his activities and observations? Jane Austen's Addison's disease probably ran too rapid a course to be apparent in her writings, but this cannot be assumed without further elucidation. Goethe held that talent is born in the stream of life, and genius in quiet solitude; were Darwin's emotional difficulties a shield for his sheltered life? That all these questions arise only illustrates that medical biography is not an end in itself. Apart from their intrinsic human interest, accurate diagnoses raise questions that the medical biographer must pass on to the historian and critic.

There is clearly a difference in the effects of debility on the life of the man of action as contrasted with the man of thought, and this may well be an important issue today. In an age when we have to think in terms of continents and centuries, the responsibilities for far-reaching decisions affecting the whole of our future are steadily becoming more and more concentrated in fewer hands. Is such concentration of power devoid of physical and mental consequences in those burdened with power? In the less strenuous fields of aca-demic life and civil service, age limits prevent the emergence of a gerontocracy and procedures exist for responsibilities to be removed tactfully from those no longer able to shoulder them for physical or mental reasons. In contrast, there are no such safe-guards in the all-important field of political decisions. At Yalta in 1945 three ailing men—two known to suffer from cerebral arteriosclerosis and the third from possibly this and further disorders—shaped the future which has become our bewildering present. It is possible that their disabilities were in part the result of the immense burden they bore and one may well ask whether such responsibilities should be imposed on anyone without in-built safeguards being provided. Medical biography raises with increasing urgency the old and woe-laden question: *quis ipsos custodes custodiet*?

Inevitably, the essays—some more than others—are occasionally rather technical, even when abbreviated and edited. Editorial notes preface some of the essays and technical and medical terminology is explained in the glossary. For fuller references to sources the original essays should be consulted. Editorial notes and some technical passages are indented.

Acknowledgements

I am indebted to the editors of the following journals from which the essays have been taken for permission to reprint, as also to Messrs. Henry Kimpton, the successors of Hirschfield Brothers, the original publishers of Chaplin's study on Napoleon.

Noah—an albino
British Medical Journal, 1958; ii, 1587

Job's illness—pellagra
Archives of Dermatology and Syphilology, 1942; 45, 371

The medical problems of Henry VIII
Centaurus, 1956; 5, 339

Shakespeare's skull and brain
British Medical Journal, 1914; i, 461

The evidence of disease in Shakespeare's handwriting
Proceedings of the Royal Society of Medicine, 1920; 12, Section on the history of medicine, p. 12

Milton's blindness
British Journal of Ophthalmology, 1930; 14, 339

Swift's deafness and his last illness
Journal of Irish Medical Science, 1939; No. 162, p. 241

Samuel Johnson's medical experiences
Annals of Medical History, 1929; New Series 1, 540

The 'insanity' of King George III: a classic case of porphyria
British Medical Journal, 1966; i, 65

Jane Austen's last illness
British Medical Journal, 1964; ii, 182

Beethoven's deafness
Journal of Laryngology and Otology, 1930; 45, 529

The illness and death of Napoleon
Hirschfield Brothers, London, 1913

Darwin's health in relation to his voyage to South America
British Medical Journal, 1965; i, 745

Abraham Lincoln's Marfan syndrome
Journal of the American Medical Association, 1964; 187, 473

CHAPTER 1

Noah—An Albino

Arnold Sorsby

EDITORIAL NOTE:

In albinism there is a pathological absence of pigment in the body. The affection occurs in all races, and the affected individuals are unmistakable to the ordinary observer. (The normal European has a considerable degree of pigmentation in the hair, skin and eyes.) Outstanding among the features of albinism is the lack of pigment in the iris and in the interior of the eye; there is considerable diminution of vision and there is also intolerance to light (photophobia).

Albinism is a hereditary affection, recessive in type. In recessive disorders both parents are clinically normal, but both carry the abnormal gene, and 1 in 4 of offspring receive this gene from both the parents and are affected.

Noah, with his wine, his ark, and the animals that came two by two, is probably the first vividly human figure in the Biblical account of the early days of man. In this he differs from the weak and gullible Adam, the milksop Abel, the stage villain Cain, and Methuselah, whose main distinction was not to have died young. Amongst Noah's shadowy progenitors his father, Lamech, has persisted as little more than a name. The birth of Noah is recorded in Genesis briefly, with an indication that he was called to a high mission[1]: 'And Lamech lived an hundred eighty and two years, and begat a son: And he called his name Noah, saying, This *same* shall comfort us concerning our work and toil of our hands, because of the ground which the Lord hath cursed.' The subsequent account of the Flood and the emergence of Noah as the first boat-builder and sailor in the world's history reveals the nature of the mission to which he was born.

ENOCH'S RECORD OF THE BIRTH OF NOAH

A fuller account of the birth of Noah is contained in the Book of Enoch the Prophet, one of the more significant volumes in the

Noah making a sacrifice. A. Koch (The Mansell Collection).

16

Pseudoepigrapha.[2] It appears to have been written in the second and first centuries B.C., and greatly influenced the writers of the New Testament, in which it is quoted by name in several passages. Possessing at first the weight of a canonical book, it gradually declined in importance and finally fell under a ban of the Church. It does not appear to have received much attention after the ninth century, and came to be regarded as lost till three manuscripts in Ethiopian were brought from Abyssinia by Bruce in 1773. The Book of Enoch, like the rest of the Apocalyptic literature, is heavy with primitive mythological and cosmological traditions. It relates in considerable detail of 'the Watchers of heaven, who have deserted the lofty sky, and their holy everlasting station, who have been polluted with women. . . . And the women conceiving brought forth giants.' The birth of Noah is recorded in similar mystical terms:

> After a time, my son Mathusala took a wife for his son Lamech.
> She became pregnant by him, and brought forth a child, the flesh of which was white as snow, and red as a rose; the hair of whose head was white like wool, and long; and whose eyes were beautiful. When he opened them, he illuminated all the house, like the sun; the whole house abounded with light.
> And when he was taken from the hand of the midwife, opening also his mouth, he spoke to the Lord of righteousness. Then Lamech his father was afraid of him; and flying away came to his own father Mathusala, and said: I have begotten a son, unlike to other children. He is not human; but, resembling the offspring of the angels of heaven, is of a different nature from ours, being altogether unlike to us.
> His eyes are bright as the rays of the sun; his countenance glorious and he looks not as if he belonged to me, but to the angels.
> I am afraid, lest something miraculous should take place on earth in his days.
> And now, my father, let me entreat and request you to go to our progenitor Enoch, and to learn from him the truth; for his residence is with the angels.
> When Mathusala heard the words of his son, he came to me at the extremities of the earth; for he had been informed that I was there: and he cried out.
> I heard his voice, and went to him, saying; Behold I am here, my son; since thou art come to me.
> He answered and said; On account of a great event have I come to thee; and on account of a sight difficult to be comprehended have I approached thee.
> And now, my father, hear me; for to my son Lamech a child has been born, who resembles not him; and whose nature is not

like the nature of man. His colour is whiter than snow: he is redder than the rose; the hair of his head is whiter than white wool; his eyes are like the rays of the sun; and when he opened them he illuminated the whole house.

When also he was taken from the hand of the midwife, he opened his mouth, and blessed the Lord of heaven.

His father Lamech feared, and fled to me, believing not that the child belonged to him, but that he resembled the angels of heaven. And behold I am come to thee, that thou mightest point out to me the truth.

Then I, Enoch, answered and said; The Lord will effect a new thing upon the earth. This have I explained, and seen in a vision. I have shown thee that in the generations of Jared my father, those who were from heaven disregarded the word of the Lord. Behold they committed crimes; laid aside their class, and intermingled with women. With them also they transgressed; married with them, and begot children.

A great destruction therefore shall come upon all the earth; a deluge, a great destruction, shall take place in one year.

This child which is born to you shall survive on the earth, and his three sons shall be saved with him. When all mankind who are on earth shall die, he shall be safe.

And his posterity shall beget on the earth giants, not spiritual, but carnal. Upon the earth shall a great punishment be inflicted, and it shall be washed from all corruption. Now therefore inform thy son Lamech, that he who is born is his child in truth; and he shall call his name Noah, for he shall be to you a survivor. He and his children shall be saved from the corruption which shall take place in the world; from all the sin and from all the iniquity which shall be consummated on earth in his days. Afterwards shall greater impiety take place than that which had been before consummated on the earth; for I am acquainted with holy mysteries, which the Lord himself has discovered and explained to me; and which I have read in the tablets of heaven.

In them I saw it written, that generation after generation shall transgress, until a righteous race shall arise; until transgression and crime perish from off the earth; until all goodness come upon it.

And now, my son, go, tell thy son Lamech.

That the child which is born is his child in truth; and that there is no deception.

When Mathusala heard the word of his father Enoch, who had shewn him every secret thing, he returned with understanding, and called the name of the child Noah; because he was to console the earth on account of all its destruction.

The version in Genesis, and that in the Book of Enoch, are thus supplementary. Both stress that Noah was born to a dedicated life, as is testified by his name, which is derived from the Hebrew verb signifying to comfort. The Book of Enoch, with its emphasis on his unusual appearance at birth, merely builds up a supernatural background to a worldly mission.

A RECONSTRUCTED FRAGMENT

A totally different possibility is suggested by the deciphered fragment of Column II of a particularly badly preserved scroll from the Dead Sea caves (Qumran I), brilliantly identified by Avigad and Yadin as a Genesis Apocryphon, and not the lost Book of Lamech as was first supposed.[3] Their reconstruction of this fragment shows Lamech's pre-occupation with his wife's faithfulness—a reaction noted repeatedly all through the ages in the literature on the birth of abnormal children to normal parents. It is only when Lamech is assured by his wife with considerable verbal emphasis that the unusual child is indeed his that he hastens to his father, Methuselah, and his grandfather, Enoch (who sojourns with the angels), to obtain a more complete explanation of an exceptional event.

1   Then I thought in my heart that the conception had been from the Watchers and the . . . from the holy ones or [?] the fallen angels.
2   And my heart was changed because of this child.
3   Then I, Lamech, was frightened and I came to BT'NWŠ, my wife, and [I said] . . .
4   '[. . . Swear to me] by the Most High, the Lord of greatness, King of all worlds . . . .
5   . . . . . . Sons of Heaven till thou tellest me all in truth if . . . . . .
6   [In truth?] Tell me without lies . . . .
7   By the King of all worlds till though speakest with me in truth and with no lies' . . . . . .
8   Then BT'NWŠ, my wife, spoke to me with vigour and with . . . . . .
9   And she said, 'O my brother and O my Lord, remember my pleasure . . . .
10   . . . . . . the period, and my spirit into the midst of its sheath and I in truth all . . . . . .'
11   . . . . . . And my heart then had changed within me greatly.
12   When BT'NWŠ, my wife, perceived that my countenance had changed . . .
13   Then she suppressed her wrath and spoke to me and said, 'O my Lord and O my [brother] . . . . . .

14   My pleasure, I swear to thee by the great Holy One, the King
of H[eaven?] . . .
15   that thine is this seed and from thee is this conception and
from thee was the fruit formed . . . .
16   And it is no stranger's, nor is it of any of the Watchers or of
the Sons of Heaven . . . [What]
17   has so altered and blemished thy countenance and [why] is
thy spirit so low? . . .
18   In truth I speak with thee'.
19   Then I, Lamech, hastened to Methuselah, my father, and I
[told him] all . . .
20   his father and he would of a surety learn all from him, for he
was the beloved and [. . . with angels]
21   his lot was apportioned and to him they tell all. And when
Methuselah heard . . .
22   . . . . . . to Enoch, his father, to learn all in truth from him.
23   his will. And he went to . . . . . . and found him there . . .
24   And he said to Enoch, his father, 'O my father and O my
Lord, to whom I . . . . . .
25   . . . And I shall tell thee that thou shouldst not be angered
that I have come hither . . . . . .
26   Fear . . . . . .

In the light of this fragment the account of Noah's appearance at
birth, as given in the Book of Enoch, is clearly not that of a miracul-
ous child but of an albino. A body white as snow, hair white as wool,
and eyes that are like the rays of the sun—these are the unequivocal
physical features to be considered once the laudatory commendations
are disregarded.

ORIGIN OF NOAH'S ALBINISM

The fragment also allows some conclusions on the mode of inheritance of Noah's albinism. On the strength of line 9, and their reconstruction of the last word in line 13, Avigad and Yadin hold that
BT'NWŠ, Lamech's wife, was also his sister. If this were so—and
such relationship was not particularly unusual in primitive societies—
Noah becomes the offspring of an extreme type of consanguineous
marriage, and his albinism would illustrate not only the antiquity
of the affection, but also the fact that the first recorded case showed
parental consanguinity. On this reading, Methuselah can now claim
the additional distinction of being the first authenticated carrier of
albinism—unless the distinction belongs to his anonymous wife
(fig. 1). Avigad and Yadin, however, point out that their reading is

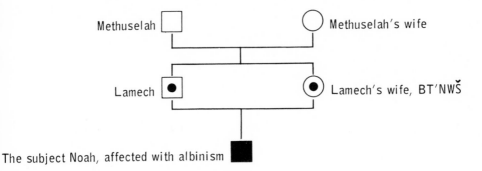

Fig. 1. Lamech and his wife, shown as brother and sister, must have inherited their recessive gene for albinism from either their father, Methuselah, or their mother.

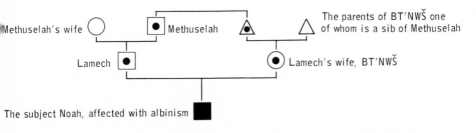

Fig. 2. Lamech and his wife are shown as first cousins. Lamech must have inherited his recessive gene from his father, Methuselah, whilst BT'NWS inherited it from one of her parents, who is recorded as a sib of Methuselah.

contradicted by the one other extant reference to Lamech's wife.[4]
The Book of Jubilees, iv, 28, refers to her as 'Bentenos the daughter
of Baraki'il, the daughter of his [Lamech's] father's brother [or
father's sister].' This would seem to show Lamech and his wife as
first cousins—the common type of consanguinity in albinism—and
would exclude Methuselah's wife as a carrier (fig. 2). On either
reading the consanguineous origin of Noah's albinism is beyond
question. BT'NWŠ and Lamech not only produced Noah but also
made genetic history. They deserve better than the oblivion that
shrouds them.

The possibility that Noah inherited his albinism from a fallen
angel need not be considered seriously. Such a supposition raises
considerable genetic difficulties. One would have to postulate that
BT'NWŠ and the angel were unrelated carriers of the gene at a time
when it could not have been widely scattered, or—alternatively and
even less plausibly—that albinism in angels is dominant and not
recessive as in man. Besides, it is not at all certain that albinism
occurs in angels, other than seraphim. And clearly fallen angels are
no seraphim.

CHAPTER 2

Job's Illness—Pellagra

Charles J. Brim

EDITORIAL NOTE

The succession of disasters—the loss of his family and his wealth and the onset of grievous disease—that Satan, with God's consent, inflicted on Job to test his allegiance is clearly allegorical. But if the prologue in Job is allegorical, bodily ailments in the text are so realistic that the signs and symptoms are recognisable clinically; they appear to have been drawn from life. The background in the prologue is clinical.

> And the Lord said unto Satan . . . my servant Job . . . holdeth fast to his integrity, although thou movedst me against him to destroy him without cause. And Satan answered Yea all that a man hath will he give for his life. But . . . touch his bone and his flesh and he will curse thee to thy face. And the Lord said unto Satan, Behold he is in thine hand, but save his life. (Job, ii, 3–6)

In the Revised version of the Bible Satan is recorded as smiting Job 'with sore boils from the sole of his foot unto his crown'. Much the same appears in the New English Bible: 'running sores from head to foot'. The Douay version is more explicit: 'And Satan . . . struck Job with a very grievous ulcer, from the sole of his foot even unto the top of his head.' These versions all overlook the actual name of the skin trouble given in the original Hebrew: 'He smote Job with sh'chin raa [literally bad skin] from the sole of the foot to the crown of the head.'

As will be seen from his essay, Dr. Brim, working from the Hebrew text regarded *sh'chin raa* not as a descriptive term but as the name of a clinical entity.

Apart from these terminological considerations, the detailed descriptions throughout Job validate Brim's assumption that Job was afflicted with pellegra—a disease of poverty. This much is thus not allegorical, though Job's recovery must be regarded as outside the clinical range, unless one forces the account of Job's latter days to read as implying that the recovery of his health came after he was restored to his wealth and had received 'a piece of money and an ear-ring of gold' from each of his brothers and sisters. This would have provided for ample nutrients and vitamins

23

to resolve the pellagra—all the more so if the alternative reading of a sheep for a piece of money suggested by the New English Bible is accepted.

A puzzling aspect is Job's soliloquy on the possibility that his affliction resulted from sexual misdemeanours in his youth. His protestations of innocence carry conviction, but they cannot be taken as evidence that venereal diseases—and only syphilis is relevant in this context—were known in antiquity, for it was not until the sixteenth century when syphilis and its far-reaching effect was first recognised. Job's disclaimer merely reflects an ancient belief that disease is a punishment from God. The prologue replaces that belief by the more subtle concept of disease as a consequence of celestial politics.

The Bible speaks of 'the botch of Egypt, whereof thou canst not be healed'[1] and the incurable skin disease, '*sh'chin raa*, that covers the knees and ankles, and involves the entire body from the soles of the feet to the crown of the head.'[2] Such a disease attacked the patriarch-philosopher Job after he had lost his fortune and had become a pauper. 'And Job was striken with a terrible skin disease, *sh'chin raa*, that involved his entire body from the soles of his feet to the crown of his head.'[3]

Job appears to have had pellagra. That the affliction results from nutritional deficiency has been recognized only in the relatively recent past. Casal in 1735, recorded his observations on 'a malignant and most peculiar sort of leprosy' which was common among Asturian peasants whose chief source of food was maize, and Frapolli in 1771 recognised pellagra as a disease entity.

It is now known that it was not maize that caused the disease, but that maize in itself does not furnish sufficient amounts of certain essential nutritional elements. When Goldberger in 1914 opened the way for the eventual conquest of this dread disease, twenty-five centuries had witnessed a chaos and confusion during which suffering pellagrins were shunned as unclean and locked up as lepers.

Pellagra is a disease due to more than one deficiency factor and is characterised by a train of symptoms localised on the skin of the body with a general involvement of the various systems and organs. The first clear manifestation of the disease is the pellagral erythema. This is followed by desiccation and exfoliation of the epidermis, which becomes rough and dry, and occasionally crusts form, beneath which there is suppuration. With these cutaneous manifestations there are digestive disturbances. In the more severe and chronic forms there are pronounced nervous symptoms such as headache, spasms, backache, paralysis and mental disturbance, for instance, melancholia or suicidal mania. Finally, there may be severe emaciation and symmetrical gangrene.

THE CASE HISTORY

Job, in his misery and without relief of his symptoms, cried out: 'O that my words were now written! O that they were inscribed in a book; that they were graven with an iron pen and lead in the rock forever!'[4] He appealed to scholars to study his physical plight and to find a remedy. He had been a happy man, a man of wealth, with a healthy family about him, more sons than daughters (sons being more esteemed than daughters), large numbers of cattle and work animals, rich pastures and a beautiful home of his own. By a cruel blow of fate, misfortune suddenly came to him. One stroke followed another; his houses were destroyed; he lost his possessions, and, as a result, his health suffered. He was stricken with a serious illness, gradual in its development, breaking out first in one part and then in another; by degrees the entire body came involved. He shunned his friends, his sole refuge being in the village dunghill or refuse heap, the only resting place of outcasts who, stricken with some loathsome disease, were excluded from the dwelling places of man.

Job was suffering from an acute, overwhelming disease that began with a severe inflammation of the skin, extending over his entire body 'from the soles of his feet to the crown of his head'. A generalised itch accompanied this condition. 'He took him a fragment of a clay vessel to scratch himself with, and he applied mud to the involved areas', which cooled the severe burning and itching caused by the dermatitis.

It is possible that he appreciated the value of the application of mud. He covered his entire body with a thick layer of mud, which made him feel as if he 'really wore nothing but earth'. The skin was soon filled with sores which crusted and formed the breeding places of maggots; these sores broke down and discharged profusely. His face became so swollen and disfigured that his friends could not recognise him. In the midst of his sufferings he appealed to the Lord: 'Thy hands have fashioned and created me, yet Thou permit me to be covered with the processes of decomposition that will ultimately destroy me.' He described the appearance of his skin as

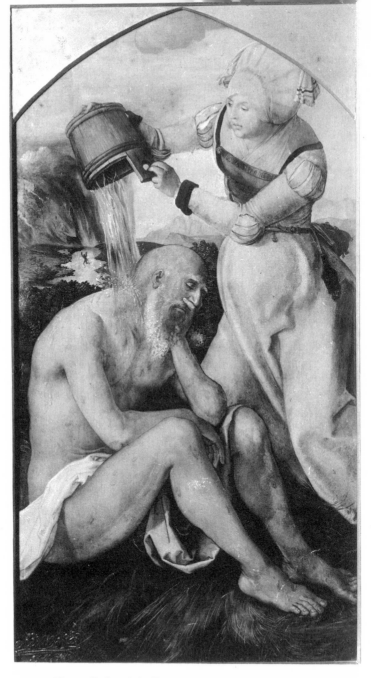

The suffering Job. Durer (The Mansell Collection).

'a moth-eaten garment that covers a worm-eaten and decomposing body'.

The pain that accompanied these lesions was so intense and so agonising that his wife, who could not bear the poor man's suffering, prayed that her husband 'be spared such agony by instantaneous death'. The pains were so severe that at times he could scarcely catch his breath. Luckily the pains were paroxysmal, with periods of slight relief.

He could not sleep through the night. He was exhausted from the tossings to and fro even until the dawn; 'before the day is done it is night again—the light is too close to the darkness.' He became prostrated from the lack of sufficient sleep. The little that he did get was troubled by dreadful dreams and the most terrifying visions, so that his soul chose strangulation or any other form of death rather than continue residing in the skeleton to which he had been reduced.

His skin began to wrinkle, and soon the emaciation was pronounced; his bones stuck to his skin. The gums were the only parts of his body that escaped emaciation. 'My garment [skin], is changed: it bindeth me about as the collar of my shirt.'[5] His body wasted and his weakness caused him to become languid and slow of movement. His abdomen sank in as a result of the wasting of the abdominal fat, so that intestinal peristalsis became visible: 'my intestines boil and cannot remain silent.' There was severe backache: 'archers shot their darts at me which split my kidneys'. His temperature was high: 'my bones are charred from the fever'. The pigmentation of his skin was explained by Job in these words: 'I have become bronzed; my skin is black upon me, not from the sun, but from the internal heat that consumes me.' His sight began to fail and his eyes lost their lustre: 'the shadow of death hovers about my eyelids.' Then followed fainting spells and attacks of palpitation.

The possibility of a venereal origin troubled him, and he chided himself for some imaginary transgression of his youth. 'Thou hast made me inherit the sins of my youth,' he cried out to God. He was led to this belief by the fact that during his illness he had become impotent: 'my desire for my wife is alienated from me.' Had he not 'made a covenant with my eyes not to even think of a maid? My heart was never enticed by a woman; upon no man's doorstep did I ever lurk; if such ever were the case then let strange men do the same to my wife.'[6] No, he never did commit such a sin, for it was carnal and lewd. He compared the consequences of illicit sexual congress with his own sick state: 'For such a sin the punishment is a loathsome and suffering sickness; adultery is a crime which is like a fire, spreading and consuming until the criminal is destroyed, and all his possessions are gone.'

The story ends with Job's cure. All his brothers and sisters and all his old friends came to celebrate his recovery and to feast with him at his home. They brought many gifts. Job regained his reproductive powers and begat seven sons and three daughters—the most beautiful in all the land. He lived to 140 years.

CHAPTER 3

The Medical Problems of Henry VIII

Ove Brinch

INTRODUCTORY

When Henry Tudor won the battle of Bosworth in 1485, he put an end to the wars which had troubled England for more than one hundred and fifty years. A few months later he married Elizabeth of York, in this way uniting the rival dynasties of Lancaster and York. According to canon law they were too closely related to marry, but the Pope granted a dispensation a few days after the wedding had taken place. With the birth of two sons to the royal couple, the danger of the revival of the War of the Roses soon vanished, and England relaxed into a deeply needed state of internal peace.

The first of the Tudor kings was shrewd and calculating. He was able to rule as an absolute monarch, since Parliament had not yet grown so powerful and so opposed to absolutism as under the future Stuart dynasty. Fines, taxes, and 'voluntary gifts' made the frugal and avaricious king enormously rich.

His eldest son, the 15-year-old Arthur, married the Spanish Princess Catharine of Aragon in 1501. She was rather untalented and no great beauty, but the young lady had a strong will and a violent temperament combined with proud self-esteem and stubbornness. It is doubtful whether the marriage was ever consummated; Arthur was a weakly boy who died a few months after the wedding. The 15-year-old widow remained in England, and Henry VII, who was a widower now, wanted to marry her, but he soon gave up this plan; it was extremely improbable that the Pope would make an exception from canon law in order to allow a man to marry his own daughter-in-law. A marriage between the younger son Henry and Catharine would not meet with the same difficulties. Canon law forbade a man to marry his sister-in-law, but in such cases the Pope was always willing to grant a dispensation, even if the marriage had

29

been consummated. Pope Julius II was asked for a dispensation, which he granted without delay, and Henry was betrothed to Catharine.

The widowhood of Catharine had been a sad one. Henry VII granted her only small sums of money, and she had to live alone and almost in poverty. In April of 1507, however, a questionable relationship developed with a Spanish confessor, a merry young dissolute Franciscan monk named Diego Fernandez. He had a bad reputation and was a lusty and domineering man of low moral standards. Catharine was much fascinated by him, and he was always with her and exercised great power over her. The Spanish ambassador, in great consternation, reported this to the King in Madrid, but he dared not write how far Catharine's intimacy with Diego had gone; he left it to the King to interrogate the messenger who brought the letter. The relationship was called intimate and extremely scandalous, but Catharine obstinately refused to give Diego up, and he remained in her household for several years until he was convicted of fornication and consequently had to resign from his office.

BIOGRAPHICAL

Henry VII died in April 1509, and Henry VIII mounted the throne of England. A few months later he married 23-year-old Catharine of Aragon. Henry was now 18 years old and a head taller than any of his people, well developed, sound and strong, vigorous and athletic, with reddish brown hair and regular features. He was well educated and could speak English, French and Latin and some Italian. He was very musical and played the lute, organ, and harpsicord, as well as being a skilled composer; some of his psalm melodies are still used in England. He was well read and a lover of the fine arts; he exchanged letters with Erasmus of Rotterdam, who was one of his sincere admirers, and being a pious Catholic he attended mass twice a day and three times on feast days. He was keen on all sports, a clever horseman and a fine wrestler, and he often won the prize at the tilts and jousts held at court. He had a winning and friendly nature; he loved beauty and splendour; he was the richest prince of all Christendom, and all people loved 'bluff King Hal'. Everything seemed to promise that England would have a splendid future under his rule.

MARRIAGES

Catharine of Aragon; (Elizabeth Blount); and Anne Boleyn

During the first years after his coronation, Henry let the statesmen carry the burdens of government and was himself occupied only with festivals and hunting and his own private life. In the beginning the young couple apparently lived a happy married life, but before the first year was over the first shadows appeared. On 31st January 1510, Catharine was delivered of a still-born daughter. As this took place seven and a half months after their wedding, it appears to have been a premature birth. A few months later Henry was carrying on an amorous flirtation with the married sister of the Duke of Buckingham. The latter, stricken with fear, removed the young lady from the court and made her take refuge in a convent, to the great annoyance of Henry. On 1st January 1511, Catharine gave birth to a fully developed boy who was baptised Henry but who died, when only 52 days old, of an unknown disease.

In 1512 Henry took part in the war of the Holy League against France and spent the time from June until October, 1513, in northern France. In September Catharine had another miscarriage. In January 1514, three months after his return from France, Henry contracted a skin disease which seems to have lasted almost two months and which caused the King to become greatly interested in the art of medicine. He experimented eagerly with plaster and liniments, which he tried on his friends and on himself. His prescriptions were said to be 'verrie goode against sores on the legges and the lykes', and it was especially noted that some of them were useful against the 'french disease'. This skin disease resulted in his terrible horror of all other maladies and often made him hurry from one place in England to another in order to avoid the plague.

In August 1514 vague rumours were heard that the king desired a divorce. They may have originated because of the three unsuccessful pregnancies of Catharine and the King's grief over lack of a male heir to his throne, and moreover, from his relations with a young woman, named Elizabeth Blount, which he did not try to conceal and which lasted at least five or six years.

The relationship between Henry and Catharine grew worse when she had another miscarriage in November 1514, and in a letter dated 1515 it is said that 'the King cares for nothing but girls and hunting'. Catharine, however, became pregnant again, and on 11th February

1516, she was delivered of her only viable child, a daughter who was christened Mary and who died at the age of 42 as the ruling queen of England.[1]

In 1519 Elizabeth Blount gave birth to Henry's only extramarital child, a boy who was christened Henry Fitzroy.[2] This made Henry realise that he could beget a boy with a woman other than Catharine, and the latter began to fear the consequences of this fact. In 1521 it is reported for the first time that Henry had malaria, and later on it is occasionally said that he suffered from similar attacks.

The King's lack of a male heir to the crown had profoundly disturbed the English nobility. The Duke of Buckingham, the greatest and richest nobleman of the realm, had uttered imprudent words concerning his own title to the throne if the King should die without leaving a legitimate male heir, and for this Henry immediately had him imprisoned in the Tower and executed for high treason (1521).

About this time Henry became intimate with Mary Boleyn, an young married gentlewoman who had spent some years at the court of France. Rumour had it that he had also had a similar relationship with her mother, which he denied.

All these years Henry's health seems to have been excellent. As mentioned before, he was an enthusiastic and skilled sportsman, and of course it was inevitable that now and then he was exposed to injuries. In 1524 it is reported that a lance was broken against his helmet; this does not seem to have resulted in a serious lesion, since he continued the joust without any interruption.

In the following years Catharine's situation became worse and worse. In November 1518 her pregnancies had ended with a still-birth. The King ceased to cohabit with her in 1524, and his growing coolness towards her made her bitter and reserved. When she ceased menstruating two years later at the age of 42, she felt lonely and deserted. This feeling was intensified when Henry made his son, Henry Fitzroy, Duke of Richmond and Somerset. The first of these titles had once belonged to Henry VII, and the second to the father of Henry VII. Catharine feared that her husband would name his illegitimate son as heir apparent.

In the spring of 1527, Henry wanted to betroth his young daughter Mary to the French Dauphin. The Bishop of Tarbes, who headed the French delegation, expressed his doubt of the validity of Henry's marriage. The point was decisive, for if the marriage was not valid the princess must be illegitimate and therefore unworthy of the Dauphin. No doubt this question had already been discussed by the King and Cardinal Wolsey on previous occasions, but this time Henry took it up very seriously. Undoubtedly he was feeling genuine remorse over his unlawful marriage and considered Catharine's many unsuccessful pregnancies as the punishment of God for his guilt. When Catharine learnt this she was, of course, greatly excited. In June 1527, Henry told her that he felt sure that their marriage was a sacrilege because it was contrary to canon law, and he therefore wanted her to separate herself from him. As Catharine, obstinate and raging, defended herself, Henry became frightened and declared that he did not want to do her any harm, that he only wanted a plain answer to the problem which the Bishop of Tarbes had posed. He did not press the point on this occasion, but a messenger was dispatched to Rome to obtain a divorce from Catharine.

About this time Henry fell in love with Mary Boleyn's sister Anne. Like her sister, Anne Boleyn had spent some years at the French court, and she was now attached to Catharine's household. She had already had some erotic adventures in England, including some with Thomas Wyatt and Henry Percy. She was to marry Percy, but he was ordered to leave the court and renounce Anne, as the King wanted to marry her himself.

In the autumn another messenger was sent to the Pope with a new petition for a divorce from Catharine (1527). In spite of many long negotiations, postponements and counterproposals, Henry never received any answer to his petition. All sorts of arguments were employed; for instance, Henry let the Pope know that he had certain secret motives for divorcing the Queen which could not be confided to a letter, but he hinted that Catharine was 'suffering from certain diseases defying all remedy, for which, as well as other reasons, the King would never again live with her as his wife.'

During this tug-of-war which lasted several years, Anne had been clever enough to refuse Henry her favour, and the more steadfast she was, the more energetic became Henry's efforts. Cardinal Wolsey was strongly opposed to Henry's plans for marrying Anne, because she belonged to an anticlerical party of the court, and consequently he fell into disgrace and was charged with treason. Among other things, he was accused of giving the King syphilis: 'The same Lord Cardinal knowing himself to have the foul and contagious disease of the great pocks, broken out upon him in diverse places of his body, came daily to your grace, rowning in your ear, and blowing upon your most noble grace with his perilous and infective breath, to the marvellous danger of your highness, if God of his infinite goodness had not better provided for your highness.' (1529).

An open conflict with the Pope was approaching, and in 1530 Henry revived an old English law according to which the Pope had no executive power over internal matters in England. Anne was still steadfast, and not until August 1532 did she yield to Henry's love-making; by then she felt sure that in a short time she would become Queen of England. In January 1533 they were secretly married; she had just confided to Henry that she was pregnant. Shortly afterwards Henry ordered Parliament to issue a law which prohibited all appeal to the Pope and declared Henry the supreme head of the Church of England. Archbishop Cranmer, the primate of this Church, declared Henry's marriage with Catharine null and void. Parliament decided also that all incomes of the Church should fall to the King. Finally a law was passed which made the children of Anne Boleyn alone heirs apparent to the throne; Mary Tudor had to be considered illegitimate.

On 7th September 1533, Anne gave birth to a daughter who was christened Elizabeth[3] and who eventually became Queen of England. Her birth was a bitter disappointment to Henry, who had expected a boy—an undisputed male heir. He soon became tired of Anne and amused himself with other women, among others a certain Margaret Shelton. In her dispair, Anne feigned another pregnancy, but she of course soon had to admit that it was a false hope. Henry had once more been kind to her, but now he immediately turned to other women again and began to think of means of getting rid of her.

In the meantime the changes in the Church of England continued. It was still Catholic, but it was now separated from the authority of the Pope. The monasteries were dissolved and the monks were persecuted; many of them were killed and their rich estates were confiscated by the crown. A great number of Englishmen who would not acknowledge Henry as the head of the Church were tortured and executed, among them the old Bishop Fisher and Sir Thomas More.

Anne did in fact become pregnant again, but she soon had a miscarriage. A third pregnancy ended with a premature birth (January 1536), perhaps because of two psychological shocks; twelve days before the miscarriage the King had an accident in a joust when he fell and was unconscious for two hours, and some days later she surprised him in the company of one of her ladies-in-waiting, the young Jane Seymour.

After Anne's miscarriages, her relations with the King grew worse. He said that he had been seduced into marrying her, that their marriage was due to sorcery, and that now God, as a punishment, denied him the long-wanted male heir. Furthermore, he had fallen in love with Jane Seymour and wanted to marry her. For political reasons he was supported by the chancellor, Thomas Cromwell, and in an excited interview he ordered Cromwell to find a solution. The chancellor began to '*conspirer et fantaisier*', and without warning the charges fell upon Anne.

She was accused of having plotted to poison the King. This accusation was not substantiated in the proceedings and was probably pure imagination. She was further charged with adultery with a young musician and four noblemen, one of them her own brother. All the charges were pure nonsense; in one instance she was said to have had a lover one month after the birth of Elizabeth, and another one month after her second miscarriage. The charge against her brother was based upon his having spent some hours alone with her in her room. Henry's marriage with Anne was declared null and void because she had been officially betrothed to Henry Percy before the wedding, a fact which she admitted. Although she denied adultery she and the five accused men were condemned to death and executed in May 1536.

Jane Seymour; Anne of Cleves; Katheryne Howard and Catherine Parr

A few days later Henry married Jane Seymour. It would be interesting to know the feelings of this young woman on the day of her marriage. Henry had grown very fat, and he suffered from an ulcer on one of his legs. This ulcer did not generally annoy him, but it caused him severe pain when, on rare occasions, it closed over; it remained uncured till his death. He was a glutton and a hard drinker, and with the passage of time he had become more and more capricious and unreasonable. In contrast, Jane Seymour was a mild and lovely lady who kindly and affectionately took care of Henry's two young daughters. His affection for her did not go very deep: a week after their wedding he met two beautiful young women and expressed his regrets that he had not met them before he married again.

As now both Mary Tudor and Elizabeth, like Henry Fitzroy, were considered illegitimate, the succession was most uncertain.

The King therefore ordered his parliament to issue a law of succession which totally deprived the people and its representatives of any say in the matter. The law transferred to Henry absolute power to indicate the person who was to inherit 'his imperiall crowne', regardless of sex and descent.

In 1539 Henry proclaimed his 'six bloody articles'. These meant a retreat towards Catholicism, declaring the trans-substantiation of the wine and bread at the communion table; they further re-established private masses and secret confessions and ordered the celibacy of the priests. The violation of these articles was punishable by death.

The first months of Henry's third marriage were full of tension. Henry Fitzroy died at the age of 17 (presumably from lung tuberculosis which seems to have occurred previously in the Tudor family). Henry was therefore immensely satisfied when Jane Seymour became pregnant the following winter. In October 1537 she gave birth to a son who later succeeded Henry to the throne as Edward VI.[4] All England mourned when the queen became ill after the rather fatiguing christening ceremony and died twelve days after her delivery (probably from puerperal fever).

Although Henry abhorred Luther and his doctrines, political conditions dictated a rapprochment with the protestant princes of northern Germany, and accordingly Cromwell proposed marriage with a daughter of one of those princes. He showed Henry the portrait of Anne, daughter of the prince of the little duchy of Cleves, and on this basis the marriage was decided. Henry became desperate when he saw her; the 24-year-old girl was plain and angular; she was pock-marked and had a sallow complexion. Nevertheless, the whole case was so far advanced that Henry could not retire, and the wedding took place in January 1540.

Decidedly this fourth marriage was not happy. Anne roused the greatest disgust in Henry; he declared that she had cohabited with other men before the wedding, and he refused to live with her. A few months later the English bishops declared the marriage to be void on the grounds that she had previously been betrothed to another prince and that this betrothal had not been officially nullified; therefore, according to canon law, Henry's marriage with her had never been valid. It was true that at the wedding Henry had sworn to love her until death separated them, but he now declared that only his tongue had sworn, that his heart had not been in the oath, which consequently was invalid. Whereupon Anne went into retirement, with great relief and an abundant pension.

During the preceding months Henry had fallen in love with one of Anne's ladies-in-waiting, Katharyn Howard, who was a lively, flirtatious and sweet girl of seventeen. They married in August 1540, one month after the divorce from Anne. What this slender young lady saw in Henry it is difficult to understand. He was now 42 years old, fat and overfed, with small wicked eyes in a round face and a festering ulcer on his leg, whimsical, domineering, egotistical and irascible. More than ever he persecuted everybody who did not comply with his 'six bloody articles' or who would not swear to his supremacy over the Church of England. The people groaned under the heavy taxes; the full treasury of his father had long been empty, and his court and wars required enormous sums of money.

The religious persecutions knew no bounds. Protestants, catholics, and anabaptists were burned at the stake side by side, while noblemen and commoners alike were executed by the hundreds if they refused to recognise Henry as head of the Church. In May 1541 a riot broke out in Yorkshire; before Henry left London with his army he summarily ordered all prisoners in the Tower to be executed. There were three at the time, and they had all been imprisoned because they denied his Church supremacy: the old countess of Salisbury, who was the last of the Plantagenet dynasty and mother of the pretender of the York dynasty, de la Pole, and also Lord Leonard Gray and Lord Dacre. For the sake of appearances a charge of murder was invented against Lord Dacre, and all three were executed without trial.

For political and religious reasons the King's counsellors were opposed to Katharyn Howard and wanted to get rid of her. In November 1541 they told Henry that they had discovered she had been living with other men before she married him, a fact which she had not told him. In the proceedings against her it was disclosed that she had also met her cousin, Mr. Culpepper, in private after the wedding. While the proceedings were in progress, Henry had periods of quiet and restraint alternating with violent fits of rage during which he called for a sword that he might put Katharyn to death himself. She and all persons implicated with her were executed in February 1542.

Henry was soon looking for another wife. In January 1543 Lord Latimer died and left Catherine Parr a widow (she was now a widow for the second time, so nobody could reasonably expect her to be a virgin). She was 30 years of age, beautiful, gentle and mild, and possessed of much human understanding; her moral standards were pure and unsullied. Soon after Lord Latimer's death Henry resolved to marry her, and their wedding took place privately six months later.

THE LAST FOUR YEARS

Henry was now shapelessly obese: 'the King was so fat that such a man has never been seen, three of the biggest men that could be found could get inside his doublet.' He was still more capricious, preposterous and testy than ever, and the ulcer on his leg remained unchanged. His religious persecutions had killed his popularity long before, and although he had acquired enormous riches by confiscating the monastic estates he was always in need of money.

In her married life with Henry, Catherine Parr displayed all her understanding of the human mind. She was kind to his three children, who in turn also loved her. In her letters to Henry and in her conversations with him she flattered the vainglorious man, and she always spoke well of him when talking with others. She herself was modest and kind, tractable and tactful.

In spite of his bad health, Henry was at this time waging war with France and Scotland. This war was a rather strange enterprise. According to plan, Henry was first to help the Emperor in France, and then, when Francis I had been defeated, the Emperor was supposed to support Henry in his efforts to force the Scottish lords to accept the marriage of the infant Mary Stuart with Prince Edward of Wales. It is strange that Henry could not foresee what would happen. When the Emperor had obtained what he wanted in France with Henry's support, he made a separate peace with Francis I and left Henry alone. For this reason Henry was forced to abandon the war with Scotland.

Although the relationship between Henry and Catherine was excellent, rumours in the spring of 1546 told of another impending royal divorce. At court and among the King's advisers there were two parties. One tended towards protestantism and included the Queen and the Archbishop, and the other, led by Stephen Gardiner, the Lord Chancellor, inclined towards catholicism. The near death of the King was expected, and both parties tried to obtain ascendancy before he died. The physical weakness of the King was characterised by his extreme obesity, the ulcer on his leg, and certain recurrent attacks which cannot be exactly described. In the intervals between these attacks he could be reasonable and clear-headed, but at other times he had violent paroxysms of rage, apparently over trifles. Finally he could walk only with such difficulty that he had to be transported in a sedan chair or in a 'device' which is supposed to have been worked with block and tackle.

Henry loved discussions, especially of religious problems, and once the catholic party, represented by Gardiner, made use of this to attack the Queen. On a certain occasion Gardiner led Catherine into a discussion of protestantism. For once her carefulness and tact failed her when she spoke in favour of the protestant doctrine, and when she had gone Henry got one of his paroxysms. On the spot Gardiner put down an indictment against her with orders to arrest her and carry her to Tower, and, foaming with rage, Henry signed the document. When Catherine was told she was deeply distressed; she collapsed in tears and nearly gave up all hope. The following day Henry heard of her despair; overnight he himself had completely forgotten the incident, and with great difficulty he went to her room, consoled her with kind words and soothed her before he returned to his bed.

A little later Catherine went to his room, accompanied by a lady-in-waiting. He received her kindly and as usual began to discuss religious questions with her. But by now Catherine was wise enough not to enter into a discussion, and declared that women did not understand such intricate problems which it required a man's sagacity to solve, and that now as always she was convinced that the King, being the wisest of all men, was completely right in his opinion. But the King declared that she was as learned as any doctor and was well able to instruct him as she had done before. Catherine answered that when she on previous occasions had mentioned religious questions it had only been meant as a pastime for him and for the purpose of being instructed by his learned words—for which the King praised her and told her of his joy in their good friendship.

Later on, as they were sitting in the garden and talking merrily with each other, the chancellor arrived with the guard to arrest Catherine. When it dawned upon the King what he had come for, he abused Gardiner with terrible invectives and ordered the perturbed chancellor to be off with his soldiers. He suddenly remembered signing the order for the Queen's arrest, which he had completely forgotten, and this gave him another violent fit of rage. Later in September Henry had another 'attack'. Although he was in bed for a long time, and everybody thought that he would die, he recovered, as he had after the previous attacks.

However, at the end of December, Henry had yet another 'attack' and it was evident that he was approaching death. His forgetfulness increased, as was demonstrated by his written orders to respect the French fortifications of Boulogne which were issued simultaneously with his oral orders to demolish them. He dictated his last will, the contents of which were the result of wise forethought: successors to the throne were to be Edward and his children, then Mary Tudor and her children, and finally Elizabeth and her children. He declared himself a good catholic and ordered requiem masses to be held in case there should be a purgatory. The regency which was to rule during the minority of Edward was to include men of both the protestant and the catholic court parties.

In spite of his weakness he intervened with great energy when the Earl of Surrey and his father Norfolk conspired against the succession. Surrey had planned to arrest the Prince of Wales after Henry's death and mount the throne of England himself. Henry immediately ordered him to be imprisoned in the Tower, where he pleaded guilty. According to the King's sentence of death he was beheaded on Tower Hill (19th January 1547). Norfolk, too, admitted his guilt but asked for grace. Henry was now so weak that he could not comprehend anything. The chancellor maintained that Henry had ordered Norfolk to be executed on 28th January, and in the name of the King he signed the death sentence.

Until the middle of January, Henry had been carried to the council chamber where he received foreign ambassadors, and periodically he seems to have been quite sensible. But the last eight days of his life he spent in bed, unable to move his legs or to carry a glass of wine to his lips. In the afternoon of 27th January 1547, he became unconscious, and in the evening he died. The constable of the Tower refused to carry out the death sentence of Norfolk, which was not signed by the King himself. Thus the death of the King saved Norfolk's life.

DIAGNOSTIC

We have listed, in so far as it was possible, all of Henry VIII's physical and mental symptoms of disease and deviations from the normal.[5] An attempt will now be made to summarise and examine these symptoms in order to procure a clear picture of his diseases and mental peculiarities.

PREVIOUS STUDIES

A number of different theories of the diseases of Henry and of his family have been set forth. In 1888 the obstetrician Currie was the first to suggest that Henry suffered from syphilis and that this was why Catharine of Aragon had her miscarriages and still-births. This was written at a time when it was still maintained that a sound woman could bear syphilitic children, and Currie did not think that Catharine herself had had syphilis.

In the 1920's the gynaecologist MacLaurin, apparently without knowing Currie's article, was of the opinion that Henry had had syphilis. He founded this theory on Catharine's miscarriages and still-births, the bad health of most of Henry's children, the ulcer on his leg, his 'terrible mental, moral and physical degeneration' during the last seventeen years of his life, and his comparatively early death in stupor.

The English psychologist Flügel in 1920 published a psycho-analysis of Henry VIII. He states that Henry was influenced by an Oedipus complex and refers to the many instances where he was surrounded by incest (canonically). He states the opinion that the King was partly attracted, partly repelled by incest, and that although he demanded chastity and fidelity in his wives, he was, nevertheless, stimulated by the idea of their relations with other men. This article was written in the infancy of psychoanalysis, and Flügel's theories cannot be maintained in the light of modern critical opinion.

The surgeon Kemble, writing in 1931, is of the opinion that Henry had syphilis, but offers no scientific documentation. According to Kemble, Henry's ulcer had started with a gummatous osteitis with perforation to the marrow cavity, and eventually resulted in a common osteomyelitis by secondary infection with pyogenic cocci.

In 1932 the historian Chamberlin wrote a book in which he carefully noted from contemporary letters and documents everything that, according to his conception, could be considered as indicating ailments and recoveries in Henry and his queens. These statements he submitted to four physicians, a surgeon, a gynaecologist and two obstetricians. They all emphasised the fact that there was nothing to indicate syphilis in the medical history of the royal family.

Appleby, in an article dated 1934, assumes, without offering any proof, that Henry was a syphilitic.

In 1947 Ellery proposed the theory that Catharine's unsuccessful pregnancies were due to her being a rhesus-negative woman. This theory cannot be accepted because if it were true, she must have started with a natural birth or two, and continued thereafter with still-births.

MacNalty in 1952 wrote a book on Henry's diseases and was of the opinion that a number of brain concussions, acquired in jousts, were the cause of his eventual mental changes. According to MacNalty, Henry was not a syphilitic.

In the same year, the bacteriologist Shrewsbury published an article to defend Henry against the charge of 'voluntarily acquiring and knowingly transmitting a dangerous disease (syphilis) that has the most serious implications' to Catharine. The intention of Shrewsbury's article is to prove that Henry was not a syphilitic; in this he certainly has not succeded.

It must be expressly stated that no specialist in internal diseases, venerology, neurology or psychiatry, has ever pronounced a written opinion of the diseases of Henry VIII, and no iconography and no study of his holograph letters has ever been attempted.

THE PRESENT STUDY

The possibility of syphilis

As to the important point of syphilis, the first question to examine must be the possibility of his contracting this disease. From the historical biographies we learn that he was of a rather moderately sexed nature, and that he only had extramarital cohabitations with three women (Elizabeth Blount, Margaret Shelton, and Mary Boleyn), and that he did not cohabit with Anne of Cleves and Catherine Parr. This surprising estimate of Henry's sexual life is based upon the fact that there is no contemporary account of his relations with other women. The contemporary accounts that do exist are principally the reports of foreign ambassadors to their respective masters (contemporary Englishmen would not venture to write letters on such subjects), and historians without doubt will feel obliged to relate only facts that can be verified. In that case they will easily run the risk of drawing wrong conclusions.

Of course the ambassadors were only interested in Henry's extra-marital relations, if there was a chance that they might result in political complications. It was not worth mentioning in their reports when the King had transient relations with casual women. Henry VIII matured early and was a strong, athletic youth with a great appetite for the pleasures of life, and it is extremely improbable that he had his first sexual experience at the age of 18 when he married Catharine, who was 5 years his senior. In any case, any indignation about the idea of Henry's possible relations with other women before and after his first marriage is irrelevant.

Just when he was sexually mature the syphilitic infection was ravaging all Europe, and the danger of infection was extremely great, especially in casual relations. Moreover, the primitive hygiene of those days offered copious chances of infection by common use of goblets, etc. (syphilis insons). Consequently, the young prince was very much exposed to syphilitic infection. It is true that no contemporary account has mentioned any early syphilitic infection or any anti-syphilitic treatment, but it must be taken into consideration that a primary syphilitic ulcer in the mouth may have been mistaken for a common angina or a labial herpes. Such mistakes would have been especially possible in cases of syphilis insons; but there are other possibilities of a syphilitic infection.

Henry married Catharine of Aragon in 1509. Two years before she had had a relationship mentioned above, which was called intimate and extremely scandalous, with the immoral and domineering Diego Fernandez. One must consider the possibility that he had given her syphilis by sexual intercourse or syphilis insons. The latter mode of infection was hardly known at that time; knowledge of the ways of infection was rather limited, which appears from the charge against Wolsey as late as 1529 of having tried to infect the King with syphilis by means of 'rowning' in his ear.

Fever and skin trouble

In the summer of 1513 Henry was making war against Francis I in France. He returned to England in October, and in January 1514 he contracted a skin disease; he was then twenty-three years old. According to one account the King had a fever, and it was feared that it would develop into 'such pustules which are called variolae'.

Another account tells that 'the King of England has had a fever; the doctors were afraid of his life, but it ended in small-pox.' The Venetian ambassador, however, wrote to the Doge that Henry had measles. Presumably these reports originated directly from court. Nothing is known of the treatment of this disease, which lasted a month or two. In 1529 the new Venetian ambassador, Falieri, in a written report to the Doge gave a thorough description of Henry's external appearance, his education and abilities, etc. Falieri emphasises Henry's face and features, which he describes as being very handsome and beautiful, 'like an angel's'. He does not mention the face being pock-marked, and no other description of Henry gives any hint of pock-marks.

We may conclude that in January and February of 1514 the King suffered from a disease which involved a skin eruption, the nature of which was not evident to the physicians. It could hardly have been variolae, for an attack of small-pox lasting for two months, would certainly have left well-known marks which are not mentioned later. It might, however, have been a syphilitic skin eruption; that it was not acknowledged as great pocks might be explained by the probable fact that doctors, only twenty years after the beginning of the great epidemic, could hardly have been familiar with the various skin eruptions which follow in the wake of that disease. The knowledge of differential diagnosis of skin diseases was very limited; there was no differentiation, for instance, between measles and scarlatina, and it seems probable that doctors did not differentiate sharply between varicellae and variolae.

Leg Ulcer

In March 1537 Lord Montague was put on trial and said: '. . . I dreamed that the King was dead, but one day he will die suddenly; his leg will kill him, and then we will have jolly stirring.' This seems to be the first time that Henry's leg ulcer is mentioned. Montague's expression 'his leg will kill him' tends to show that the fact was well known, since it is not described further. The ulcer must have existed for a certain length of time, perhaps several months. Furthermore, Montague must have considered it a severe disease, since he thought that Henry might die from it.

Only a little is known of this ailment. Contemporary accounts call it an ulcer, a sinus and a fistula, but nothing is said of the localization on the leg. It remained unhealed until his death, but it is repeatedly mentioned that on several occasions when the fistula was closed, Henry suffered severe pain until the ulcer opened again.

Shrewsbury maintains that the ulcer was due to uric arthritis of the knee joint. This diagnosis is based on the fact that Henry VII suffered from 'gout', and on the gluttony and drinking habits of Henry VIII. The foundation for this diagnosis is rather slim and must be compared with the statement of the Spanish ambassador Chapuis: 'Henry's malady was only by chance and has no certain return like the gout, the proper season of which is the autumn.' It seems that the 'gout' of the days of Henry VIII cannot be identical with the same ailment of modern terminology. The supposition of Shrewsbury that the fistula might originate from a staphylococcal infection, which he thinks was a widespread disease of those days, must be considered pure conjecture.

The ulcer may well have started as a syphilitic gumma which, as Kemble thinks, had penetrated to the marrow cavity and caused a secondary streptococcal osteomyelitis with permanent secretion, giving the patient violent pains when the fistula was closed for one reason or another. In 1538 it is reported that the King 'has had stopped one of the fistulas on the leg, and for ten or twelve days the humours which had no outlet were like to have stiffled him, so that he was sometime without speaking, black in the face and in great danger, but now the King is so well again as nobody had dared to hope.' This seems to indicate that a therapeutic attempt to close the fistula had been successful and caused a retention of the 'humours' in the marrow cavity until the outlet had been re-established. The ulcer cannot be supposed to originate from varicose veins, because the healing of a varicose ulcer is not painful, but rather quite the contrary.

Difficulty in walking

It is reported that in 1546 Henry was not able to walk any more, but had to be transported in a 'device' which is supposed to have been a sort of elevator with block and tackle; it may have perhaps been only the sedan chair, which is mentioned in the inventory of the castle. Both interpretations may be right: he may have been carried from one room to another and hoisted or lowered from one storey to another. At that time he was enormously fat, but apparently his walking difficulties were due to the weakness of his legs. In this connection one must of course think of tabes dorsalis, and further-

Fig. 1. Painting of Henry VIII by Holbein, 1536. Reproduced from Ganz: *The Paintings of Holbein the Younger,* London, 1950.

more of the paintings which represent the King standing with straddled legs. He may have chosen this position because it gives good support to ataxic legs, but it might just as well be what etholog-ists call an 'imposing attitude.'

Evidence from portraits: development of a nose deformity

When contemplating this question, it is of interest to compare various contemporary pictures of Henry VIII. Holbein has painted several portraits of the King which are of some significance in this connection. The first is from 1536 and shows the King in three-quarters view with the right side of the face turned towards the observer (fig. 1); it is remarkable that the nose of this portrait is quite normal. All later portraits are facing to the front; most of them are supposed to be contemporary replicas of an original which no longer exists. On one of these copies (1537) which belongs to the collection of Windsor Castle (fig. 2) a deformity of the nose is distinctly noticeable as a slight circumscript swelling about the form and size of an almond, reaching from the lower part of the nasal bone to the wing of the nose. In 1540 Holbein made a chalk sketch of Henry's face (fig. 3), and in the place of the swelling a corres-ponding circumscript depression of about the same size is distinctly visible on the sketch. On a portrait of Henry in the National Gallery in Rome, which Holbein is supposed to have painted in 1539–40, neither a swelling nor a depression is seen on the nose.

But in 1544 Cornelys Matsys made an etching of Henry which deviates greatly from all other portraits. In this etching he is depicted with an oblique glance in the small, screwed-up wicked eyes and cruel lines around the mouth. The extremely repulsive face is flat and fat, and on the right side of the nose the depression is shown (fig. 4). It is the size of a nut. Size and localisation are unchanged but there is now in addition a marked deviation of the nasal septum which is specially remarkable between the nostrils.

In the personal psalm book of Henry an artist has painted or drawn a miniature of him in his last year. He looks now very much aged, weak and furrowed, and his hair and beard are white. It seems that his right eyelid hangs lower than normally, while the left eye appears more open than is natural (fig. 5). It must, however, be remembered that the original is a miniature and one must not attach too great importance to details of small single strokes of the artist's brush or pencil.

Fig. 2. Replica of a painting of Henry VIII, 1537. (The Collection of Windsor Castle). Reproduced from Ganz: *The Paintings of Holbein the Younger*, London, 1950.

The deformity of the nose is of great importance. It cannot be ascribed to a traumatic lesion, in the first place because this generally deforms the nasal bone, which is not altered in Henry's case; secondly because a post-traumatic swelling will soon vanish and the result of the lesion will then remain stationary. A deformity that begins with a swelling and ends with a depression can, practically speaking, only be caused by an inflammatory subcutaneous process and a consequent cicatricial shrinkage of the soft tissues. Such a process is characteristic of a syphilitic gumma. It must presumably have begun some time before 1537, when it was depicted for the first time; it may even have started in the last months of 1536. In that case it would have appeared simultaneously with Henry's leg ulcer, and this fact strongly supports the supposition that the ulcer was of syphilitic gummatous origin. Some contemporary reports suggest that Henry had ulcers on both legs; if these reports are reliable this would give a still stronger support to the diagnosis of multiple gummata.

The absence of the deformity of the nose on the Rome portrait, on the wedding portrait from 1539–40, and on the well-known painting of the barber-surgeons' guild (1542–43) is easily explained. Presumably Henry ordered the artist to leave the deformity out; on the portraits which would remind coming generations of 'the King's Majesty' he wished to appear as favourably as possible. In order to increase the majestic effect, his clothes have been given quite un-naturally broad shoulders, and his hands and feet and the straggling legs have assumed a carriage which is highly imposing. This carriage corresponds to what ethologists call imposing attitude in animals, and therefore the straddling legs do not necessarily indicate ataxy.

Generally speaking the observer gets the impression that the paintings of Henry VIII tend to beautify and idealise the King, while drawings and etchings seem to be more realistic than the painted portraits. Presumably Henry never saw the etching by Cornelys Matsys; if he had, he certainly would have had the plate destroyed. As to the miniature portrait two things should be remembered: it is a three-quarters view, but it is the left side of the face which is turned towards the observer; Henry has taken care not to show the ugly side of his nose. And moreover the miniature was painted in his personal psalm book where it would be concealed from other people.

Fig. 3. A chalk sketch of Henry VIII by Holbein, 1540. (Munich Collection).
Reproduced from Shrewsbury: *Henry VIII. A Medical Study.* Journal of the
History of Medicine, Vol. VII, number 2, 1952.

Evidence from holograph letters: inebriety

Nothing is known of Henry's walk, nor of his voice, speech, sight or hearing. In the biography by Pollard (1902) two holograph letters are reproduced in facsimile, one from 1518 and the other from 1527 (figs. 6 and 7). The present writer has had two additional holograph letters photographed, the originals of which are preserved in the Cotton Library of the British Museum; one dates from 1539, the other from 1544 (figs. 8 and 9).

On comparing these four letters it is seen that No. 1 and No. 4 are easily legible and the contents easily understood in spite of an almost complete absence of punctuation; the sentences are sensibly constructed and tolerably clearly formed. No. 2 and No. 3 are quite different; their handwriting is crabbed and the words are repeatedly struck out and corrected. No. 2 is a love letter to Anne Boleyn, written in French and with an almost incomprehensible sentence construction. Only by means of suitable punctuation and much imagination can one discover that the letter contains a reproach to Anne Boleyn because she would not become his mistress, and an entreaty for an answer as soon as possible. No. 3 is a very learned theological interpretation of a sentence of S. Chrysostomus which Henry considers in favour of the timeliness of the special sort of confession which he had ordered. This letter, like No. 2 has a number of corrections but no punctuation at all, and the sentences are formed so obscurely that their intent is almost incomprehensible. If an observer had only this letter (from 1539) he would rightly conclude that the writer must have suffered from a disease of the central nervous system (in this case the so-called third stage of syphilis). However, on comparing this letter with No. 2 (from 1527), one must admit that the one is just as disorderly and incoherent as the other. Considering that letter No. 4 from 1544 is just as clear and easily understood as No. 1 from 1518, it cannot be assumed that the writer of these four letters suffered from a syphilitic cerebral disease. The shortcomings of the second and third letters must be due to other reasons, and it is an all but obvious assumption that the writer was under the influence of alcohol when he wrote these two letters; Henry habitually consumed great quantities of wine, beer and gin.

Progressive deterioration in character and mentality

In studying the mental state of Henry VIII one is confronted by great

Fig. 4. Henry VIII, 1544. An etching by Cornelys Matsys. Reproduced from Chamberlin: *The Private Character of Henry VIII*, London, 1932.

difficulties. Only one fact is commonly agreed upon: in about his 40th year an alteration in his character sets in; this does not begin suddenly but leads eventually to progressive deterioration during the last 17 years of his life. However, this alteration of character is differently interpreted by different historians and by the physicians who have studied his case.

As a prince and as a young king, Henry was highly intellectual, talented, cultured and well educated; he was friendly and sociable, beloved and a great favourite with everybody, a Prince Charming and an elegant man of the world. In the course of the last 17 years of his life he changed into an ugly, obese tyrant deprived of all popularity, who recklessly and with horrible cruelty terrorised his people, respecting no one, with the sole purpose of increasing and consolidating his power.

During the first 20 years of his reign Henry was politically shrewd and cunning. In the great political struggle on the Continent he knew how to stake his little English kingdom to the best advantage, thereby being able to change the great political balance of power as he willed by supporting now one group of states, now another. In England itself conditions were quiet, orderly and peaceful. The first sign of anxiety and lack of mental balance occurred in 1521, when Henry had Buckingham executed for aspiring to the throne. Six years later he began to consider a divorce from Catharine because his marriage with her was contrary to canon law. It must be emphasised that he petitioned the Pope for the divorce *before* he fell in love with Anne Boleyn, and consequently his pangs of conscience were probably sincere.

The alteration in his character and mental faculties began at the time when he wanted to marry Anne Boleyn. He then committed one of a number of seemingly irrational actions. In the autumn of 1527, when he was 36 years old, he despatched a messenger to Rome with two petitions. First of all the Pope was asked for a declaration that his predecessor had had no power to exempt from the provisions of canon law the prohibition against marriage between a man and his brother's widow. Secondly, the Pope was asked for an exemption from the same canon law's prohibition against a man's sexual relations with two sisters (Mary and Anne Boleyn). These petitions of course only entangled matters even more; they were too much even for the very amenable Pope, who in addition was not free because of his dependence on the Emperor, who was Catharine's

Fig. 5. Henry VIII. Enlarged reproduction of a miniature in the personal psalm book of the King. Reproduced from Chamberlin: *The Private Character of Henry VIII,* London, 1932.

nephew and who was keeping the Pope imprisoned in Castel San Angelo.

Henry committed his next irrational action in the case against Anne Boleyn (1536). She was accused of adultery, and Henry made the archbishop declare the marriage null and void. Consequently the charge of adultery ought to have been dropped, but nevertheless she was sentenced for this crime (and for having attempted to poison the King, a charge which seems to have been pure nonsense). Henry's intention of declaring the marriage invalid is supposed to have been inspired by his desire to have Elizabeth, like Mary Tudor, considered illegitimate, thereby excluding her from the succession. This explanation, however, cannot be accepted, as no woman up to that time had been crowned as a ruling queen of England.

Henry's action during the trial of Katharyn Howard was equally irrational. Katharyn was accused of having known other men before her marriage with Henry, and the trials made it evident that she had also had secret meetings with Mr. Culpepper after the marriage. This, however, was not included in the charge: presumably Henry did not wish to be declared a cuckold a second time. Consequently the whole charge was based on a foundation so weak that Parliament, in other cases always compliant, hesitated to sentence Katharyn. As a matter of fact, she was charged only with having tainted Henry's Blood-Royal by her premarital relations with other men. As the trial dragged on, Henry constructed an additional charge of treason, and Parliament did not dare to hesitate any longer; no evidence was demanded, and Katharyn was sentenced to death.

Patients suffering from cerebral syphilis are generally very extravagant and absurd in financial matters and in the management of their affairs; they display signs of megalomania and are inclined to forget important actions a short time after they have committed them. Eventually they become slack and apathetic (dementia paralytica). The extravagance of Henry VIII is not easily estimated. It was part of his royal dignity to wear silk and velvet, to adorn himself with gold and precious stones and to scatter about him costly presents of ready money, fine jewellery and rich estates. In his youth he was the richest monarch of all the world, and after the Reformation he confiscated almost 800 monasteries along with their estates and riches. While in this regard his covetousness knew no bounds, he was hardly more extravagant than other kings of his time and for several centuries to come. His extravagance perhaps

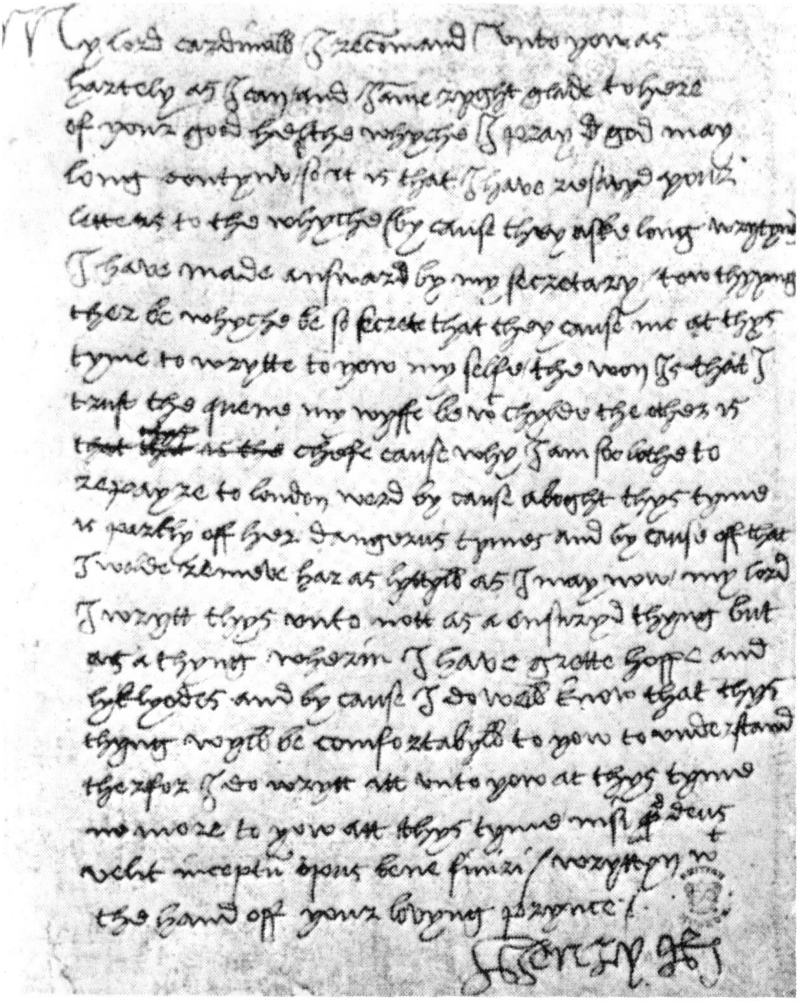

My lord cardinall I recomand unto you as
hartely as I can and I ame ryght glade to here
of your good helthe whyche I pray god may
long contynu. so it is that I have vewyd your
letters to the whyche by cause they aske long wrytyng
I have made answard by my secretary. two thyngs
ther be whyche be so secrete that they cause me at thys
tyme to wrytte to you my selfe the won ys that I
trust the quene my wyffe be with chylde the other ys
~~that that is the~~ chefe cause why I am so lothe to
repayre to london ward by cause abought thys tyme
is partly off her dangerus tymes and by cause off that
I wold remove her as lyttyll as I may now. my lord
I wrytt thys unto you not as a ensuryd thyng but
as a thyng wherin I have grette hoppe and
lyklyodes and by cause I do well know that thys
thyng wyll be comfortabyll to you to understand
therfor I do wrytt it unto you at thys tyme
no more to you at thys tyme nisi quod deus
velit inceptum opus bene finiri. wrytyn wt
the hand off your lovyng prynce
Henry R.

Fig. 6. Holograph letter from Henry VIII to Cardinal Wolsey, 1518. (Letter No. 1). Reproduced from Pollard: *Henry VIII,* Edinburgh, 1902.

was a reaction against his father's well-known economy, and, in any case, cannot be attributed to cerebral syphilis.

The question of his megalomania is equally difficult to answer. Considering such background factors as Henry's age and his power as an absolute King, it must be presumed that his megalomania would assume expressions rather different from those of a common person of today. A megalomaniacal King of the period probably would have believed that he was Emperor, Pope, or God himself. No one else could have been his superior. The words 'empire' and 'imperial' are frequently employed in contemporary documents. Henry's greatest man-o'-war was christened 'Harry Imperial', his throne was called his 'Imperial See', and he speaks of his 'imperial crown'. He wanted to unite Ireland and Scotland with England and to realise his right of inheritance to France, so creating an Empire which might come up to that of Charles V. But this cannot be considered megalomania; it is nothing but a violent craving for power.

Moreover, there is a linguistic explanation of the matter. Contemporary statesmen expressly defined the word 'imperial' as being identical with the modern words 'independent' and 'sovereign.' In Law No. 24 of the Parliament session of 1532, for instance, it is pronounced: 'This realm of England is an Impire . . . gouerned by one supreme head and kynge, hauing the dignitie and royall estate of thimperiall crowne of the same.'

In the conflict with the Pope, however, the case was different. When the Pope would not grant a divorce from Catharine, and since he wanted to marry Anne Boleyn, Henry could see no other way out than to detach England from papal authority. At the same time he made Parliament declare him supreme head of the Church of England with all the power of the Pope and entitled to all the riches and incomes which had previously belonged to the Pope. He boasted that he was King, Emperor and Pope all in one person. A comparison with Luther is natural: Luther detached Northern Germany from the authority of the Pope, but he did not himself aspire to the supremacy of the Protestant Church with the position of a Pope.

Henry, on the other hand, enforced his spiritual supremacy with terrible cruelty. Priests, monks and laymen, protestants, catholics and anabaptists were hanged and burned at the stake by the hundreds, only because they would not recognise him as the head of their Church. In comparison with the atrocities of the Spanish

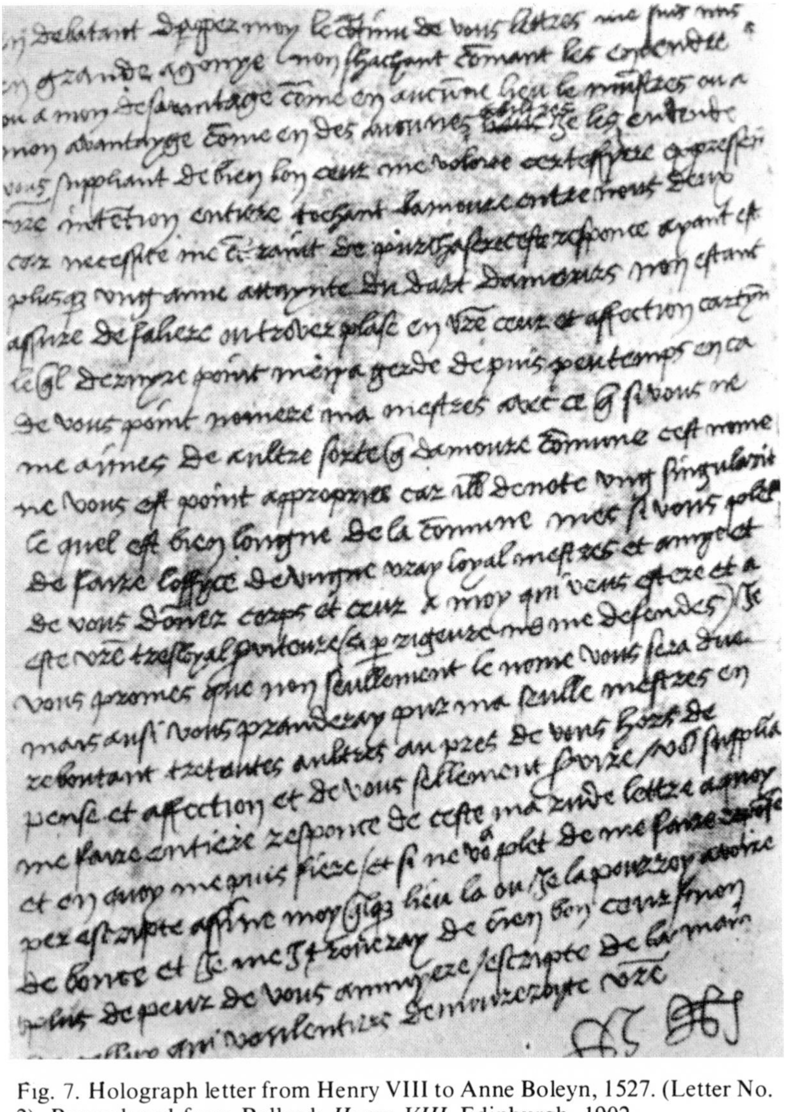

FIG. 7. Holograph letter from Henry VIII to Anne Boleyn, 1527. (Letter No. 2). Reproduced from Pollard: *Henry VIII,* Edinburgh, 1902.

Inquisition and the burning of heretics in France an obvious fundamental difference will appear. Neither in Spain nor in France were the heretics killed by the rulers for their own glorification, but *ad majorem dei gloriam* and because they would not belong to the Catholic Church and recognise the Pope as their spiritual lord. In England Henry VIII ordered people of all confessions to be executed because they would not recognise himself as the head of the Church, as their Pope. Certainly this cannot be considered megalomania. Patients with dementia paralytica fancy that they are something very great, which they are not in reality. But Henry did not fancy that he was Pope; he decreed himself Head of the English Church, decreed himself its Pope, just as he tried to create an empire. In both cases his actions resulted from a violent craving for power.

The question of Henry's relations with the Church leads directly to the question of his relations with God. In certain periods he adhered to catholicism, acknowledging his own self as the Pope of England; at other times he swung towards protestantism. One must not attach too much importance to these shifting beliefs; they were the result of political ambitions as in the case of many other princes. The principal basis of his religion was always catholic, but independent of Rome, a position which was violently maintained in the six bloody articles of 1539 in which he gave sovereign orders as to religious worship.

In December 1545 Henry made his last address to Parliament. This address, which has been called his political testament, is generally dealt with very emotionally by his biographers. This is rather surprising, since the text is a tissue of self-glorification, hypocrisy, unction and boasting. He emphasises his love and goodness to his people and his subjects' confidence in and affection for himself; he reproaches them for their ardent discussion of the question as to which creed or which learning was right. He is moved to tears and weeps openly as he humbles himself before the face of God; he mentions his small and poor faculties, but towards the end of the address he asserts himself when he calls himself 'your supreme head and sovereign Lord'. He reproaches his people with their lack of fraternal love and brotherhood and tells them to love each other and not to quarrel over God and religious problems in ale-houses and taverns. If anybody is of opinion that a priest or a bishop does not preach the right learning he ought not to quarrel over it but to report the case to the king's councillors 'or to us, to whom is com-

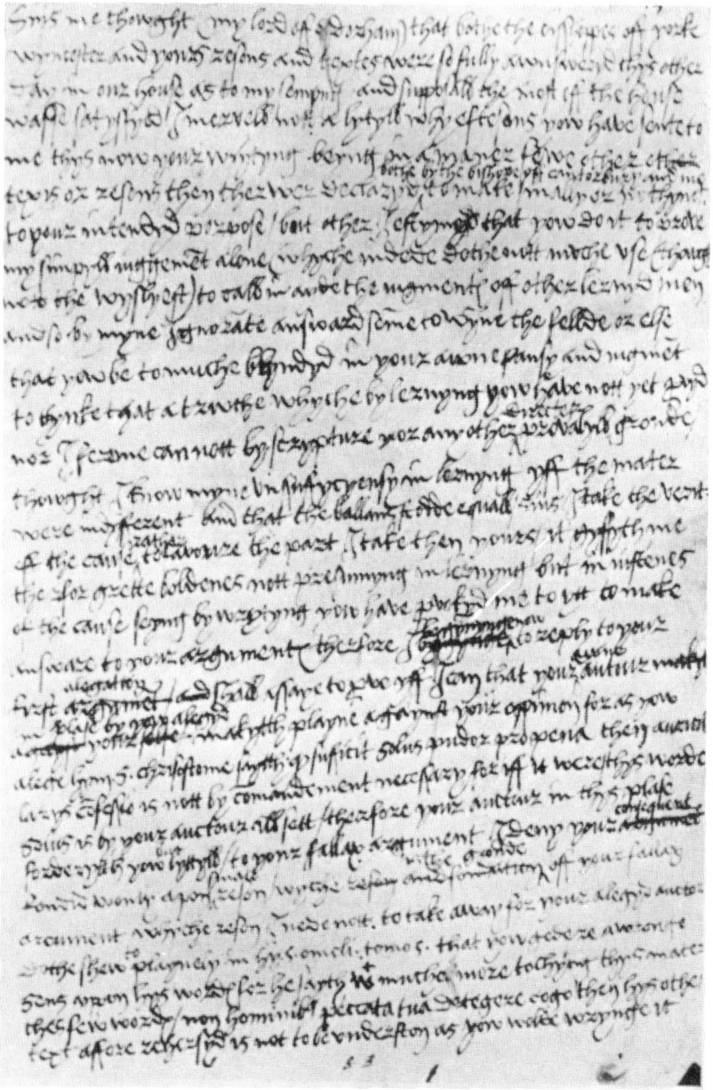

Fig. 8. Holograph letter from Henry VIII to the Bishop of Durham, 1539. (Letter No. 3). Photograph of an original letter preserved in the Cotton Library of the British Museum, London.

mitted by God the high authority to reform such causes and behaviours.' And he ends by repeating his sermon on brotherly love.

This address repels the reader, not only because one can almost smell the gin on his breath, but also, and not least, because of the background of Henry's own egotism and lack of altruism, his brutality and despotism, and his repeated shifts from orthodox catholicism towards his private English catholicism, over the boundaries of protestantism and back again to English catholicism. What Englishman could feel certain which creed he ought to embrace in order to be in harmony with the supreme head of the Church? Without doubt Henry considered himself the specially appointed deputy of God in spiritual and worldly affairs, and Luther may have hit the mark when he said: '*Der Junker Heinz glaubt, er ist Gott und kann alles machen.*'[6] On this point one may perhaps consider his opinions and actions expressive of megalomania.

As mentioned above, patients with cerebral syphilis are inclined to forget important actions a short time after they have committed them. In Henry's case there are certain such episodes, as for example when he in a violent fit of rage, signed an order for the arrest of Catherine Parr on a charge of heresy, and immediately proceeded to forget it until the following day when the chancellor came to arrest her and was turned out in another fit of rage. Another instance of his forgetfulness in his last years is seen in his written orders to tear down the French forts around Boulogne, which were issued simultaneously with his verbal orders to leave them untouched.

An attempt to trace the character of Henry VIII during the last seventeen years of his life demonstrates that he, in the first place, is recklessly egotistical. Every personal consideration is put aside in favour of his selfishness; even his queens and his daughters are not spared. He demands unconditional surrender and obedience from everybody irrespective of rank and station in life. Anyone who will not swear to recognise his spiritual and temporal supremacy, or who otherwise violate his six bloody articles, is subjected to the most terrible torture and executed in the most horrible way in order to satisfy his craving for self-glorification.

It has been said of Henry that he never broke the law. This may be true, but it is explained by the fact that he controlled elections to Parliament and compelled it to issue such laws as he demanded. From 1511 until 1529 no Parliamentary elections took place. Generally Parliamentary sessions lasted only a few weeks. It is true

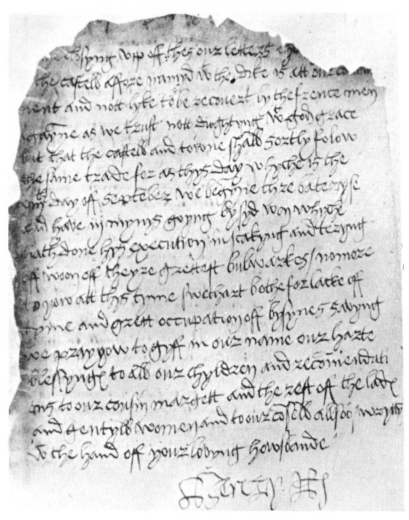

Fig. 9. Holograph letter from Henry VIII to Catherine Parr, 1544. (Letter No. 4). Photograph of an original letter preserved in the Cotton Library of the British Museum, London. The margin of the letter has been damaged by an incendiary.

that the nature and the functions of the Parliament of the XVI century cannot be paralleled to those of our time. But it must be remembered that Parliament never even tried to oppose Henry. When it at rare intervals refused to obey the King's orders, it was always on the matter of the imposition of taxes. In other respects Parliament was very obedient; it did not even scruple to issue penal codes with retroactive effect when Henry ordered it to do so. At last however, even the most obedient Parliament became too troublesome, and in 1539 Henry made it issue a decree which gave his proclamations the validity of law.

Henry, like most other perpetrators of violence, was always a coward. It is true that he was bold enough in tilts and jousts, but in his wars he never personally took part in battle. In addition, he was also a psychical coward. When he wanted to divorce Catharine and on some occasions was met with her stiff resistance, he kept himself in the background and made his statesmen act in his place. Later on, when he wanted to part with his other queens and his statesmen, he always made others act on his behalf in order to avoid personal annoyance.

His egotism was strongly evident in his craving for power and his desire to appear in a favourable light to other people, in his appearance and manners as well as in ethical respects. That is why he ordered Wolsey to invent the crimes with which Anne Boleyn was charged; that is why he did not charge Katharyn Howard with adultery, and that is why he ordered Holbein and other artists to make replicas of an old portrait, which demonstrated' the King's Majesty', at the expense of true likeness.

SUMMARY AND CONCLUSIONS

THE AVAILABLE DATA

(1) At the age of 22 and four years after his marriage with Catharine of Aragon, he had a skin disease which could hardly have been small-pox.

(2) At the age of 33 he had his first attack of malaria.

(3) At the age of 37 he began to suffer from severe headaches which returned at varying intervals throughout his life.

(4) During the last seventeen years of his life he was increasingly obese.

(5) From about his forty-fourth year he suffered from an ulcer on one leg (or on both legs) which was never permanently healed and which was not painful except when the fistula, at varying intervals, was temporarily closed.

(6) At the age of 44 or 45 he acquired a deformity of the right side of the nose, at first consisting of a circumscript swelling, eventually resulting in a corresponding depression, located in the region between the lower end of the nasal bone and the wing of the nose, and causing a deviation of the nasal septum.

(7) The last half or whole year of his life he could not (or could only with great difficulty) walk and had to be transported from one place to another. From 1535 he is depicted with his legs astride.

(8) The last months before his death he had a number of 'attacks' which are not described in detail, and between these he had periodical violent paroxysms of rage.

(9) His character and appearance during the last seventeen years of his life underwent a remarkable alteration, which set in a few years before his leg ulcer is first mentioned and his nose deformity is first observed.

(10) The psychological alteration shows an increasing egotism, self-glorification and absence of inhibition in his personal affairs.

(11) On certain occasions during his last year he totally forgot important dispositions shortly after he had made them.

(12) In 1518 as well as in 1544 he was able to write letters of high quality, sensibly constructed and easily understood. Between these dates his letters could be incoherent, irrational and almost unintelligible.

(13) Finally, the miscarriages and still-births of Catharine of Aragon must be taken into consideration.

INTERPRETATION

All these are indisputable facts. As to their interpretation one must admit that most of them, taken one by one, do not prove a syphilitic infection; his leg ulcer may have been a common osteomyelitis, the skin disease in 1514 may have been a furunculosis; his egotism and craving for power, his recklessness and cruelty, may have been expressive of psychopathy; his difficulty in walking may have been caused by prolonged alcoholism; the straddled legs in the paintings may correspond to the imposing attitude of animals; his supposed ptosis of the eyelid may have been an unintentional stroke of the miniaturist's brush with no foundation in reality; his 'attacks' may have been due to arteriosclerosis of the cerebral arteries; his forget-fulness may have resulted from alcoholic intoxication, and Catharine's unsuccessful pregnancies may have been due to habitual miscarriages.

It should be noted that eleven of these symptoms are only based on second-hand evidence, derived from contemporary reports made by people without medical knowledge and experience. There are two first-hand pieces of evidence which will bear objective examination: the portraits of Henry VIII and his holograph letters. As to the portraits it must be admitted that if the deformity of the nose can be recognised as a gumma, the diagnosis is evident, of course, at once; as a matter of fact, it can hardly be interpreted in any other way; it will furthermore be seen that several other symptoms might without difficulty fit the picture; his leg ulcer (or ulcers), his head-ache, his skin disease, the ptosis of the eyelid, Catharine's mis-carriages and—perhaps—a hint of megalomania.

In the complex of symptoms one has of course no clinical or laboratory examinations to go on. No examination has been made of Henry's skeleton which would confirm or dismiss the diagnosis of syphilis with absolute certainty. In favour of the diagnosis of juvenile syphilis the age must first of all be considered. It was a period in which the new infectious disease was extremely widespread, in which its character as a venereal disease had hardly been generally understood, in which the secondary and tertiary symptoms, especially the skin eruptions and the gumma, had hardly been attributed to syphilis, and in which extragenital primary syphilis had scarcely been recognised. It must furthermore be remembered that although syphilis was from the beginning treated with mercury, this treatment was so ineffective that the infectious skin eruptions might reappear many times. The sources of infection were so numerous that the early developed, virile and vital young man with an abounding appetite for the pleasures of life must have been highly exposed to syphilitic infection.

There is nothing to indicate definitely that Henry had tabes dorsalis or dementia paralytica. (If he had syphilis he may have escaped medullar and cerebral complications, like most other syphilitics). His holograph letters and the absence of any possible apathy and distinct signs of megalomania seem to contradict these diagnoses. Besides, a patient with dementia paralytica could hardly have lived for seventeen years; he would presumably have died from his cerebral disease after a few years.

To an ordinary physician without special psychiatric training the development of the mental peculiarities of Henry VIII seems to follow a certain line. Throughout his youth he was always successful, in his wars as well as in internal English affairs. At that time he was friendly and tractable, beloved by all and a great favourite with everybody. In his middle age, when he met with adversity, his character gradually deteriorated, or perhaps merely revealed its true colours; the unsuccessful pregnancies of Catharine, his consciousness of guilt over the unlawful marriage with his brother's widow, the resistance against his desire for divorce and for the marriage with Anne Boleyn, the successive matrimonial calamities and the resistance of his people against his usurped authority of the supremacy of the Church of England, combined with many other sorrows and troubles that beset him, aggravated the alteration of his character. The egoistic, brutal and reckless features of his character prevailed, and eventually he appears a psychopath of the boasting, swaggering, self-maintaining and self-glorifying type who, with transparent hypocrisy and meanness, calls upon everybody to inform him of other people's supposed heresy with the sole purpose of advancing his personal aims.

The difficulty of estimating the psychological and mental diseases of Henry VIII is due not only to the scantiness of the available evidence, but also to the very different outlook and attitude towards life that prevailed as compared with modern times. At that time the fact that high prelates and noblemen as well as common citizens could be tortured and executed without legal process and without evidence of their crime was accepted by the people with little or no protest. Everybody submitted to the supreme will of the King without attempting to complain so long as taxation was not involved. It is therefore very difficult for modern people to enter into the mentality of the time of Henry VIII and to comprehend the reactions—or absence of reactions—of his contemporaries against the tyranny and the cruelty of the sovereign.

SELECTED REFERENCES

Anonymous: *Some Royal Deathbeds*, Brit. Med. Journ., 1910.
Appelby, L. H.: *The Medical Life of Henry VIII*, Bulletin of the Vancouver Medical Association 1934, X, 87–101.

Currie, A. S.: *Notes on the Obstetric Histories of Catherine of Arragon and Anne Boleyn*, Edinburgh Medical Journal, 1888, I, 34 pp.

Ellery, R. S.: *Must Syphylis still serve?* Medical Journal of Australia, 1947, I, 86 pp.

Flügel, I. C.: *On the Character and Married Life of Henry VIII*, Internat. Journ. of Psychanalysis, 1920, I, 1 p.

Kemble, J.: *Henry VIII, a Psychological Survey and a Surgical Study*, Annals of Med. Hist., New Series 1931, III, 78.

MacLaurin, C.: *The Case of Anne Boleyn* (in: *Post Mortems of Mere Mortals*, New York, 1930), 11–32.

MacLaurin, C.: *The Tragedy of the Tudors* (in: *Post Mortems of Mere Mortals*, New York, 1930), 50–102.

MacNalty, S.: *Henry VIII, a Difficult Patient*, London, 1952.

Shrewsbury, J.: *Henry VIII, A Medical Study*, Journ. of the Hist. of Medicine, 1952, VII, 141–185.

SUMMARY OF DISCUSSION AT THE DANISH MEDICO-HISTORICAL SOCIETY[7]

Chief physician *Paul Reiter*, M.D., specialist in psychiatry:

The numerous pathological manifestations in Henry VIII may in the most natural way be put under the common denominator of syphilis with tertiary manifestations throughout the last seventeen years of his life (the leg ulcer, the nose disease, the ptosis of the eyelid, the straddling legs, his coarse psychological deterioration paroxysms of rage and other 'attacks'), and I believe that he had a tabo-paralysis with protracted or stationary development. Although the classical picture of dementia paralytica includes euphoria and megalomania and a rapid ending, it is well known that it may often develop slowly and intermittently with long stationary intervals. This form of dementia paralytica is especially characterised by the moral coarseness of the patient whose finer mental qualities generally degenerate and deteriorate, and who becomes the victim of the most frantic paroxysms of rage. Originally he must presumably have been a talented psychopath. The diagnosis of Flügel, published in the infancy of psycho-analysis, cannot be maintained, but probably the psychopathy must have constituted a disposition for the syphilitic mental disease. It is not necessary to consider Catharine of Aragon as the source of his infection, as other sources were abundant, and Catharine's 'scandalous relationship' with Diego Fernandez is unproved.

Professor *Ejnar Jarløv*, M.D., specialist in internal diseases: The theory of the remarkable psychical déroute of Henry VIII being due to dementia paralytica seems so obvious that it is only natural that several medical writers have considered it to be a fact, in spite of some English authors' attempts to prove other diagnoses. On account of the very careful study of Dr. Brinch one may appreciate his doubts on this point—a doubt upon which I agree. That the King had syphilis I look upon as a fact according to the evidence available. As to the diagnosis dementia paralytica I have my doubts, because, for instance, of his ability to write sensible letters in his later years after having written unintelligible and incomprehensible letters some years before. I think that his mental condition might well be explained as a dementia alcoholica, especially because the clinical picture of the patient is characterised not so much by dementia as by the alteration of his character, which to a high degree resembles that of a habitual alcoholic, displaying wickedness, accusations against those around him, self-pity, etc. Henry's consumption of alcohol—like that of many of his contemporaries, was very great, and his occasional forgetfulness may very well be explained by intermittent *abusus spirituosorum*. His failing ability to walk may be due to alcoholic neuritis ('pseudo-tabes'), and the 'attacks' may have been alcoholic eclampsia.

Chief physician *C. E. Jensen*, M.D., specialist in venerology: If we presume that Henry VIII suffered from syphilis there are a number of facts in his case history which fit very well into the picture: Catharine's miscarriages; Henry's headache; his skin disease after the return from France in 1513, which may very well have been a secondary syphilitic skin eruption; his straddling legs; and finally, his leg ulcer and the disease of his nose. These latter diseases may very well be considered as multiple simultaneous gummatous processes, of which that of the nose healed with cicatricial shrinking without any ulceration, whereas the leg gumma has ulcerated either because of unsufficient treatment or because of secondary infection with pyogenic cocci. The violent pain when the fistula was closed seems to indicate a secondary osteomyelitis, as the uncomplicated gumma is indolent. To diagnose syphilis with absolute certainty, however, is not possible on this foundation alone, especially because of the insufficient description of the skin disease in 1514; it may have been a furunculosis or an ecthyma. The idea of the leg ulcer and the nose disease being gummata is almost certain, and it must be considered as the most probable solution of the question.

Reply by *Ove Brinch*: From the facts stated by other medical writers, as well as those put forward by myself and the opinion of the specialists expressed in the present discussion, it is possible to make the following diagnoses of the diseases of Henry VIII: 1) malaria, 2) obesity, 3) inebriety, 4) alcoholic polyneuritis, 5) tertiary syphilis (with multiple gummata), 6) secondary osteomyelitis, 7) alcoholic dementia and/or general paralysis of the insane, 8) psychopathy.

Obviously it is impossible to diagnose syphilis with absolute certainty on the symptoms and descriptions available. It would, however, be possible to prove or disprove the correctness of this diagnosis by means of an examination of the skeleton of the King. A scientific study of his bones would reveal the truth without any possible doubt.

CHAPTER 4

Shakespeare's Skull and Brain

An Anthropological Study

Arthur Keith

EDITORIAL NOTE

Shakespeare's head was unremarkable in both the shape of the skull and the size of the brain. The steps by which Sir Arthur Keith established this on scanty data are a good example of the scientific method used with imagination.

In sharp contrast to these rigidly controlled conclusions are his two stark assertions that Shakespeare was a descendant of the Bronze Age invaders of England and that his shorthead (or roundhead in the more commonly used nomenclature) was typical of the stock or race that has produced the world's finest artists. The first of these assertions is doubtful, the second preposterous. Anthropologists no longer attach much importance to the shape of the skull as a racial characteristic and many question the very concept of race. In the endless invasions, conquests and dispersals throughout recorded and in prehistoric times, there were many complex factors other than the shape of the skull.

Mr. M. H. Spielmann has recently been engaged on a systematic examination of the evidence relating to the history of the monument at Stratford-on-Avon, and to the authenticity of the numerous portraits of Shakespeare. His final opinion is that only the monument (fig. A) itself and the Droeshout portrait (fig. B) can be regarded as well authenticated—as having been in existence soon after Shakespeare's death in 1616. As regards the monument, even Mr. Spielmann has reservations; he is of opinion that its sculptor, Gerrard Johnson, 'evolved' the head and neck, and that there is an inconsistency between the proportions of the head and face. In his exciting book entitled *Bacon is Shakespeare*, Sir E. Durning-Lawrence refuses to regard either the monument or the Droeshout portrait as an authentic document. As regards the portrait, he has written:

Fig. A. Shakespeare: Droeshout Portrait.

'It is almost inconceivable that people with eyes to see should have looked at the so-called portrait for 287 years without perceiving that it consists of a ridiculous, putty-faced mask fixed upon a stuffed dummy, clothed in a thick coat.'

The monument, in Sir Edwin's opinion, represents a flat-headed Chinaman, and was made, he believes, more than a century after Shakespeare's death. The doubts cast on the authenticity of the monument, first by Mrs. Stopes, and later by Sir Edwin Durning-Lawrence, have been cleared away by the late Mr. Andrew Lang, and by lectures given at the Royal Institution by Mr. M. H. Spielmann in the same year. Anything we can know concerning the personal appearance, and of the racial character of the greatest Englishman has to be gathered from these two sources: the monument at Stratford-on-Avon, and the Droeshout portrait.

The monument in particular is important for it enables us to measure those characters of the head which are of particular interest to students of the human body.

THE SKULL

THE MONUMENT

If the bust represented on the monument is largely imaginary, then the blunders of the sculptor will become manifest when we apply to it the various criteria which are used when heads and skulls are examined by modern anthropological methods. The remarkable dimensions which the sculptor of the Stratford bust has given to Shakespeare's head become manifest when an exact drawing is made of the crown from above (fig. 1). Within a drawing of the crown I have placed a drawing of a skull of a modern Englishman— poised in the same position and drawn to the same scale as the Shakespearean bust. It is at once seen that there is a double contrast —one of shape and one of size. The skull of the Englishman, slightly under average dimensions, is 188 mm long; when covered with flesh the head would have been 8 mm more—196 mm. Shakespeare's head is 212 mm long; his skull should have measured 204 mm—a long skull—reaching well towards the maximum limit of cranial length. In width, there is a much greater difference; the modern skull is 137 mm wide; in life, the width of the head would have

Fig. B. Shakespeare: Monument at Stratford (The Mansell Collection)

measured 10 mm more—147 mm. The width of Shakespeare's head, as represented in his bust, is 168 mm. His skull should have measured 158 mm—a wide skull—reaching well towards the limits of maximum width. In the modern skull the width represents 73 per cent of the length; in Shakespeare's bust the width represents 77·5 per cent of the length. As tested by measurement the Shakespeare head falls neither into the long-headed group nor into the round or short-headed, but within the intermediate group. Yet, when we come to examine the bust in profile all the features which characterise the short-headed type of men become manifest.

To those who have given no special attention to the form of human heads it may seem that the short-headed and the long-headed are but variants of one type. The difference is much greater than a mere individual variation; it is a radical difference. Robert Burns was a good representative of the long-headed type of man. In fig. 2 the profile of his skull is contrasted with a drawing made from the skull of the short-headed race which reached England for the first time at the close of the Neolithic period— some 2,000 years before the time of Christ. A glance at those two figures reveals an essential difference in conformation—a difference which is chiefly confined to that part of the head which lies behind the ear-holes. In Burns, the long-headed, the occiput forms a backward, projecting eminence; in the short skull the occiput is flattened, as if it had been compressed from behind by the application of a board during infancy. There is another difference between these two types of heads: in the long head the vault is low and flat; in the round head the vault wells upward to a crown, as if the brain, when compressed from behind, had forced up the middle part of the roof of the skull. How it has come about that there is this radical difference between the two prevailing types of human heads in Europe we do not know; there is a secret buried here which has not been discovered as yet. All we are certain of is that the long heads are the offspring of one line of human descent—the round heads, of the type here described, of quite a different line. They must have sprung originally from a common stock.

When we come to study the Shakespeare bust in true profile there can be no doubt as to the type of man it represents; he is depicted for us in the Stratford monument as a representative example of the short-headed type. All but in one respect, the dimensions exceed those of any skull of this type known to me. We have seen that, in length and breadth measurements, Shakespeare's head approaches

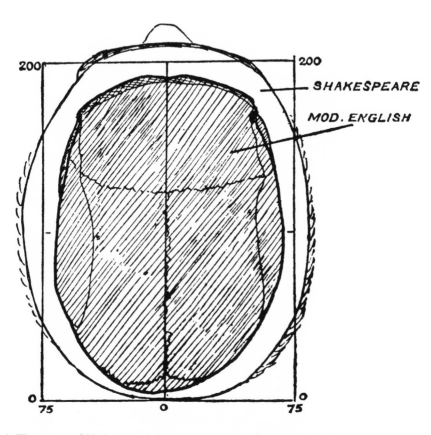

Fig. 1. The crown of Shakespeare's head as represented in the Stratford bust, with the corresponding view of a skull of moderate size. Both are drawn to the same scale.

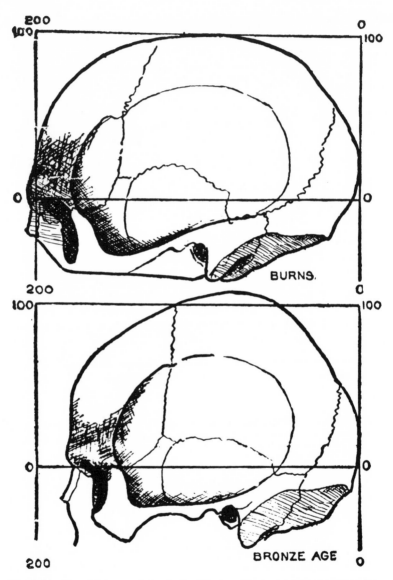

Fig. 2. Profile of the cast of the skull of Robert Burns, a representative of the long-headed type of man, contrasted with a skull of the Bronze Age – a representative of the short type.

the maximum head. This is also true of its height. The bust represents the crown as rising 150 mm above the level of the ear-holes—for, although the ears are covered by the ample side-locks of hair, the position of their passages can be fixed approximately. The 'auricular' height of the skull—deducting 7 mm for the thickness of the scalp on the crown—should have measured 143 mm—almost a maximum amount. When I first noted those maximum dimensions of the head of Shakespeare as portrayed by Gerrard Johnson, I was inclined to suppose the good sculptor had wished to give the poet a head which would be in keeping with the brain of marvellous power. Either that, or he had taken a sculptor's licence with the absolute dimensions of Shakespeare's head, and enlarged them to give to his subject that imposing dignity which increased size can give a modelled head. The width of the forehead, at the level of the eye-brows, is represented in the Stratford bust as 120 mm—quite 10 mm beyond what a forehead, shaped as Shakespeare's is, should measure. The face is 15 mm longer than one would expect. If we suppose that the sculptor had added 8 to 10 per cent to the actual measurements of the head he really portrayed, then, in every respect, the head represented in the Stratford monument as that of Shakespeare becomes a representative specimen of the short-headed type. I had reason, when seeking for an explanation of certain features of Shakespeare's forehead, to measure Chantrey's bust of Sir Walter Scott in the National Portrait Gallery. I found in that case—and it is so in many others—the sculptor had modelled the head about 10 per cent above the actual dimensions. I think Gerrard Johnson took a similar liberty.

In fig. 3 I have taken the skull of a man who lived in Kent during the Bronze Age—the period which succeeded the Neolithic—and have done, in regard to the dimensions, what I suppose Gerrard Johnson did to Shakespeare's features—enlarged them 10 per cent. It will be seen how accurately the skull—thus enlarged—fits within the Stratford bust. From the accuracy of the fit, we may be certain that the man who wrought the Stratford bust did not portray an imaginary head, but had before him an actual subject or model, and that subject was of the short-headed type. Was it Shakespeare's head which was portrayed? Mr. Spielmann assures us that the men who paid for the monument knew Shakespeare's features and were satisfied with the likeness. They would not be satisfied, we may presume, with a radical alteration of the shape of the head. We cannot suppose that the sculptor gave the poet a typical short head to satisfy those who had paid him for a true likeness.

It is not only from the side that the Bronze Age skull fits within Shakespeare's bust, the fit is equally good when we view its inset from above and from the front (figs. 4 and 5). The poet is thus represented—if we allow a reduction of 10 per cent in face and head—as a man with facial features of average dimensions. The face, when so reduced, measures from the root of the nose to the lower margin of the chin just over 120 mm; its width, from the zygomatic arch of one cheek to that of the other, is a little over 130 mm. The mean length of the face of a modern Englishman is 120·7 mm; its width 132 mm. Indeed, if we presume that the sculptor added about 10 per cent to the actual dimensions, then, in size of head and face, Shakespeare might be regarded as a representative individual of the short or round-headed type.

If there is any truth in the Stratford bust—if it represents the features of Shakespeare—then there is no doubt that our national poet is a product of the round-head stirp of humanity. We are certain at least that Shakespeare does not belong to the early British breed, for not a trace of a 'round-head' has been found in England earlier than the age at which men began to replace their stone weapons with implements made of bronze. In the Neolithic period we have evidence that the 'round-heads' were pushing their way westwards through Central Europe towards the coasts of the North Sea. In the Bronze period, commencing about 2000 B.C. they began to arrive in Britain. They gradually permeated every part of the country—England, Wales, Scotland, and Ireland—but at no period did they form the majority of our population.

Shakespeare is a descendant of the Bronze Age invaders. That is a remarkable fact, for it is this same short-headed stock—spread abroad in Central Europe, through Germany, France and Italy—which has produced the world's finest artists.

THE DROESHOUT PORTRAIT

I shall deal briefly with Shakespeare's features as represented in the Droeshout portrait. I feel certain that it is a rather crude engraving made from some previous portrait or drawing which was placed at Droeshout's disposal five or six years after Shakespeare's death. Such a portrait as that known as the 'Felton', might well have served

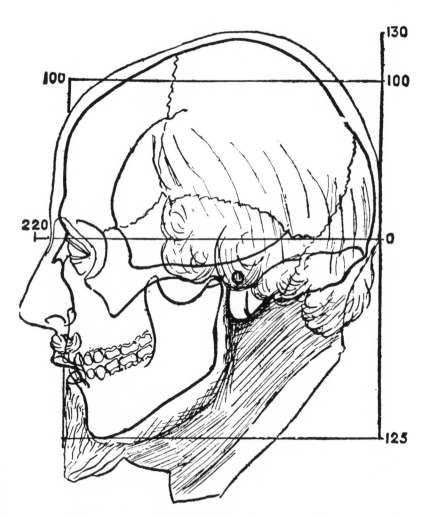

Fig. 3. Profile of Shakespeare's bust with drawing of skull of a Bronze Age man inset; the dimensions of the skull being enlarged ten per cent.

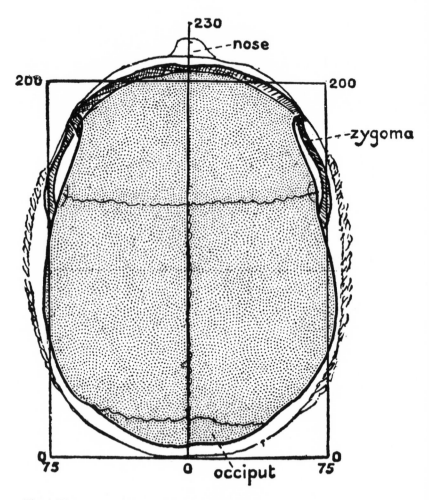

Fig. 4. The crown of Shakespeare's bust from above, with the corresponding outline of a Bronze Age skull inset. The skull has been enlarged ten per cent.

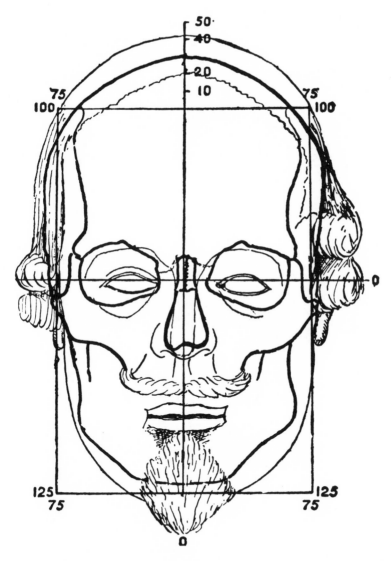

Fig. 5. Full-face view of Shakespeare's skull with similar view of a Bronze Age skull inset. The skull is enlarged ten per cent.

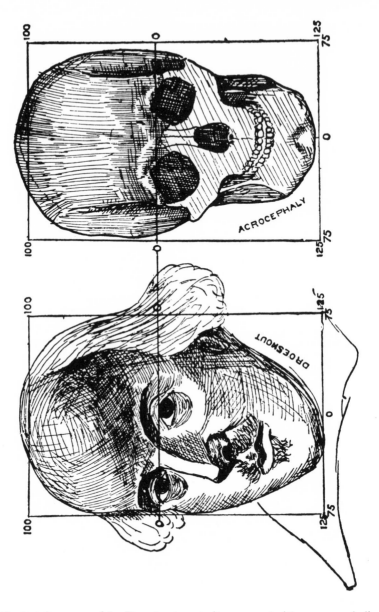

Fig. 6. A free copy of the Droeshout portrait compared with an acrocephalic skull.

as the original from which Droeshout worked. The Droeshout portrait is simply the Felton portrait with certain marks of age superadded—loss of hair and bagginess beneath the eyes. The loftiness and the modelling of the forehead in the Felton and Droeshout portraits suggests an abnormal development of Shakespeare's head (fig. 6). In every race of mankind there occasionally appear individuals with remarkably high heads—individuals in whom the vault rises up to form a 'tower' or 'sugar-loaf'. The condition is due to a mal-development in the base of the skull. The front part of the base is prematurely arrested in its growth, with the result that the developing brain, in order to find room, has to raise up the crown into the characteristic sugar-loaf form. The condition is now recognised as a distinct kind of maldevelopment known as *acrocephaly*. Sir Walter Scott was certainly the subject of this condition—at least to a mild degree. Was Shakespeare also a subject of acrocephaly?

If the Droeshout portrait be set side by side with a skull which shows the acrocephalic condition, it is seen that the vault of the skull rises higher than does the dome of the Droeshout head. When the acrocephalic skull is viewed in profile and placed within the outline of the Stratford bust (fig. 7) it is seen that all grounds for suspecting acrocephaly in Shakespeare disappear. The most characteristic feature of the acrocephalic head is its shortness from back to front. The head of Shakespeare's bust is relatively long.

THE BRAIN

Looking away for a minute from the question of type, it is of interest to see what size of brain the Stratford bust suggests for Shakespeare. If we accept the dimensions of the bust as real and not enlarged, we must estimate the dimensions of the skull as follows: Length 204 mm; width 158 mm; auricular height 143 mm. Employing one of the formulae invented by Miss Lee and Professor Pearson for estimating the size of the brain from the dimensions of the skull, we find that Shakespeare's brain capacity was a little over 1,900 ccm—not an impossible amount. Curvier's brain capacity was over 1,900 ccm; Cromwell and Byron are said to have had brain capacities well over 2,000 ccm. The average Englishman has to be content with a capacity of 1,477. If we suppose—and I think we must accept the supposition

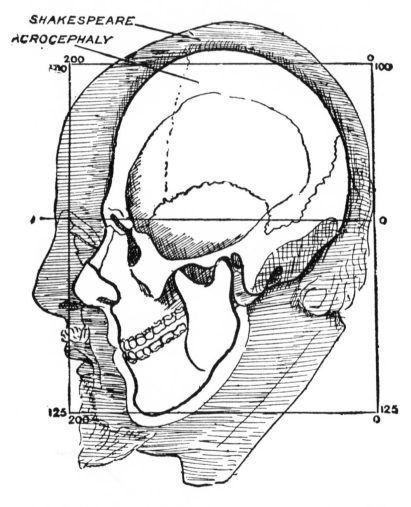

Fig. 7. Skull showing the malformation known as acrocephaly set within a profile of the Stratford bust. Both are drawn to the same scale.

—that the Stratford head has to be reduced by about 10 per cent to find the true dimensions of Shakespeare's brain, then the power of the poet's brain must be ascribed to quality rather than quantity. In the reduced scale, the length of the head would be 184 mm; width 143 mm; auricular height 129 mm; the brain capacity 1,540 ccm.

CHAPTER 5

The Evidence of Disease in Shakespeare's Handwriting

Ralph W. Leftwich

EDITORIAL NOTE

Dr. Leftwich, in his essay on Shakespeare's handwriting, holds that his genius was crippled by a commonplace minor ailment. This may well be true, but here, as frequently elsewhere, an answer to one question only raises another. In the discussion on Leftwich's paper (read at the Royal Society of Medicine on 19th March 1919) Dr. F. G. Crookshank, himself subject to writer's cramp ('scrivener's palsy'), made these pertinent observations:

> Very probably what we call 'writer's cramp' is susceptible of different pathogenic explanations in different cases: but it may be not without relevance to the question of Shakespeare's disability (for disability there undoubtedly was) to recall that, in certain cases at least, the exhaustion is definitely cortical rather than 'peripheral', and that writer's cramp, like other professional cramps, palsies and spasms, is apt to obtain when there is a greater measure of conscious cerebration accompanying the carrying out of what, like writing, may be at other times a more or less automatic act, or series of acts. It is the concomitance of (1) attention to writing and (2) thought in composition that exhausts: moreover, writer's cramp, like other so-called neuroses, sometimes manifests itself, almost without precedent warning of overstrain or over-exhaustion, in those who are the subject of worries and anxieties. One other point: it is a little curious that exhaustion of the cortical writing centres should so frequently, if not always, first show itself by illegibility of the signature—almost the most 'automatic' act of calligraphy.

Shakespeare's scrivener's palsy would thus not necessarily be a professional disease, but the physical expression of mental exhaustion. If the term psychosomatic disease did not exist in 1919, the condition itself was no less prevalent then than it is today.

THE MATERIAL

We have in all six signatures of Shakespeare (fig. 1): that on the Mountjoy deed, discovered by Professor Wallace and preserved at the Record Office, dates from 1612; that on the Blackfriars purchase deed at the Guildhall, and one of a mortgage deed of the same property, at the British Museum, date from 1613; while three on the will at Somerset House date from 1616. Consequently, they are all specimens of his writing late in life. Besides these, the name occurs in two books: an Ovid's *Metamorphoses* (1502) and a Florio's *Translation of Montaigne* (1603). These, if genuine, might have been written earlier, and this would explain why they show no sign of the disease with which I shall deal later. But as the best authorities do not believe that they are genuine I shall leave them out of consideration. Now, although these signatures have been closely examined and scrutinised by palaeographists and others, they have never been systematically examined and analysed by any one with a medical training; and nothing but speculative suggestions have been made with regard to their association with disease.

In Shakespeare's times, two styles of writing prevailed, the Gothic and the Italian. He had been taught the Gothic, which bears a close resemblance to German cursive script. It was gradually ousted by the Italian for the good reasons that this was easier both to read and to write.

Before going farther I must mention a peculiarity, which has been no doubt noticed by all of you, the abbreviation of the second syllable of the surname as shown in the signatures of 1612 and 1613. The practice seems extraordinary to those who are unfamiliar with the subject; but, as a matter of fact, it was quite common, at that time, with persons whose names ended in 'per' and the like, such as Couper, Draper, Roper, and even Shepherd.

Next, I will draw your attention to points which have been commented upon by lay palaeographists, and especially by Sir E. Maunde Thompson. In an article in 'Shakespeare's England', he says that the curve of the capital S in the full will-signature is 'angular'. He also noted

(1) The capital 'S' of the signature on the second page of the will is made in two sectional strokes with a gap between them.

(2) The first 'a' in the 1612 autograph is open at the top: to ordinary eyes, however, the fact is hidden by the unwieldy loop of

Specimens in facsimile of Shakespeare's signature. The top signature was written on May 11, 1612; the next two on March 10, 1613; the fourth signature is on the first sheet of the will; the fifth on the second sheet of the will; and the sixth on the third sheet of the will, which was executed on March 25, 1616.

the 'h' preceding it, and I think the point is still more evident in the second 'a' of the full will-signature.

(3) The last syllable of the surname on the third page of the will (1616 [c]) suggests 'almost a breakdown.' The 's' in the 1612 signature has been omitted.

In the absence of a knowledge of medicine, on the part of these observers, no particular significance was attached to the peculiarities; but when they are recognised signs of a certain diseased condition, such evidence, unbiased as it was by technical knowledge, becomes of much increased value. It would lighten my task very much if we possessed a specimen of the writing before disease had set in. Unfortunately this is not the case; but in compensation, we have two testimonies to its excellence. In the introduction to the first folio, the editors, Hemyng and Condell, say: 'His mind and hand went together, and what he thought he uttered with that easiness that we have scarce received from him a blot upon his papers'— (i.e., even a blot). Five years earlier, Ben Jonson, in conversation with Drummond of Hawthornden, said: 'I remember that the players have often mentioned it as an honour to Shakespeare that in his writing (whatsoever he penned) he never blotted out a line.' Now, a bad writer makes both blots and corrections; but we are not dependent upon the testimony of others for we have under our own eyes a proof that he was able to write at least a word or two well. Look at the 'By me, William' of the full will-signature. It cannot be denied that this is exceedingly well written, and I have no doubt that it represents the standard of writing to which the editors alluded. Further, his large output shows that he was a rapid writer, and the combination of speed with clearness accentuates his skill in penmanship. Lastly, whereas, up to 1610 he wrote hundreds of pages of MS with scarcely a blot, in those before us he made, as you can see, four blots in writing fourteen words.

Do the six signatures in general confirm the favourable testimony of the actors? It must be confessed that they do not; and the verdict must be that had Shakespeare supplied them with their parts written in the general style of the autographs, no such appreciation would have been shown. Moreover, every signature appears so laboured and consequently so slowly executed that it is impossible to believe that the writer of them could have penned with his own hand the great volume of work of which he was the author if his earlier writing had been no better.

CLINICAL CONSIDERATIONS

The idea that the signatures show signs of disease is very old. In considering the question of morbid influence we are handicapped by two difficulties. First, that Shakespeare wrote in a script that is strange to us. Secondly, that we have to base our conclusions upon three capital and eleven small letters. For this drawback, however, we have the very great compensation that the writing extends over a period of no less than four years. Consequently, it represents different stages of the malady and yields us many more symptoms than any letter of a single date however long. The signature on the first page of the will is so damaged as to be nearly useless to us, and not much importance can be attached to the copy of it made by George Steevens in 1778, since it is impossible that the first stroke of the W could ever have been shorter, or the other strokes finer, than they now are. As far as it goes, however, its characters confirm the conclusion to which I shall come later. There can be no doubt that the full will-signature on the third page was signed first, as indeed is the case even now with testators.

The idea that the signatures show signs of disease is very old. Some have gone so far as to evolve or concur in a pathetic little account of the scene that took place when the will was signed. It had already been drawn up two months when the poet is said to have developed alarming symptoms; witnesses were hurriedly summoned, and in an almost dying condition he just managed to append these trembling signatures. Now, there is not a shadow of foundation for all this. Shakespeare survived the signing a whole month; two witnesses would have sufficed, yet five attended; no solicitor's presence was necessary, yet to bring Francis Collins there, the messenger would have had to travel sixteen miles! Lastly the other signatures would be still unexplained.

POSSIBLE CAUSES

PHYSICAL AND MENTAL DISABILITIES

Some have suggested that the defects in his writing may have been due to locomotor ataxy, or one or other form of chronic paralysis; but the preamble to Shakespeare's will negatives constitutional illness. The will begins thus: 'In the name of God, amen! I, William

Shakespeare, of Stratford-on-Avon, gentleman, in perfect health and memorie, God be praised.' The only account of his death, which took place a month after signing—that of the Rev. John Ward, a later Vicar of Stratford—states that it was due to a fever—i.e., a disease of short duration. We can exclude as causes of bad writing such conditions as defective education, disablement of the hand through rheumatism or injury, as well as such diseases as are characterised by rhythmic tremor by the fact that the writing is not *uniformly* bad or tremulous (see the William at the end of the will). Many diseases also can be excluded by considerations of age, duration, and association with impaired mental capacity. As regards the last, there is no sign of it during the years that remained to him. Our knowledge of him at that period is very limited, but we know that in 1612 he was a competent witness, that in 1613 he received from the Earl of Rutland a good fee for designing (but not drawing) a symbolic tournament-badge or 'impresa' and also bought and mortgaged house property; that in 1614 the Town Council of Stratford directed their clerk to ask Shakespeare to support their action in the matter of the Welcombe enclosures; that in 1615 he not only associated himself with some neighbours in an action to protect their joint rights in the Blackfriars freehold, but that he was specially consulted in London by the solicitor to the Stratford Corporation. We know that in 1616 he was of testamentary capacity and there is no evidence of gradual mental deterioration in his works. *The Tempest* was produced in November 1611, about six months before the date of the earliest signature, and far from showing any falling off this play is perhaps unsurpassed in the realm of pure imagination by any other. It is not known when he last acted.

SCRIVENER'S PALSY

Now, is there any morbid condition in which the handwriting exhibits the abnormalities shown in the Shakespeare autographs without being barred by any collateral considerations? There is one, and only one: scrivener's palsy or writer's cramp. I have seen a considerable number of cases in my time, but, since the introduction of the typewriter, the condition has become rarer. Fortunately, we have very close and accurate descriptions of the handwriting of the victims by outstanding medical authorities, and we can thus draw up a perfectly clear picture of the changes that take place and seek for their presence in the Shakespeare signatures.

Gowers divided writer's cramp into four varieties: spastic, tremulous, neuralgic and paralytic; but it is generally agreed that the classification involves much overlapping. Shakespeare suffered essentially from the spastic form. In this, the pen is not completely under the control of the writer. Against his will, it makes little jerks, unduly long strokes or unintended marks; and though a good beginning may perhaps be made, the hand very soon tires and refuses to write at all. Sir William Gowers says that the general effect is that of a letter written in a jolting carriage, and this you will agree, is precisely what Shakespeare's writing suggests.

The recognised signs of writer's cramp are very numerous. We will take first the signs derived from predisposing causes:

(1) Age and sex. Smith-Jelliffe scheduled 194 cases of writer's cramp, and of these forty-five, or about one-fourth, were between 40 and 50; Gowers, in 151 cases, found thirty-two between these ages. Now Shakespeare was 46 or 47 at the onset. The preponderating sex is of course male.

(2) Writer's cramp is commonest in those who have written habitually in a cramped hand. In writing Gothic characters the hand is necessarily cramped.

(3) It affects those who have written voluminously. Shakespeare did. The first folio alone contains 1,000 double-column pages and, in addition, there were the sonnets, the poems, and the actors' parts.

(4) The condition may persist for many years. Poore mentions a case of ten years' duration and Gowers one of twelve. In Shakespeare's case, it is still present at the end of four.

(5) The general bodily and mental health is unaffected.

We will take the signs of writer's cramp as exhibited in the specimens of the handwriting before us. And, here, let me add that even in the living subject there are few other objective signs.

(6) The writing is sprawled across the paper (Head, Gowers). This is very marked in the 1612 and 1616 *a* and *b* signatures.

(7) The letters are coarsened (Robins, Erb, Campbell Thomson). The feature is evident in the 1612 and 1616 *a* letters as well as in the initial letters of 1613 *a*.

(8) The downstrokes are thickened (Gowers, Oppenheim, Thomson). Notice the 'W' and the two 'll's of the 1612 autograph.

The next four signs are important because they were pointed out by lay palaeographists:

(9) The upper part of 'a' or 'u' may be open (Robins, Head, Thomson). We have no 'o' but an uncompleted 'a,' according to Maunde Thompson, occurs in the 1612 autograph, following what looks like a great 'O'. This may not be clear to inexpert eyes, but the open 'a' in the surname of the full will-signature is clear enough.

(10) A curve may be made in two strokes instead of one (Poore). This point is clearly shown in the capital 'S' of the second will-signature, where it consists, according to Maunde Thompson, of two sectional strokes with a gap between them. The initial 'S' of the 1613 *b* signature is also suspicious.

A curve may be made by a succession of short strokes (Robins, Poore, Gowers, Church). Maunde Thompson says that in trying 'to accomplish the outer curve' (of the capital 'S'), 'he failed, the curve becoming angular.' William Martin, is much more explicit. He counted in the capital 'S' eight distinct little strokes, which, combined, formed the curve. Now, how does this compare with a medical description of writer's cramp? Thus: the American neurologist, Dr. Robins, with no thought of Shakespeare present to his mind, says that he counted thirteen of these little strokes in a capital N and fourteen in a capital T. The coincidence is remarkable. The peculiarity is not however confined to this instance for it can also be recognised more or less throughout.

The letters at the end of a word may get more and more slurred till they become illegible (Head, Romberg, Campbell Thomson). Gowers and others describe this as the 'sign of the tired hand'. The following is the description given by Thompson: 'By me William', he says, 'is good; but the hand then begins to fail, the first three letters of the surname are still clearly legible, but are somewhat deformed; then ensues almost a breakdown, an imperfect "k" and a long "s" ending in a tremulous finial.' This feature, which is perhaps the most striking characteristic of all the signs of writer's cramp and is all but pathognomonic, is especially evident in the full will-signature.

Some further signs call for consideration:

(i) The spasm drives the nib through the paper (Gowers, Wilfred Harris, Meige, Bury, Smith-Jelliffe and Aldren Turner). Now, a quill would not succeed in penetrating parchment and the result would be a blotted letter or a splutter. This sign is plainly visible in the last letter but one of the 1612 signature, in the 'W' of 1613 *a*, and in the bottom loop of the 'h' in the full will-signature.

(ii) A stroke may be too high or too low (Gowers, Erb). The point is not of much importance, especially in this script; but it is too low in the first I of 1616 *a*, both here and in the drawing made by George Steevens in 1778 when it was less damaged; while it is too high in what looks like a colossal 'O' in the 1612 autograph, but which is really the upper loop of a Gothic 'h'.

(iii) An unintentional mark may be made (Gowers, Wilfred Harris, Erb). There is one below the 'S' of the 1612 signature. It is not a blot, for if you examine it closely, you will see that it is semicircular. The dot within the 'W' is not a displaced dot of the 'i' as some have thought, for it is found where an 'a' follows the 'W'.

(iv) The effects are not uniform; a word or two may occasionally be fairly well written and the same letter may be written sometimes well, sometimes ill (Gowers, Erb, Oppenheim, Campbell Thomson). This feature excludes a large number of conditions in which the handwriting is defective. It is seen in the difference between the 'William' and the 'Shakespeare' in the third page signature and in that between the two 'll's in the 1612 and the first 1613 signature.

(v) A letter is often unlinked to the next (Meige, Campbell Thomson, Oppenheim). This feature is not of much importance. I do not mind confessing that I am sometimes guilty myself; but unlinked letters can be seen in the second 1613 and the second and third page will-signatures.

(vi) Tremor. Tremor is more or less evident everywhere; but is best seen in the second 1613 signature. It is of the spastic variety, for passive tremor is practically absent and its absence excludes a large number of diseases.

(vii) Omitted letters. None of the medical writers I have referred to mentions this point as a feature of writer's cramp; but considering the labour of writing in these cases, it is only what one might expect. Certainly Shakespeare sometimes omitted letters; for the small 's', which in this script is represented by a long straight or curved line, as in the two 1613 autographs, is absent in the full will-signature; but this is not the case, though the shaky 's' and the 'k' are mixed up together.

(viii) The pen is dropped (Wilfred Harris and many others). This may or may not have happened, but at any rate the blur over the 'I' in the first page will-signature is consistent with its occurrence.

Few people are familiar with the Gothic script of the period and to meet the objection that other Elizabethan writers may show the same caligraphic peculiarities, I have examined the writing of Ben Jonson, Marston, Peele, Bacon, Daniell, Donne, Massinger, Stowe, and many others, and I am certain that none of them suffered from writer's cramp. Nor is there any evidence of it in the writing of the Warwick solicitor who drew up the will, Francis Collins.

I submit that a diagnosis of writer's cramp is unimpeachable. Every condition precedent, whether of age, of occupation, of chronicity, or of freedom from bodily or mental disease is fulfilled in the history of the case and every objective sign in the handwriting has been demonstrated.

THE IMPLICATIONS OF THE DIAGNOSIS

In our days, the victim of this disorder sometimes succeeds in teaching himself to write with the left hand; but the rule is that this soon shares the same fate as the right and it would be frankly impossible with Gothic script. I may be also asked: Why did he not dictate his plays? Well, it is not given to everyone to dictate even a letter with any facility and many that we receive and that read so well and so glibly, have had as much editing as a parliamentary speech; and you may remember that Goldsmith, having engaged an amanuensis for this 'Animated Nature,' found himself mute when he wanted to start dictating. Apart from that, only a very clumsy and unreliable form of shorthand was available in Shakespeare's time. Thus John Heywood, complaining of the piracy of his plays, wrote in 1605: 'Some by stenography draw the plot, put it in print, scarce one word true!' And it is one thing to dictate a letter and quite another to dictate a play; for a play, with its frequent changes of scenes and players, presents something like a maximum of difficulty. Possibly Shakespeare tried and failed and incidentally this may be the explanation of the fact that when the masque portion of *The Tempest* was added in 1613, it was written by another, probably Chapman. Milton's task, that of dictating an epic was far easier and he, moreover, had had the advantage of secretarial training.

This, then, is the explanation of the mystery as to why a healthy man who had devoted himself with the greatest regularity to play-writing suddenly and finally gave it up at the age of 46, notwithstanding that his business interests in the theatres continued.

CHAPTER 6

Milton's Blindness

Arnold Sorsby

EDITORIAL NOTE

The fairly extensive literature on the causation of Milton's blindness centres essentially around two possibilities: glaucoma and detachment of the retina. Glaucoma is fairly common; it is an affection in which the pressure in the eye is raised and this generally develops in eyes that are otherwise normal; the raised pressure induces blindness from damage to the retina and the optic nerve. Detachment of the retina is relatively rare, but is a frequent complication of the more severe forms of myopia (shortsight); the retina dies after becoming separated from its underlying blood supply.

> '. . . Thus with the year
> Seasons return, but not to me returns
> Day, or the sweet approach of even or morn,
> Or sight of vernal bloom, or summer's rose,
> Or flocks, or herds, or human face divine;
> But cloud instead, and ever-during dark
> Surrounds me, from the cheerful way of men
> Cut off, and for the book of knowledge fair
> Presented with a universal blank
> Of Nature's works to me expunged and rased,
> And wisdom at one entrance quite shut out.'
> *Paradise Lost*, III, 40–50.

THE EVIDENCE

Milton's blindness is enmeshed in the texture of his writings.

Such evidence as is available on the nature of his blindness comes mainly from scraps of autobiographical detail left by Milton; these are supported and extended by the early biographies extant. That his blindness came on rather early in life is well known from the opening lines of the sonnet on his blindness:[1]

> 'When I consider how my light is spent
> Ere half my days . . .'

Some clue as to its nature is found in the other sonnet dealing with his blindness, the one addressed to his friend Cyriack Skinner.[2]

> 'Cyriack, this three years' day these eyes, though clear,
> To outward view, of blemish or of spot,
> Bereft of light, their seeing have forgot;'

That his eyes though blind were 'clear to outward view, of blemish or of spot', is again asserted by Milton in his prose writings. Answering a personal attack he says[3] that but for his eyes he has not changed in any respect and as for these they 'are externally uninjured. They shine with an unclouded light, just like the eyes of one whose vision is perfect. This is the only point in which I am against my will, a hypocrite.'

A further reference to his eyes is found in 'Paradise Lost.' In a glorious paean on light[2] he says:

> 'Thee I revisit safe,
> And feel thy sovran vital lamp; but though
> Revisit'st not these eyes, that roll in vain
> To find thy piercing ray, and find no dawn;
> So thick a drop serene hath quenched their orbs,
> Or dim suffusion veiled.'

Drop serene and dim suffusion are not so much alternate diagnoses as different names for very much the same thing, for *gutta serena* was the name for blindness with a transparent (i.e., non-obscured) pupil and *suffusio nigra* stood for blindness in which the pupil was black (and not grey). Both these names, therefore, agree with the statements made by Milton elsewhere to the effect that in his blindness his eyes were normal in appearance. Milton has also left us information on the state of his eyes during his childhood, and expressed the opinion that his early studies had harmed his sight. On this subject he says:[3]

'From the twelfth year of my age I scarcely ever went from my lessons to bed before midnight; which indeed was the first cause of injury to my eyes, to whose natural weakness there were also added frequent headaches.' That excessive work led to his blindness was the belief of himself and his medical advisers. He records the circumstances under which he undertook to write a defence of the republican cause:[3]

'When I was publicly solicited to write a reply to the defence of the royal cause; when I had to contend with the pressure of sickness and with the apprehension of soon losing the sight of my remaining eye; and when my medical attendants clearly announced that if I did engage in the work, it would be irreparably lost—their premonitions caused no hesitation and inspired no dismay.' Indeed Milton found the yoke of blindness tolerable through his belief that he sacrificed his eyes in the service of his cause:[4]

> 'Yet I argue not
> Against Heav'n's hand or will, nor bate a jot
> Of heart or hope, but still hear up and steer
> Right onward. What supports me, dost thou ask?
> The conscience, friend, to have lost them overplied
> In Liberty's defence.'

Most important information of the nature of his blindness is preserved for us in a letter written by Milton[5] to his friend Philaras, a Greek diplomat who had asked Milton to give him an account of his blindness, so that he might consult Dr. Thevenot, a Parisian oculist of great repute. What Thevenot did, or indeed whether the letter reached him is not known. In this letter Milton gives an account of the subjective symptoms he experienced during the development of his blindness. The letter is dated 28th September 1654, and by this time Milton had been blind for about three years.

'It is 10 years, I think, more or less since I felt my sight getting weak and dull, and at the same time my viscera generally out of sorts. In the morning if I began as usual, to read anything, I felt my eyes at once thoroughly pained, and shrinking from the act of reading, but refreshed after moderate bodily exercise. If I looked at a lit candle, a kind of iris seemed to snatch it from me. Not very long after, a darkness coming over the left part of my eye (for that eye became clouded some years before the other) removed from my vision all objects situated on that side. Objects in front also, if I chanced to close the right eye, seemed smaller. The other eye also failing perceptibly and gradually through a period of three years, I observed some months before my sight was wholly gone, that objects I looked at without myself moving, seemed all to swim, now to the right now to the left. Inverterate mists now seem to have settled in my forehead and temples, which weight me down and depress me with a kind of sleepy heaviness, especially from meal-time to evening. [Here follows an allusion to classical literature]. But I should not forget to mention that, while yet a little sight remained when first I lay down in bed, and turned myself to either side, there used to shine out a copious glittering light from my shut eyes; then that as my sight grew less from day to day, colours proportionately duller would burst from them,

as with a kind of force and audible shot from within; but that
now, as if the sense of lucency were extinct, it is a mere blackness
or a blackness dashed, and as it were interwoven with an ashy
grey, that is wont to pour itself forth. Yet the darkness which is
perpetually before me, by night as well as by day, seems always
nearer to a whitish than to a blackish, and such that, when the
eye rolls itself, there is admitted, as through a small chink a
certain little trifle of light.'

It is worth noting that this document so careful in its details is
confined entirely to subjective symptoms: the physical appearance
of his eyes is not touched upon. In view of the fact that this letter is
a personal statement intended for an oculist it is hardly likely that
Milton would have suppressed any obvious external change in the
appearance of his eyes, and this letter must therefore be taken as
lending further support to his statements elsewhere that his eyes
were free from blemish or spot.

There is therefore no reason to doubt the diagnosis of *gutta serena*
which Milton gives of his case in *Paradise Lost*.

Apart from these autobiographical details there is some further
evidence bearing on the subject in the contemporary portraits and
sketches of Milton and in the lives of him by his contemporaries.

As for the portraits and sketches, there is unfortunately little of
any importance to be obtained in this direction. Though very many
etchings are available which are claimed to represent Milton at
some time or other, it would appear that there are only two undoubted contemporary portraits.[6] Obviously but little significance
can be attached to copies of later dates, and in so far as the present
writer has seen them they are entirely negative for the appearances
of the eyes in all of them are normal. The two undoubted portraits
of Milton have been inaccessible to the writer but good photographs
of them show nothing abnormal about the eyes. The subject of
Milton's portraits is a highly complicated one and open to considerable dispute[7]—and to draw positive conclusions from any of them
would be a procedure of doubtful wisdom. All that can be said is
that there is nothing in the available representations of Milton to
disprove his statement as to his eyes during his blindness, and
presumably earlier on, being of normal appearance.

The evidence as to Milton's appearance and his mode of life as
retailed by biographers who were his contemporaries are in the main
but confirmations of his own autobiographical notes dispersed

through his writings. Thus the earliest *Life of Milton* extant,[8] generally ascribed to his friend and physician Nathan Paget, tells of his 'sitting up constantly at his study till midnight' in his early years. The onset of his blindness is thus related:

> 'Whilst he was thus employed [writing the Second Defence] his eyesight totally failed . . . from a weakness which his hard nightly study in his youth had first occasioned and which by degrees had for some time before deprived him of the use of one ey: And the Issues and the Seatons made use of to save or retrieve that, were thought by drawing away the Spirits, which should have supply'd the optic vessells, to have hastened the loss of the other. Hee was inded advised by his Physitians of the danger in his condition, attending so great intentness as that work required.'

The following extract is of interest:

> 'He was of a moderate stature, and well proportioned, of a ruddy Complexion, light brown Hair and handsome Features; save that his Eyes were none of the quickest. But his blindness, which proceeded from a Gutta Serena, added no further blemish to them.[9] His deportment was sweet and affable, and in Gate erect and Manly . . . on which account hee wore a Sword while hee had his Sight, and was skilled in using it.'

Milton's later biographers add but little to these pen-pictures. In fact the later *Lives* appear to be based on this first biography and the details supplied by Milton. One noteworthy remark appears in the *Life* by Aubrey,[10] who knew Milton personally:

> 'His father read without spectacles at eighty-four, his mother had very weak eies and used spectacles presently after she was thirty years old.'

Of the other contemporaries who have written about Milton, none throws any further light on the subject; but the following remark taken from the *Life* by his nephew Edward Philips[11] shows that the resignation with which Milton took his blindness, when at length it fell on him, was not the spirit in which he took the catastrophe during the long years it was preparing.

> 'His sight, what with his continual study, his being subject to head-ake, and his perpetual tampering with physick to preserve it, had been decaying for about a dozen years . . . the sight of one for a long time clearly lost.'

The information obtained from the original sources as to Miltons' eyesight and the possible causes of his blindness may therefore be summarised as follows:

(1) Milton's eyes had a 'natural weakness'. 'His eyes were none of the quickest.'

(2) His vision in his early days could not have been defective to a very high degree for 'Hee wore a Sword while he had his Sight, and was skilled in using it.' 'I was won't constantly to exercise myself in the use of the broad sword, as long as it comported with my habits and my years.'[3]

(3) The exact date of his blindness is not known with certainty. By 1654, the year that Milton wrote to Philaras the letter giving details of his case, he speaks of his blindness as though it were not a recent calamity. In a state paper, a letter from the Hague dated 20th June 1653, Milton is spoken of as being blind. The writer of *Regii Sanguinis Clamor* which was published in 1652 makes a personal attack on Milton, upbraiding him with his blindness, selecting for the motto of his work Virgil's description of the eyeless cyclops: *Monstrum horrendum, informe, ingens, cui lumen ademptum*—A monster horrid, hideous, huge and blind. Masson[12] holds that Milton's blindness was complete by March or April 1652—and this date is generally accepted.

(4) Milton was therefore only 43 at the onset of his blindness, and from his letter we know that his sight had been 'getting weak and dull' for about ten years before 1654, that is from his thirty-fifth year.[13] 'Not very long after a darkness coming over the left part of my left eye (for that eye became clouded some years before the other) removed from my vision all objects on that side.' It would therefore appear that the left eye had failed when Milton was not very much more than 35. The right eye does not seem to have failed so suddenly. 'The other eye failing perceptibly and gradually through a period of three years. I observed some months before my sight was wholly gone, that objects I looked at without myself moving, seemed all to swim.'

(5) Milton's blindness seems not to have been associated with any external signs; the eyes 'are externally uninjured. They shine with an unclouded light, just like the eyes of one whose vision is perfect.'

(6) Milton's 'father read without spectacles at 84, his mother had very weak eies and used spectacles presently after she was thirty years old.' In addition there is also the account of the subjective sensations felt by Milton in the terminal stages of his developing blindness.

THEORIES AS TO THE CAUSE OF MILTON'S BLINDNESS

A vivid sidelight is thrown on the age in which Milton was living that his enemies should publicly ascribe his blindness to a divine punishment for his transgressions—and that Milton found it necessary to deny such charges. And not only Milton but his biographers too.[8, 9] In an impassioned defence of himself Milton says:[3]

'. . . I have accurately examined my conduct and scrutinised my soul, I call Thee, O! God, the searcher of hearts to witness that I am not conscious either in the more early or in the later period of my life, of having committed any enormity, which might deservedly have marked me out as a fit object of such a callamitous visitation. But since my enemies boast that this affliction is only a retribution for the transgressions of my pen, I again invoke the Almighty to witness that I never at any time wrote anything which I did not think agreeable to truth, to justice and to piety. This was my persuasion then and I feel that same persuasion now. Nor was I ever prompted to such exertions by the influence of ambition, by the lust of lucre or of praise; it was only by the conviction of duty and the feeling of patriotism, a disinterested passion for the extension of civil and religious liberty.'

The cause of Milton's blindness was touched upon by two writers before the era of the ophthalmoscope. According to W. Lawrence[14] Milton suffered from 'suffusion'; Mackenzie[15] held that the blindness was caused by 'amaurosis' due to congestion or inflammation of the optic nerve secondary to a chronic disease of the digestive organs.

More recent writers have been more definite in their diagnosis, and four different suggestions have been advanced.

1. GLAUCOMA

That Milton's blindness was due to glaucoma seems to be a popular view. This view first was advanced in 1879 by Alfred Stern[16] who says in his classical *Life of Milton*, that he consulted a 'distinguished ophthalmologist' on the nature of Milton's blindness and that according to this authority some of the features tended to a diagnosis of glaucoma, though others were against such a view. The reasons for this conception are not given. Glaucoma is also suggested by Hirschberg[17] in a footnote in his monumental *Geschichte der Augenheilkunde*. Again no reasons are given. In an article on the subject in the *American Encyclopedia of Ophthalmology*, T. H. Shastid[18] also suggests glaucoma—and again no reasons are advanced.

Apparently the main reason for the diagnosis of glaucoma is the fact mentioned by Milton in his letter to Philaras, that if he 'looked at a lit candle, a kind of iris seemed to snatch it' from him. That this symptom led Hirschberg to the diagnosis of glaucoma is vouched for by Mutschmann[19] who declares that Hirschberg says so in a personal letter to him.

On the face of it there is much to support the view that glaucoma was responsible for Milton's blindness. Here is a progressive deterioration of sight extending over a period of years (somewhere between eight to twelve years), associated with the phenomenon of iridescent rings around naked lights, and ultimately leading to complete blindness though the external appearances of the eyes are normal. But the diagnosis of glaucoma only holds good when the bare outlines are considered: the details do not fit in.

To begin with Milton was first troubled with his eyes at about the age of 35 according to his own account, at about the age of 31 according to the account of his nephew Philips. 'Not very long' afterwards the 'left part of the left eye' had failed. This certainly does not mean contraction of the nasal half of the field—nor can it mean the deterioration of vision following an acute attack of glaucoma, for such deterioration does not pick out particular parts of the fields. Besides its presupposes the glaucomatous process to have started very early in life if by the early thirties the sight of an eye could have been lost. By 43 Milton was totally blind. It is uncommon for chronic glaucoma—and it must have been chronic if it was glaucoma, as the 'right eye was failing perceptibly and gradually for a period of three years'—to lead to complete blindness by 43.

Thus if it is true that the chronic nature of the deterioration suggests glaucoma, the age of the victim is all against it. The objection to glaucoma is strongly fortified by an analysis of the symptoms as related by Milton. Chronic glaucoma is essentially a symptomless disease; it is true that vision deteriorates steadily but because central vision is unaffected till late the patient is not aware of it. Glaucomatous patients do not describe loss of field such as Milton describes. The metamorphopsia of which Milton speaks, the micropsia, the illusion of objects moving, the 'copious light glittering from shut eyes' are all symptoms that are never met with in glaucoma. The one outstanding symptom that is present in glaucoma is the seeing of iridescent rings, and because other symptoms are absent in glaucoma this symptom has usurped quite an unmerited place in the diagnosis of this disease. It certainly is not pathognomonic of glaucoma: it is met with in a number of other conditions, and in view of the fact that everything else points strongly against glaucoma, the presence of this symptom is insufficient evidence for such a diagnosis. It must also be remembered that when Milton was blind, he could still get 'a certain little trifle of light' with his eyes in certain positions. The blindness from glaucoma is usually absolute.

Two further facts throw doubt on the diagnosis of glaucoma. One is our knowledge that Milton's eyesight was naturally weak. It may therefore be that this 'natural weakness', if its nature could be ascertained, was ultimately the cause of the blindness. The other is the fact that on the one symptom on which one is tempted to diagnose glaucoma Milton appears to have been an unreliable witness. The iris around a candle of which Milton speaks may merely have been a play of colours, for it is said[20] that Milton only saw three colours in the rainbow. A play of colours around a light is decidedly more feeble evidence of glaucoma than a display of rainbow colours.

2. DETACHED RETINA

In a short communication Dufour[21] of Lausanne advanced in 1909 the suggestion that Milton's blindness was due to detachment of the retina in both eyes. He bases his conclusions on an analysis of the letter to Philaras and on the fact that Milton's eyes were normal in their external appearances. Dufour stresses the illusions of deformity and mobility of objects looked at, the subjective sensations of light persisting after loss of sight, the facts of 'dimness of the visual field coming on first on the left side and then at the top; the sensation of steam before the eyes, showing the well-known picture of the narrowing of the visual field from above.'

As to the cause of the detachment, Dufour holds that it was due to myopia, and in support of the theory that Milton was myopic he points out that Milton was an ardent student since childhood, and this would cause him to be myopic. As further proof is given the fact that though Milton travelled extensively, crossing 'some of the most beautiful parts in the world' there is not in his work 'one description, one line referring to the beauties of Nature.' 'Although in the seventeenth century no thought was given to the beauties of Nature, this attention to things heard, and indifference to things seen, appears to be the chief characteristic of the short-sighted.'

In criticism of Dufour's view it must be said that though his analysis of the letter to Philaras makes out a strong case for detachment, his proof that Milton was myopic is not very convincing. Whether close work, even by poor candle light, can bring on myopia, is to say the least, very much in question, and to say that Milton was insusceptible to the charms of Nature is an overstatement. It is enough to quote the opinion of Walter Savage Landor on Milton's treatment of Nature: 'If ever there was a poet who knew her well and described her in all her loveliness, it was Milton.' That Milton should not have spoken of the natural beauty that he must have seen during his travels is readily explained by the fact that none of his contemporaries ever spoke of such things. Appreciation of the beauties of Nature is a remarkably recent acquirement—and only two hundred years ago Switzerland was regarded as a country full of hideous and inconvenient mountains. Milton may have been, and probably was, myopic, but the evidence advanced by Dufour is by no means convincing.

3. CONGENITAL SYPHILIS

In 1924 Saurat and Cabannes[22] advanced the suggestion that Milton suffered from congenital syphilis and that this affection was the cause of his blindness. They reject the suggestion of detachment, because they are not satisfied that Milton was myopic; indeed they hold that Milton was not the subject of myopia, basing their conclusion on the fact that Milton had good colour vision. In arriving at the conclusion as to Milton's good colour vision they base themselves on the work of Squires[20] whose opposite conclusion, viz., that Milton had poor colour vision they do not mention. They therefore argue against detachment on this hypothetical good colour vision. They also say that such of the symptoms described by Milton as are suggestive of detachment may also be met with in the last stages of chronic inflammatory processes of the retina and optic nerve. Excluding detachment (they say nothing against glaucoma) they therefore suggest neuro-retinitis, and hold that it was of syphilitic origin on the strength of some facts concerning Milton's health and that of his family. The chief of these are the mortality in Milton's family, and the fact that Milton suffered from joint trouble (affecting the fingers and diagnosed as gout by his physicians). The further proof advanced is that Milton had feeble eyes in his childhood and that his mother's eyes were weak—and also that Milton's oval face suggests congenital syphilis to a physician.

This is remarkable evidence on which to diagnose congenital syphilis. Nothing at all is said of the fact that Milton was one of six children—of whom three survived—and that Milton was the third, the two others who survived being the second and the sixth. The survival of the second, third and sixth does not suggest syphilis, and the death of three out of six children is nothing unusual in mediaeval chronicles and certainly poor evidence for the diagnosis of syphilis. How the fact that Milton's mother had weak eyes is a support for this theory is by no means obvious. Supposedly she was suffering from syphilitic inflammation of the eyes and we are to believe that it was for this that she took to wearing glasses. Such a belief lacks nothing in boldness. The other evidence as to Milton's congenital syphilis is the mortality among his children and grandchildren, and also the fact that his brother lost three children in their childhood. Congenital syphilis with such widespread influences persisting for generations is indeed a remarkable phenomenon. The immediate progeny of a congenital syphilitic usually show no strain of syphilis: in Milton's case his grandchildren were still dying from it. His exceptional qualities were apparently not confined to his writings: the congenital syphilis ascribed to him by Saurat and Cabannes is even more exceptional. One of Milton's daughters and his first two wives died in childbed. This apparently was also due to Milton's congenital syphilis, for these deaths are recorded in the list of catastrophes for which congenital syphilis is the explanation.

The symptoms that Milton describes during the onset of his blindness are said to fit with the suggestion of a disturbance of congenital syphilitic origin. In a world where everything is possible, this of course cannot be ruled out, though most oculists expect a different type of clinical picture for congenital syphilis. Interstitial keratitis and iritis are, with their obvious external lesions, more common conditions in congenital syphilis than lesions which could give rise to obscuration of particular parts of the visual fields and distortion in the appearances of objects. It must be admitted that some—and only some—of the symptoms described by Milton can

John Milton (The Mansell Collection).

be explained on the hypothesis of disseminated choroiditis. But any other chronic lesion would do as well. The fact that Milton's eyes were 'weak' since childhood is important evidence, but in itself no evidence at all that he suffered from congenital syphilis.

Milton's oval face we are also told suggests congenital syphilis. Milton's face must have possessed highly suggestive properties: to his fellow students it suggested the nick-name of the Lady of Christ College,[8] to a contemporary lampooner it suggested 'a horrid monster'; to a modern critic[19, 24] who thinks that Milton was an albino it suggests albinism.[23] And no doubt it has suggested other things to other critics besides Saurat and Cabannes.

Milton's family history is definitely against congenital syphilis and the nature of Milton's eye trouble does not contain one shred of evidence in favour of such a view. Congenital syphilis as the cause of Milton's blindness is not only a far-fetched theory, but one that flies in the face of all established facts. A rather less painfully laboured case could be made out for acquired syphilis—less painfully laboured but no less obviously impossible.

4. ALBINISM

The theory that Milton was an albino is really outside the scope of the present article, for the author of that theory—H. Mutschmann,[19,24] is a professor of literature and not a medical man—does not claim that albinism was the cause of Milton's blindness. He accepts Hirschberg's view that glaucoma was responsible for the final catastrophe.

Mutschmann's views are, however, of interest as they touch upon the nature of the 'natural weakness' of Milton's eyes. It must be added that Mutschmann has no interest in this question apart from the fact that it is part and parcel of a theory of his that Milton was a physical and moral degenerate, and that all his life and work was only a striving after power, that he was a potential criminal inhibited only by his cowardice, and so on and so forth. It is not surprising that Mutschmann should think that some of the accepted views concerning Milton are 'impertinent concoctions' (*eine freche Erfindung*). Those who are interested in the remarkable *tour-de-force* by which all this is 'proved' can refer to the voluminous efforts of their author—both in German and in English.

That Milton was an albino is argued on two lines: evidence is advanced from the biography by Aubrey and this is supported by internal evidence from Milton's writings. Milton, according to Aubrey had brown hair: marginal note makes the brown into 'abrown'; furthermore Milton was 'exceeding faire'. The fact that Milton's hair was 'abrown' means to Mutschmann that it was not brown, that is white. White hair being proved, the 'exceedingly faire' complexion proves albinism. That his eyes according to the same biographer (who knew Milton) were a 'darke gray' does not upset Mutschmann very much. That Milton had white hair is further proved to Mutschmann's satisfaction by the reddish tinge of his hair seen in some portraits.

The fact that the earliest life of Milton extant, the one ascribed to Nathan Paget, speaks of Milton as having a ruddy complexion and light brown hair is not even mentioned by Mutschmann. On the 'evidence' that Mutschmann has collected he has reared a colossal superstructure of albinism—and as if it were a natural corollary—of physical and moral degeneracy. Milton's albinism is further proved by reference to his writings from which Mutschmann is satisfied that Milton among other phobias had photophobia and was a nyctalope. On the literary merits of this criticism Mutschmann can be left to the recognised authorities on Milton. He has been dealt with faithfully by Stern, the veteran Milton scholar of Germany, amongst others. Here it is only necessary to point out that there is no disproving Mutschmann's evidence as to Milton's albinism, for there is no evidence to consider. What he says about Milton's appearance are not facts but distortions.

Mutschmann has drawn up an elaborate chronology of Milton's works on the hypothesis that Milton betrays his photophobia in his writings up till 1644. In that year he suffered his 'first attack of glaucoma' and that 'would have the effect of suddenly reducing the sensibility of the retina so considerably, as to cause the disappearance of existing photophobia without however completely destroying the sight.'

Glaucoma which acts by 'suddenly reducing the sensibility of the retina' cannot but be acute glaucoma. And unless Milton had acute glaucoma in both eyes in 1644 (and there is no evidence of involvement of the right eye till much later) we must believe that it was only the left eye that was albinotic. As albinism is a generalised disorder, albinism confined to one eye is a decidedly interesting subject.

DISCUSSION

It is clear that the most important document available, the letter to Philaras, does not in itself solve the problem of Milton's blindness. The two views deserving attention that have been advanced on the strength of this letter are that the blindness was due to glaucoma, or to detached retina. The reasons for rejecting glaucoma have been advanced: glaucoma only explains the broad outlines but not the details that we have, and some of these details go decidedly against glaucoma.

Against detachment the arguments are that no satisfactory proof is advanced by the exponent of this theory that Milton was myopic and that he ignores the question of iridescent rings of which Milton speaks. As to these rings it has already been pointed out that they do not by any means always argue for glaucoma, and certainly cannot be taken to mean glaucoma when as in this case all the other symptoms described by Milton may therefore be taken to mean detachment if the pre-existing condition of myopia can be proved. The graphic description of obscuration of the left side of the left eye and ultimately complete failure of that eye, strongly suggest detachment leading to disorganisation of the eye, particularly if taken together with the description of the failure later on of the right eye. 'I observed some months before my sight was wholly gone that objects I looked at, without myself moving seemed all to swim.' Perception of light and some functioning retina remained, as it almost invariably does in such cases: 'The darkness which is perpetually before me by night as well as by day, seems always nearer to a whitish than to a blackish, and such that when the eye rolls itself, there is admitted as through a small chink, a certain little trifle of light.'

It is, of course, possible that the right eye was suffering from a progressive inflammatory choroido-retinitis which would explain most of the symptoms, though hardly the swimming of objects looked at. The difficulty of detachment as a diagnosis in the case of the right eye is that it was 'failing perceptibly and gradually through a period of three years.' Detachment is usually abrupt in onset though the deterioration it causes is progressive for a considerable time before complete blindness sets in. In view of the fact that the swimming of objects only set in some months before the sight was wholly gone, and at the time when 'inverterate mists' made their

appearance, it is not unlikely that detachment was the culmination
of active myopic degeneration which had been going on for some
years.

MYOPIA AND DETACHMENT

Abrupt detachment in the left and detachment in the right following
on progressive myopic changes in that eye seems to be a likely
diagnosis on the strength of Milton's letter, and not an unlikely
diagnosis from what we know of myopia. It therefore remains to
consider what evidence there is for the view that Milton was myopic,
and in attempting to establish myopia it is not at all necessary to
presuppose a high degree of myopia, for detachment is as prone—
if not more so—to attack the medium myope as the high myope.
This brings us back to the question of the natural weakness of his
eyes to which Milton testifies. Was this natural weakness myopia?

On the available evidence it is not possible to come to a definite
conclusion, but there is a strong presumptive evidence that it was
indeed myopia which was the cause of his weak eyes and led ultimately to his blindness. It should, however, be added that though
the presence of myopia makes the diagnosis of retinal detachment
more probable, the absence of myopia does not exclude it. Bilateral
detachment in eyes devoid of myopia is not particularly uncommon.
The evidence that Milton was a myope comes from varying sources:

(i) MILTON'S HEREDITY

Milton's mother 'had very weak eies and used spectacles presently
after she was thirty years old.' We have no nearer definition of her
defect than this statement. It could not have been astigmatism for
which she took to glasses, for an astigmatic correction was first
made use of by Airy in 1827. Thirty is too young an age for presbyopia, so that the choice is left between hypermetropia and myopia,
and of these myopia is much the more likely condition, for hypermetropia rarely gives rise to such a severe visual defect as is implied
in Aubrey's statement. Of course it is possible that the 'weak eies'
were not visually defective but subject to chronic conjunctivitis or
blepharitis, but it is unlikely that glasses were worn for such conditions at that time. 'Weak eies' in all probability means a high
degree of myopia.

There is also a strong probability that Milton's father was a
myope. Aubrey says that he could read without glasses at eighty-

four. Only a myope can do that, though the myopia need not be of the axial type. It is just possible that this myopia of Milton's father at eighty-four was not of the axial type but due to incipient cataract. But again axial myopia is the more likely.

Thus if Milton's father and mother were both myopic, it is not at all unlikely that Milton too was a myope, for the strong hereditary tendency in myopia is well known.

(ii) MILTON'S HABITS

Milton tells us that his eyes were 'naturally weak'. Whether this weakness means in Milton's case what it meant in his mother's we do not know, for there is no record of Milton taking to glasses. We know he was an ardent student from his early days, with brilliant scholastic attainments; he shunned society and was not popular with his gay fellow-students. He was what is colloquially known as a 'bookworm,' exhibiting all the characteristics popularly ascribed to the spectacled student. His habits are in agreement with the suggestion that he was of myopic stock and that the weakness of his eyes was indeed myopia.

(iii) THE INTERNAL EVIDENCE FROM MILTON'S WRITINGS

The support based on the internal evidence of Milton's writings comes from a disinterested source. N. P. Squires[20] in analysing Milton's treatment of Nature shows—and this is generally accepted —that Milton was none too good an observer, and the following extract gives the conclusions reached on the careful analysis he makes of Milton's references to Nature.

'This lack of intimate knowledge sometimes caused him to make mistakes as in his allusion to the pine tree in 'Paradise Regained', IV, 416–17, and in 'Lycidas' where he groups together flowers of different seasons which could not possibly be found in bloom at the same time. Another fact which forces us to this conclusion is his lack of fine distinctions in colours. He mentions green and blue, but never refers to their various shades. In Wordsworth, for instance, we find not only green, but olive green, pear green, dark green, etc., not only blue, but pale blue, dark blue, sable blue, black blue, etc.

'These failures to be exact may possibly have been occasioned by near sightedness. We do not have a record that Milton was thus afflicted, but we do know that he had some trouble with his eyes, that he strained them by overstudy in his youth, and that they were a continual source of anxiety to him. Excessive study in youth nowadays usually tends to myopia,[25] and so it is not unreasonable to suppose that this was the nature of Milton's ailment. The effect of myopic vision is to render outlines indistinct, and hence to make impressions indefinite. It is impossible to distinguish one sort of bird from another or one sort of tree from another, altho' the observer is fully aware that a bird or tree is before him. This seems to have been precisely the case with Milton. He mentions definite birds very rarely, except the nightingale and this is always spoken of in connection with its singing at night, when of course it could not be *seen*. The failure to make nice distinctions in colour also could be explained by the same theory, as could the fact that he saw three colours in the rainbow. Another bit of evidence is his fondness for bright glittering objects.'

One piece of autobiographical detail must be considered as going against the conclusion that Milton was a myope, and this is Milton's statement supported by his first biographer that he wore a sword and had skill in using it. It must, however, be remembered that these statements were written in defence against attacks on Milton's character, and to wear a sword and use it was a necessary equipment of a gentleman's character in those days. Besides, a myope of medium degree, as Milton probably was, might very well be able to use a sword, for sword play after all takes place at fairly close quarters, and should not be impossible to one not very highly myopic.

But all these speculations are only about the man and not about the creator of the polysyllabic splendour of 'Paradise Lost'. To attempt to trace the influence of Milton's eyesight and of his blindness on his life and work is an idle task, for Milton, whose soul was like a star that dwelt apart, is like Shakespeare, free—though others abide our question.

CHAPTER 7

Swift's Deafness and His Last Illness

T. G. Wilson

In August 1846, Dr. W. Mackenzie, a well-known Glasgow oculist, wrote to the Editor of the *Dublin Quarterly Journal of Medical Science*, raising the question of Dean Swift's last illness. At this time the journal was edited by Dr. (afterwards Sir) William Wilde, the famous Dublin surgeon who for a long time was principally remembered as an archaeologist and as the father of Oscar Wilde, but who is now considered by competent authorities to have been one of the greatest pioneers of otology in this country.

The general opinion at this time was that Swift lived, as he died, insane, decaying at the top first like the famous elm he saw while walking outside Dublin. It was also thought that the attacks of giddiness and deafness which he suffered from youth upwards, eventually brought on lunacy and death. Wilde went into the subject very thoroughly, and eventually published a book about it, which went into two editions. His conclusions were erroneous, but the book is important, as in it all the data are marshalled in such a careful and complete manner that it has been the standard work of reference ever since, in so far as the signs and symptoms of Swift's diseases are concerned.

The next publication of importance was written by Bucknill in 1882. This was a scholarly article, and is on the whole correct, but as Bucknill did not examine Wilde's evidence at its source, he also fell into errors, which will be described later.

Since then many full-length biographies of Swift have been published by non-medical authors. Six have been written in the last few years alone. In almost all of them considerable attention has been given to the Dean's health, but they have all made many gross mistakes, and many different diagnoses. The chronic illness from which he suffered throughout life has been ascribed to many causes.

Stephen Gwynn has diagnosed otosclerosis. Others call it 'epileptic vertigo'. It has been ascribed to over-eating, sexual excesses, and drink. The theory that the Dean was insane is still held. Hone and Rossi, who go deeply into the subject, have the correct label for the disease, but their account is full of inaccuracies and curious errors. For instance, they say that it is easier to transmit degeneration from the left ear to the right than *vice versa*. I have, therefore, attempted to clear the matter up, as far as our present knowledge goes.

For this purpose, I propose to divide the patient's history into two periods. The first of these is before, the second after, he had reached the age of 72.

CLINICAL HISTORY

UP TO THE AGE OF SEVENTY-TWO

Giddiness and deafness

We can take the history of the first period from Swift's own writings. Disregarding intercurrent affection such as shingles and gout, most of his complaints refer to *giddiness* and *deafness*, which attacked him intermittently, and sometimes were accompanied by sickness. He himself ascribed these symptoms to eating too many apples, in the year when he was twenty-two or twenty-three. Writing to Mrs. Howard, he said: 'About two hours before you were born, I got my *giddiness* by eating a hundred golden pippins at a time, and when you were five years and a quarter old, bating two days, having made a fine seat about twenty miles farther in Surry where I used to read— and there I got my *deafness*; and these two friends have visited me, one or other every year since: and being old acquaintance, have now thought fit to come together.'

On 1st September 1711, he says: 'My head is pretty well, only a sudden turn at any time makes me feel giddy for a moment, and sometimes it feels very stuffed, but if it grows no worse I can bear it very well.'

His deafness was first in one ear. 'Did I ever tell you that the Lord Treasurer hears ill with the left ear, just as I do? . . . I dare not tell him that I am so too, for fear that he should think I counterfeited to make my court.'

On 24th October 1711: 'I had a little turn in my head this morning,

Dean Swift by C. Willison (The Mansell Collection).

which though it did not last above a minute, yet, being of the true sort, has made me as weak as a dog all this day.'

On the 10th May 1712, he wrote: 'My left hand is very weak, and trembles, but my right side has not been touched.' This is puzzling: paresis, or tremors, of the limbs is not a sign of Ménière's disease. It was hardly due to a stroke, as Swift lived another thirty-four years.

In 1720 we get definite confirmation of the intermittent nature of Swift's trouble. 'What if I should add, that once in five or six weeks I am deaf for three or four days.' Melancholy and depression always made him worse, and after the death of Vanessa he suffered for weeks.

In 1727 he had an attack brought on by 'cider, fruit and champagne'. This time he found the disease very hard to shake off. 'I believe this giddiness is the disorder that will finally get the better of me,' he wrote. He moved to Pope's house at Twickenham, but now Stella was dying of tuberculosis, and the sad account of her last illness quite unmanned him: 'my weakness, my age, my friendship, will bear no more.'

Later he said: 'I walk like a drunken man, and am deafer than ever you knew me. . . .' This is a remark any doctor might hear in his consulting room, and it is typical of Ménière's disease.

On 29th June 1731, he wrote to Gay: 'The giddiness I was subject to, instead of coming seldom and violent, now constantly attends me more or less, though in a more peaceful manner, yet such as will not qualify me to live amongst the young and healthy.' And again, in 1733 he writes: 'I am just recovering two cruel indispositions of giddiness and deafness after seven months. I have got my hearing; but the other evil still hangs about me, and, I doubt, will never leave me until I leave it.' Here, one notes, a chronic giddiness remains, but the deafness has disappeared, although the illness had first occurred forty-three years before.

The following year Swift visited Howth Castle, and while there was unlucky enough to suffer an attack. One of the worst features of Ménière's disease is the way in which attacks come at the most inopportune moments, and extremely suddenly. On this occasion the Dean had to lie down for two hours, but he was then able to proceed back to Dublin, so that evidently it was not a particularly bad attack. About this time he complained that he was 'never wholly free from giddiness and weakness, and sickness in his stomach.'

Swift was now getting old and gloomy, more eccentric and

depressed. In his own words: '*vertiginosus, inops, surdus, male gratus amicis.*'

Shortly after this he wrote the famous verses on his own death:

> 'For poetry he's past his prime
> He takes an hour to find a rhyme.'

> 'See how the Dean begins to break:
> Poor gentleman, he droops apace,
> You plainly find it in his face;
> That old vertigo in his head
> Will never leave him till he's dead;
> Besides, his memory decays,
> He recollects not what he says.'

In 1736 Swift suffered another severe Ménière attack and, writing to Pope, said that he was unable even to make conversation. In November of this year, he wrote his last literary work, the 'Legion Club'. It was directed against the Irish Parliament, and a more savage satire was never written. It is a conclusive proof that his brain was still fully active when he was almost 70 years old.

It was a bitter attack on the Irish House of Commons in College Green:

> 'Not a bowshot from the college,
> Half the globe from sense and knowledge;'

He would like to see it totally destroyed:

> 'Could I from the building's top
> Hear the ratt'ling thunder drop,
> While the devil upon the roof
> (If the devil be thunder-proof)
> Should with poker fiery-red
> Crack the stones, and melt the lead;
> Drive them down on ev'ry scull,
> While the den of thieves is full;
> Quite destroy that harpies' nest,
> How might then our isle be blest!'

As it was difficult to destroy the house, however, it should be converted into a mad-house:

> 'Let the club have right to dwell
> Each within his proper cell,

With a passage left to creep in,
And a hole above for peeping.
Let them, when they once get in,
Sell the nation for a pin;
While they sit a-picking straws,
Let them rave of making laws;
While they never hold their tongue,
Let them dabble in their dung.'

In spite of old age, the labyrinthine attacks still troubled him. 'My giddiness and deafness are more frequent,' he wrote in 1737. In the same year he wrote to Dr. Sheridan a letter which gives us a most valuable key to his deafness. 'In England, before I was 20, I got a cold which gave me a deafness I could never clear myself of'— a phrase which seems to point to a deafness from a Eustachian or middle-ear catarrh. This idea is confirmed by the fact that Swift had a marked deflection of the septum, with considerable deformity of the vomer. 'Although it came but seldom and lasted but a few days, yet my left ear has never been well since.' 'When the deafness comes on,' he adds, 'I can hear with neither ear, except it be a woman with a treble, or a man with a counter-tenor. This unqualifies me for any mixed conversation: and the fits of deafness increase.' This is the typical complaint of sufferers from high tone deafness.

Insanity

Let us now examine the evidence brought forward to prove that Swift was insane. It is well known that he always dreaded the onset of mental disease, but that does not mean that he ever experienced it. We may disregard his last five years of senility.

What do we find? That there is, in fact, no evidence whatever. Swift was, it is true, neurotic and eccentric all his life, a prey to gloomy forebodings, a valetudinarian constantly preoccupied with his health. But nowhere in his biographies, or in his own writings, is there any indication of insanity whatever. He did, it is true, chase his friends around the Deanery in order to exercise himself, but this is no evidence of lunacy. He did, also, commit a public assault upon the Revd. Dr. Wilson, one of his chapter, but from all accounts the Revd. Dr. Wilson richly deserved it. The popular idea that Swift was mad seems to originate from the biographies by Johnson and by Sir Walter Scott. Both these *Lives* contain phrases such as 'madness . . . compounded of rage and fatuity', and 'frantic fits of passion', but neither adduces any real evidence to show that Swift's mind was diseased. Swift, therefore, was not mad. The idea seems to have arisen in the first instance from Swift's habit of referring to his attacks of giddiness, deafness and sickness as 'fitts' . . . 'fitts of deafness, a small giddy fitt and swimming in head—M.D. and God help me.'

Epilepsy

This constant talk of 'fitts' also led to the theory being put forward that the Dean suffered from epilepsy. There is nothing degrading in suffering from the disease which afflicted St. Paul, Caesar and Mohamed; but Swift was no epileptic. It is quite obvious, from reading his journals, that he used the word as we would use 'attack.' For instance, he says: 'Hearing that my ill stomach, and a giddiness I was subject to, forced me in some of those fits to take a spoonful of usquebagh, he sent me a dozen bottles.'

The cause of his deafness

Wilde dismissed the idea of epilepsy, and put forward his own theory that the trouble was due to 'cerebral congestion' of a periodic nature. We must remember than Ménière did not describe his classical case until 1861, and that the functions of the labyrinth were still largely unknown. Under the circumstances, Wilde's effort was not bad. Since he wrote, although our knowledge has increased enormously, Swift's symptoms have been attributed to at least three other diseases.

(i) One of these, otosclerosis, suggested by Stephen Gwynn, is obviously wrong, and may be dismissed without further discussion. It would account for the deafness, but for little else.

(ii) The second is syphilitic labyrinthitis. The suggestion that the Dean suffered from syphilis is a hardy perennial. It has been used to explain why he did not marry Stella (if, indeed, he did not). In its congenital form syphilis of the labyrinth causes great destruction of the delicate perceptive mechanism of the ear, and most patients are very deaf when first seen, usually in infancy. But if Swift's ear troubles were due to the spirochaete, the infection was almost certainly acquired. Here we are still in difficulties, for it is very hard to get a clear clinical picture of acquired syphilitic internal otitis.

Syphilis manifests itself in a no less protean fashion in the ear than elsewhere.

There are, however, a number of facts which are against a diagnosis of acquired syphilis:

(*a*) Syphilitic labyrinthitis is usually a late manifestation, although Politzer has recorded a case which occurred on the seventh day. Swift's first symptoms occurred at the age of twenty.

(*b*) In my experience, mainly of cases from the Venereal Diseases Department of Dr. Steevens' Hospital, deafness arising from this cause is not subject to fluctuations in severity. Ground lost is never recovered.

(*c*) Syphilitic deafness is progressive, and in most cases eventually severe in degree. It may progress slowly for a time, and then suddenly become much worse. Swift did not complain of his deafness in his old age nearly as much as he did in earlier life. His giddiness was, perhaps, his most annoying symptom in his old age.

(iii) Ménière's syndrome. This was first suggested as the true disease by Bucknill in 1882, but has been strangely forgotten since. It fits very well. First of all, we have the Dean's gloomy introspective mentality and neurotic temperament, exactly what we have come to expect in these cases. We have the continual linked up attacks of giddiness, deafness, and vomiting, although Swift did not himself realise that these three symptoms were related. After all, why should he? Giddiness is apparently an ocular manifestation, and vomiting an abdominal one, and it was not suspected for a century after Swift's death that the three symptoms were really caused by a single disorder, and that an affection of the internal ear.

In view of the malignant way in which water and 'waterlogging' pursued the Dean, even after his death and burial, it is with regret that one is compelled to discount the possibility that he might have suffered from Barany's syndrome. This condition causes intense vertigo, deafness, and severe headache, and is due to a collection of fluid in the posterior fossa between the cerebellum and the petrous. It is probably caused by a cystic degeneration of the saccus endolymphaticus. It is unlikely to have been the trouble in Swift's case, because it is usually caused, or accompanied, by suppurative middle ear disease, and also because headache was not a prominent feature in Swift's illness.

We return, therefore, to the diagnosis of Ménière's disease. It is interesting to speculate as to the influence of the disease upon his temperament. Would the Dean have had that fierce, extroverted indignation, that savage introspective gloom, without it? If those minute changes were not present in his internal ears would his genius have remained the same, or would his have been the gentler muse of a Barrie or a Lamb? Or, on the other hand, did his temperament affect his disease? We cannot affirm that it did not. Most Ménière subjects are highly strung and nervous, like asthmatics and other allergic subjects. Perhaps if they were not so constituted they might not be susceptible to the disease.

It is quite likely that posterity is profiting by Swift's sufferings, for illness which comes on so suddenly with such extremely unpleasant manifestations is bound to leave an impression, particularly upon a man so stamped with personality as Swift. A disease in which one can fall out of a chair, which may make it necessary to lie prostrate to avoid injury through falling, while a world whirling in giddy circles mingles with a background of violent nausea, will leave its mark on any man. Plunged periodically into this violent illness, and immobilised physically and mentally; gradually crawling back to health only to suffer sudden relapse when he felt fully recovered, it is no wonder the Dean became gloomy and morose. But no Ménière's patient is stupid, and Swift's brain seemed to have been sharpened rather than dulled by his experiences; warped it may have been, but not blunted.

Remedies

His habits of life do not seem to have borne much upon his illness, except in that excitement, or activity in public affairs, tended to bring on his trouble. This he himself fully realised. He also certainly drank more than can have been good for him, particularly in his later days.

His diet he kept very low, at times subsisting on rice and gruel, and cutting out tea, coffee and fruit, of which he was very fond. 'I take no snuff, and will be very regular in eating little, and the gentlest meats. . . . I drink little, miss my glass often, put water in my wine, and go away before the rest.'

He was violently, perhaps fanatically, fond of exercise, riding, rowing, and walking. After he was sixty (1734) he used to pursue his friends round the Deanery, up and down stairs, round tables and from room to room. This was his *Medicina Gymnastica*, and some writers considered it a proof of impaired mentality: I prefer to call it a manifestation of the eccentricity of genius. Many a modern author would do the same, if he could get publicity thereby.

Swift was never a believer in bleeding: 'Fig for your physician and his advice, Madame Dingley. . . . I will trust to temperance and exercise.' He did, however, take many medicines—snuffs, pills, and potions. 'I am deep in pills with assafoetida, and a steel bitter drink. . . . I take eight pills a day, and have taken, I believe, a hundred and fifty already'. He also took, on Arbuthnot's advice, 'cinnabar of antimony and castor, made up into boluses with confect of alkermes.' Another favourite recipe was the 'Tinctura Sacra', which was made up with aloes, cardamon, ginger, and Spanish white wine.

'The physicians are merciless dogs in purging and vomiting,' said Mr. Forde. 'I heartily wish you would try the Bath waters which are allowed to be the best medicine for strengthening the stomach.' But the Spa waters were unsuccessful, for they increased his vertigo and brought on swelling of the legs.

In 1730 he was put on a strict regimen by Dr. Arbuthnot, who advised him to take 'emetics first; then an electuary every morning, chiefly composed of conserve of orange and abysinth, with some tincture of bark'; which latter was to be repeated in the afternoon. Lavender drops, antispasmodics, and bitters all show us that the doctors thought his illness originated in the stomach. 'The liver, spleen and other viscera have had their day since,' said Wilde, 'but in Swift's time all diseases were referred to the stomach.'

THE LAST FIVE YEARS

It is quite clear, therefore, that the Dean, like Martin Luther, was a lifelong sufferer from Ménière's disease, of which the exciting cause was probably Eustachian obstruction caused by a badly deflected septum. It is also clear that no evidence has been brought forward which would even suggest that he was insane before he reached the age of seventy, or that he ever suffered from syphilis. Let us now examine the closing years of his life, from 1740 onwards until the end of 1745.

Swift dreaded the onset of senility. 'I believe I shall say with Horace *non omnis moriar*, for half my body is already spent.' He refused to wear spectacles, and spent the time he should otherwise have occupied in reading in taking violent exercise. 'The truth is,' wrote Delany, 'his spirit was formed with a strong reluctance to submission of any kind; and he battled almost as much with the infirmities of old age as he did with the corruptions of the times. He walked erect; and the constant and free discharges by perspiration, from exercise, kept him free from coughs and rheums, and other offensive infirmities of old age. . . .

'This incessant and intemperate exercise naturally wasted his flesh, and exhausted the oil of his blood, and his lamp of life was then in the condition of an ill-tempered candle, which frets and flames at once, and exhausts itself as it frets.'

After the summer of 1740 Swift gradually sank into a stuporose condition, in which he remained more or less until he died. He made a couple of entries in his account books in 1742, but after this came a final silence. 'His understanding was so much impaired, and his memory so much failed, that he was utterly incapable of conversation. Strangers were not permitted to approach him, and his friends found it necessary to have guardians appointed to take proper care of his person and estate. Early in the year 1742 his reason was totally subverted, and became absolute lunacy.' (Faulkner.)

The Dean had now come very near the end of the journey. He was for the most part bedridden, in

'Second childishness and mere oblivion
Sans teeth, sans eyes, sans taste, sans everything.'

Records of his last three or four years are very scanty. There are, however, two points about his last illness which must be considered, as they have been interpreted by Bucknill as part of the proof of the theory that the Dean had a right-sided hemiplegia. The first is a statement that his food was cut for him. This is contained in a letter of Swift's cousin, Mrs. Whiteway, who says: 'His meat was served up ready cut, and sometimes it would lie an hour on the table before he would touch it.' She adds, however, that he would 'then eat it walking.' The second point is contained in a letter of another cousin, Mr. Deane Swift. 'He endeavoured, with a good deal of pain to find words to speak to me; at last, not being able after many efforts, he gave a heavy sigh, and, I think, was afterwards silent.' Another biographer said: 'He would attempt to speak his mind, but could not recollect words to express his meaning.' From these statements we learn that the Dean suffered from aphasia.

The letters from which these two extracts have been made are the only authentic records of the last three years of Swift's life which have come down to us.

He died on 19th October 1745. His end was 'easy without the least pang or convulsion,' said Lord Orrery. 'He died in very great agony, having been in strong convulsive fits for thirty-six hours before,' said Faulkner, the publisher.

POST-MORTEM EXAMINATIONS AND EXHUMATION

Autopsy

An autopsy was performed by Mr. Whiteway, surgeon to Steevens' Hospital, and nephew of the lady one of whose letters I have just quoted. It was, perhaps, very incomplete, for there is no evidence of the brain having been opened. All that we learn was 'that he opened the skull and found much water in the brain.' Dr. Lyon later commented on 'the sinus of his brain being loaded with water'. Old Brennan, the Dean's servant, who held the basin in which the brain was placed after it was removed, said that 'there was brain mixed with water to such an amount as to fill the basin, and by their quantity to call forth expressions of astonishment from the medical gentlemen engaged in the examination.'

I fear, however, that all this waterlogging of the brain must be dismissed as being due to senile atrophy of the brain. With the advance of age, every cell in our bodies shrinks. The liver, heart, and other viscera become smaller, the skin becomes thin and satiny. The brain withstands this shrinkage longer than the other organs, as might be expected, but in the end the convolutions become narrower, and separated by wide sulci. Since the brain is enclosed in a rigid case which cannot contract, the resulting space becomes filled with fluid. This is what happened in Swift's case.

During the Dean's last illness, the Revd. David Stevens, one of his chapter, several times expressed the desire that Swift should be trephined, because he thought that he suffered from 'water on the brain.' Some years afterwards, several lunatics in Swift's Hospital were trephined on the supposition that their insanity was caused by the cerebrum having become too large for the cranium. This fashion may have been started by the result of the Dean's post-mortem.

The Death Mask

Immediately after the post-mortem examination, a plaster cast or death mask was taken from the face. This mask has been supposed since the earliest days to exhibit peculiarities which, in my opinion, do not exist. As may be seen from the photographs it represents an ordinary-looking elderly man, who is completely edentulous, and closely resembles the late Edgar Wallace. There is no doubt of its authenticity, for the depression across the forehead corresponds exactly with the saw cut in the skull where the calvarium was removed nearly two hundred years ago by Mr. Whiteway. It is almost certainly the cast which Wilde examined, for the two lines of writing across the back of the cast are just as Wilde described them, although we cannot now decipher them even as well as Wilde did, or thought he did. Wilde's transcription was:

'Dean Swift, taken off his . . . . . . the night of his burial, and the f . . . . . . one side larger than the other as in nature . . . . . . Opened before . . . . . . The mould is in pieces.'

The back part of the plaster head is not a cast, but is obviously just finished off 'according to the eye of the artist'. Wilde said the original mask (presumably the mould itself) remained in Trinity College for years until it was accidentally destroyed.

This cast has been examined curiously and minutely by very many people. Sir Walter Scott said: 'In the Museum of Trinity College, Dublin, there is a dark plaster bust, or cast, of Dean Swift. It is an impression taken from the mask applied to the face after death. The expression of countenance is most unequivocally maniacal, and one side of the mouth (the left) horribly contorted downwards, as if convulsed with pain.'

Looking at the mask, I am sure it will be agreed that this is nonsense. There is no 'maniacal' expression whatever—in fact, the face is quite placid and peaceful. Wilde thought Sir Walter had 'greatly exaggerated,' but he said 'there is an evident drag in the left side of the mouth, exhibiting a paralysis of the facial muscles of the right side.'

Wilde thought this the late outcome of the 'apoplectiform cerebral congestion'. Bucknill, however, having made a correct diagnosis of Ménière's disease as the cause of the Dean's earlier troubles, and being left with this supposed facial paralysis as a surplus symptom, naturally linked it with the aphasia and the history of food being served to the Dean ready cut up, and diagnosed a right-sided hemiplegia. Unfortunately, he apparently did not examine the bust for himself. Wilde is well known to have been a meticulously careful and conscientious observer. Nevertheless, he was certainly wrong in this case.

Looking at the cast, at first sight one is inclined to think there may have been a facial paralysis, but of the *left* side, not the right. The upper lip seems to come down lower on this side than on the right, looking at the cast from the front, and this inequality is accentuated by the sideways tilt of the nose. But, viewed from the side, the naso-labial fold and the fold at the corner of the mouth appear to correspond almost exactly on both sides. Then one notices that the jaw is tilted slightly to the right, and that the whole head is not exactly in one straight line with the neck. These points are well illustrated by photographs, and from them I have come to the definite conclusion that the death mask affords no evidence whatever of facial paralysis. If it ever existed it is not shown by the mask. The upper lip, it is true, is at a slightly lower level on the left side than on the right, but this is probably an artefact, produced when the cast was taken from the face originally.

There is, therefore, no proof that the Dean ever had hemiplegia. The aphasia is easily accounted for by senile changes in the brain, which also furnishes a good reason for serving food ready cut up.

Wilde appears to have misled us in another instance in his deductions from the cast. He states that 'the *left* eye is much less full and prominent than the right; in fact it is comparatively sunken and collapsed within the orbit.' He relates this to an attack of what may have been orbital cellulitis from which the Dean suffered in 1742, when 'in one night's time, his left eye swelled to the size of an egg' while he was suffering from crops of boils. I have failed to find any great difference between the two eyes, and here again I think Wilde is at fault. This mistake may also have arisen from the angle at which the head is tilted.

After this cast had been taken, the Dean was buried in his Cathedral, beside his beloved Stella, and there his bones remained undisturbed for almost a hundred years.

Exhumation

The River Poddle is now one of Dublin's invisible underground streams, and its very existence is probably unknown to the majority of Dubliners. In Swift's time and later the Poddle was the cause of much trouble. Floods and insufficient sewers caused frequent floodings of the Cathedral, and made it 'unsafe to assemble in.' This continued until 1835, when it was determined to take steps to end these frequent inundations.

In doing so it was necessary to expose several coffins, amongst them those of Swift and Stella, lying two and a half feet below the flags of the aisle below the monuments to their memory. The opportunity, very properly, was taken to open the coffins.

'All the bones of the skeleton,' said Dr. Houston, 'lay in the position into which they had fallen when deprived of the flesh that enveloped and held them together. The skull, with the calvarium by its side, lay at the top of the coffin; the bones of the neck lay next, and mixed with them were found the cartilages of the larynx, which by age had become converted into bone—as had the rings of the trachea.' Six dorsal vertebrae, and three lumbar, were ankylosed, and several of the costal cartilages were ossified. The whole was obviously the skeleton of an aged man, and we can draw few deductions of interest from it, except that the skull shows considerable deformity of the nasal septum.

In 1835 all forms of quackery were rife, and the phrenologists occupied a sort of fashionable no-man's-land between science and charlatanism. They tried what they could make out of the skull. The result was not impressive. Those parts of the skull marked out as accommodating the organs of *wit* and *comparison* were scarcely developed at all, while the portions assigned to *philo-progenitiveness* and *amativeness* appeared excessive.

The British Association were meeting in Dublin at this time, and here was much festivity and entertaining. Amid this gaiety the bones of both Swift and Stella were carried around the drawing-rooms of Dublin and exhibited as curiosities. In ten days they were returned to their sepulchres. Stella's skull, that 'perfect model of symmetry and beauty' as Wilde called it, was restored to its resting place, and the old bones of Swift were once more placed in that tomb, *ubi indignatio ulterius cor lacerare nequit*. They were returned, that is, all but the ossified thyroid cartilages, which were stolen, and were last heard of in New York.

While the skulls were going the rounds engravings were made of them, and casts taken from both inside and outside Swift's skull.

From the examination of these Wilde made various deductions, none of much importance, beyond noting the great capacity of the cranium, and the small size of the cerebellum. He thought it very like the long-headed skulls of the neolithic Irish aborigines, the Fir Bolgs of the ancient Irish annalists. This is scarcely a compliment, for the book of MacFirbis says, 'everybody who is black, loquacious, lying, tale-telling, or of low and grovelling mind, is of the Fir Bolg descent.' The fact that Swift was of pure English blood did not affect this theory, as skulls of this type are found all over North-West Europe.

Wilde, who was a great archaeologist, was the first to attempt a scientific classification of pre-historic man in Ireland. He followed the ancient annalists in dividing the early invaders into Fir Bolgs, de Danaans, Milesians, and Norsemen. Later it became fashionable to scoff at this tabulation. The latest authority on the subject, Dr. Cecil Martin, now of Toronto, brings forward evidence to show that Wilde and the annalists were substantially correct. He states that there were four successive invasions in pre-history of men whose physical characteristics and time-period agree with the ancient legends. We may as well call them Fir Bolgs, de Danaans, and so forth, for the old names are as good as any, and more pleasing than most.

Wilde's principal contribution, apart from a masterly marshalling of the facts, is his insistence against the general opinion of his day, that Swift, until he became senile, was not insane. In Wilde's day, the average Dubliner was quite convinced that Swift was the first inmate of his own asylum, in spite of the fact that it was not built until after his death. Wilde's theory that Swift and Stella were brother and sister is interesting, but erroneous, and not original with him.

SWIFT'S MEDICAL ATTENDANTS

Eight doctors in particular attended him during his long life. Doctors Cockburn, Sir Patrick Dun, Radcliffe, Arbuthnot, Nicholls, Grattan, Helsham and Whiteway all treated him at different times. One and all, they showed him much kindness, and he appreciated their attentions fully. The chief of them was Arbuthnot, a wise physician, a humorist and scholar, whose friendship he greatly valued. He was a Scot, the Queen's physician, the associate of Pope and Gay, and Swift's lifelong friend. 'Oh! if the world had but a dozen Arbuthnots in it, I would burn my Travels.'

There is one more attendant who must be mentioned. Let Swift do it himself:

> 'When on my sickly couch I lay
> Impatient both of night and day,
> Lamenting in unmanly strains,
> Call'd every power to ease my pains;
> Then Stella ran to my relief

With cheerful face and inward grief,
And, though by Heaven's severe decree
She suffers hourly more than me,
No cruel master could require
From slaves employed for daily hire,
What Stella, by her friendship warm'd
With vigour and delight perform'd:
My sinking spirits now supplies
With cordials in her hands and eyes:
Now with a soft and silent tread
Unheard she moves about my bed.
I see her taste each nauseous draught,
And so obligingly am caught;
I bless the hand from whence they came
Nor dare distort my face for shame.'

CHAPTER 8

Samuel Johnson's Medical Experiences

Humphry Rolleston

To admirers of Samuel Johnson's intellectual attainments it may perhaps seem a gross material sacrilege to discuss his physical disabilities. But it is hardly necessary to labour the argument that every sidelight on this great personality should be explored. Johnson was of opinion that 'all knowledge is of itself of some value. There is nothing so inconsiderable that I would rather know than not,' and spoke freely and in some detail about his ailments. Thus he remarked, 'My diseases are an asthma, a dropsy and, what is less curable, seventy-five,' and in truth he had others some of which fortunately he did not realise. About 1778 he wrote to his old friend Dr. Edmund Hector of Birmingham, 'My health has been from my twentieth year, such as has seldom afforded me a single day of ease,' and his letters to Mrs. Thrale, of which more than two hundred originals were publicly sold in January 1917, contain many references to his bodily ills, and even to his 'sarcocele'.

ATTITUDE TO MEDICINE

Acting on the principle of Terence's line, 'Homo sum; humani nihil a me alienum puto,' Johnson had a catholic interest in his fellows. He was 'a great dabbler in physic', and, being, as E. S. Roscoe says, pre-eminently a teacher of the art of living, he undauntedly invaded its sacred realms, not only by writing the proposals for, and articles now difficult to identity in, Robert James' 'Medicinal Dictionary' (1743) in three folio volumes, but by giving advice, criticising to his friends the treatment their doctors adopted, and, on occasion, by prescribing.

To the rheumatic Bennett Langton he sent a prescription for sulphur, mustard seed, sugar and infusion of the root of lovage. He

Dr. Samuel Johnson, after Reynolds (The Mansell Collection).

instructed Mrs. Thrale about the treatment of her husband in 1780, and in 1771 advised her to take the aperient waters of St. George's Spa in the grounds of 'The Dog and Duck' tavern (hence 'Dog and Duck Waters') on the site recently occupied by Bethlem Hospital' St. George's-in-the-Fields. He also gave Mr. Perkins (Thrale's manager and one of the founders of Barclay and Perkins' brewery) directions for a journey undertaken in 1782 in search of health, laying much stress on banishing all worry and anxiety, for he followed Dr. Frank Nicholls (1699–1778), in believing that mental disturbance would prevent medical treatment from attaining its object. His friend Thomas Lawrence (1711–83), President of the Royal College of Physicians of London (1767–1775) after an attack of hemiplegia and aphasia in March 1782, got edema of his paralysed hand and for this Johnson recommended electrical treatment. In 1783 he did not hesitate to write to a fellow sufferer, the Reverend Dr. J. Taylor, 'It does not appear from your Doctor's prescriptions that he sees to the bottom of your distemper,' and accordingly he went on to dictate that a regulated diet and in particular milk were more likely to be beneficial than physic. He recommended Miss Boothby to take a special mixture made from powdered dry orange peel for her dyspepsia, and, though a layman, was in advance of his medical contemporaries in disapproving of routine blood letting.

After his attack of paralysis and loss of speech, blisters were applied to the back and neck, and he 'compelled the apothecary to make his salve according to the Edinburgh Dispensatory, that it might adhere better; I have now two on my own prescription.' When at Montrose in 1773 and in need of medicine he wrote out the prescription in technical characters. On 11th December 1784, two days before his death, his legs were incised for dropsy, Johnson, always willing to suffer pain if he could thereby obtain relief, up-braided his medical friends in attendance for undue anxiety about their professional reputation; they included the famous William Heberden, the elder (1710–1801), whom on a previous occasion he had sent for as 'Ultimus Romanorum, the last of the learned physicians,' but now reproached as 'timidorum timidissimus'.

Of the words connected with medicine in his Dictionary, C. W. Burr has given an interesting account, and after quoting Johnson's definition of a surgeon, 'One who cures by manual operation: one whose duty is to act in external maladies by the direction of the physician,' adds the comment, 'Some physicians think it would be a proper penance for professional conceit if modern surgeons were compelled to read this definition daily.' The anonymous author of a pamphlet, ascribed to John Callander, the Scottish Antiquary, and printed in Edinburgh, entitled 'Deformities of Dr. Samuel Johnson Selected from his Works' fell foul of nearly everything Johnson wrote, including the medical words in the Dictionary; but this critic rather overreached himself in commenting on the definition of tympany as 'a kind of obstructed flatulence, that swells the body like a drum', in the following words, 'Flatulence is not inserted, but flatulency is said to be "windiness; fulness of wind"'. And what does he mean by an obstructed fulness of wind, or by his elegant simile of a drum.'

Johnson's acquaintance with medical men was extensive, ranging from the President of the College of Physicians, Heberden, Percivall Pott (1714–88) Master of the Corporation of Surgeons (1765) to Robert Levett, who early in life took a liking to surgery, and as a waiter in a Paris café was by the good offices of the medical clients enabled to walk the hospitals, and was for thirty-six years a member of Johnson's queerly assorted and somewhat quarrelsome household; he had a practice 'in physic among the lower people' from Marylebone to Houndsditch. The gratuitous services of Johnson's medical advisors engendered a very high opinion of the self-sacrificing generosity of the profession which he freely expressed on many occasions. It is noteworthy that medical men were well represented in the Ivy Lane Club of which he was the moving spirit and dictator, and that he defined a club as 'an assembly of good fellows meeting under certain conditions.' On the other hand in *The Idler* of 5th August 1758 he did not manifest any enthusiasm for experimental physiology in the reflections that:

Among the inferior professors of medical knowledge, is a race of wretches whose lives are only varied by varieties of cruelty, whose favourite amusement is to nail dogs to tables and open them alive . . . The anatomical novice tears out the living bowels of an animal, and styles himself physician, prepares himself by familiar cruelty for that profession which he is to exercise upon the tender and helpless . . . I know not, that by living dissections any discovery has been made by which a single malady is more easily cured.

This is very sad from such a future friend of the profession, but no doubt his tender heart for animal suffering was responsible for language which we expect from modern anti-vivisectionists.

When corresponding with his medical friends on his own ailments Johnson did so in Latin; this custom made a rather unfortunate start: in 1729 Dr. Samuel Swinfen, his godfather and probably the first doctor he consulted about his mental depression, was so struck with the ability of Johnson's exposition that he showed the letter to others and thus brought down on his head the patient's wrathful indignation at a breach of professional conduct. In his final illness he kept an account from 6th July to 8th November 1784 in Latin of his symptoms under the title 'Aegri Ephemeris'. Johnson had definite views on medical conduct; thus he insisted that a doctor should always tell his patient the truth, and that it was wrong to deceive a sick man for fear of alarming him. When he was on his deathbed he insisted on having the truth from Dr. Richard Brocklesby.

THE MAJOR DISORDERS

The most prominent features in his medical history were a lifelong tendency to melancholia, recurrent asthma in his latter years, an attack of right-sided hemiplegia with aphasia and slight agraphia, and finally dropsy.

MENTAL DEPRESSION

Mental depression, probably inherited with other characters from his father, who was of 'a large and robust body and of a strong and active mind but was addicted to a vile melancholy', pursued him throughout life, becoming intensified from time to time. In 1729, when twenty years of age, he was so seriously affected that he often walked the thirty-two miles from Lichfield to Birmingham and back in the hope of relief; in 1764, when 55 years old he suffered severely, and this recurred on and off, there being special notes in Boswell's *Life* about depression in 1766, 1768, 1773, 1776, and 1777. His dreadful bouts of melancholy were accompanied by remorse for venial or fancied sins and by fear of madness or of death; Dr. Samuel Swinfen's singularly injudicious remark made to him at the impressionable age of twenty that the melancholia would probably terminate in madness was most harmful, for it seems to have left a lasting impression, and by autosuggestion to have been responsible for the dread of insanity. He fought the infliction courageously by work, exercise, and other methods of distraction, especially conversation, which he definitely distinguished from mere talk.

In addition to these remedies he advised Boswell and other perhaps more genuine sufferers from what the great George Cheyne called the 'English malady', to be moderate in food and drink and especially to avoid alcohol at night. Johnson, it must be admitted, did not consistently set this example: sometimes most abstemious, he was at other times a voracious eater and copious drinker, and when not a total abstainer would act on his maxim 'Claret for boys, port for men, brandy for heroes,' preferring the latter as it did its work (of intoxication) most rapidly, and so, as he said, enabled him 'to get rid of myself; to send myself away.' He well described his disposition in the words 'abstinence is as easy to me as temperance would be difficult.' His strength of mind in becoming a teetotaler when advised after illness to do so was remarkable; from 1736 to 1757 and for the last twenty years of his life, except on special occasions, he confined himself to water, lemonade, and tea. It is, however, rather startling to find him described by his admirer the Reverend J. Hay as the first total abstainer.

Johnson's love of society was thus a means of getting free from his own thoughts and depression, for he felt that 'the great business of life was to escape from himself', and, as Sir Joshua Reynolds said, 'Solitude to him was a horror'; thus when at Brighton in 1782 with Mrs. Thrale and Fanny Burney he rather ungallantly explained why he accompanied them to a ball by the resigned dictum, 'It cannot be worse than being alone.' His frankly expressed fear of death not because of annihilation or of pain, for, as Hollins says, there never lived a man more fearless of pain; it was hell that he dreaded. This has been thought to be morbid, but perhaps his courage in speaking freely and his downright manner, for example in the statement that the whole of his life is 'but keeping away the thoughts of death,' may have led to an exaggerated impression of his real mental attitude.

Psychological studies of Johnson have naturally not been wanting. As early as 1854 Vieillard and Dumont dedicated a brief memoir on obsessions and hypochondriasis to Johnson as a life-long victim, and in 1857 Dumont wrote a feuilleton 'Sur l'état pathologique de Samuel Johnson' dealing rather fantastically with the morbid psychological aspects which he discovered in Johnson and explaining them by early struggles with the adverse conditions of disease, destitution and disappointment. Dumont also analysed his own prolonged sufferings from *névrose cérébrale* in a remarkable volume of 600 pages (*Testament medicale, philosophique et litéraire*) which has been compared with J. J. Rousseau's *Confessions*.

ASTHMA

In 1712, when two and one-half years old, he caught cold and had a bad cough on the way back from London where he was touched for the King's Evil or tuberculous glands in the neck; but otherwise there is not any record of respiratory trouble until 1755 when at the age of forty-six he had laryngitis and was bled three times to 36 ounces. There is then an interval of seventeen years, until 1772, when he had a winter cough which recurred in 1774 and in February 1777, his breathing in the last attack being so much embarrassed that he was bled to 36 oz. in three days,[1] and indeed repeated this on his own account by opening the venesection wound. After further attacks in 1778 he improved, and on 18th June 1779 wrote that he had got rid of the 'convulsions' in his chest which had troubled him for twenty years. But in the winter of 1781–1782 he was much troubled by asthma, and in spite of his objection to routine venesection was bled three times in February; for the remainder of his life he was frequently laid low with attacks described under the name of asthma; in the winter of 1783–84 this, combined with edema of the feet and legs, kept him in the house for many weeks. In 1783 he began on medical advice to take opium, with great relief, and at one time the dose had risen to 3 grains daily; but when a few days before his death he extracted the hopeless prognosis from Dr. Brocklesby he gave up the struggle and all medicine, including opiates.

Though speculation is tempting, it is difficult to decide about the nature of his asthma. In 1772 Johnson may have had bronchitis with asthma as a result from bacterial sensitisation, and the interval of freedom in 1780, followed in the winter of 1781–82 and for the rest of his life by difficulty in breathing, might conceivably mean that the character of the asthma had changed or become mixed and complicated by the addition of renal or cardiac asthma, possibly of both. As he almost certainly had granular kidneys, a dilating heart and emphysema, there is an organic basis for asthmatic paroxysms of more than one category.

HEMIPLEGIA AND APHASIA

On 16th June 1783 Johnson sat without undue fatigue for his portrait (which he afterwards called 'a grimy ghost') to Miss Frances Reynolds, sister of Sir Joshua, and in the evening was very comfortable and cheerful; but at 3 next morning he woke, sat up, and after a feeling of confusion and indistinctness in his head lasting about half a minute had the alarming shock of finding himself aphasic. In his fear that his mind would be affected, he prayed that however his body might be afflicted his understanding should be spared; and, much like Sir Walter Scott in similar circumstances, tested his mental capabilities by translating his prayer into Latin; this brought comfort, for though the lines were not very good he recognised this and made them easily, so that he was assured that his faculties were unimpaired. As 'wine has been celebrated for the production of eloquence' he took 2 drams but without effect on the aphasia, though he dropped off to sleep. When seen by Heberden and Brocklesby there was facial weakness on the right side, but the hemiplegia must have been slight, for next day he wrote, 'Though God stopped my speech, he left me my hand.' There was, however, some agraphia, for he added, 'in penning this note I had some difficulty; my hand I know not why, made wrong letters.' Recovery was rapid and complete, and these symptoms never recurred. Whether the attack was due to a small hemorrhage or thrombosis cannot be settled, as Johnson's brain was not examined; but a small vascular lesion cannot be excluded.

DROPSY

Dropsy was first noticed in June 1783 by Sir Lucas Pepys (1742–1830), who was afterwards described by J. F. Payne as having 'proceeded with unvarying success along the path of honour as hospital physician, society physician, and court physician.' Pepys was driven to expostulate with his strong-willed patient, saying, 'Sir, if you were tractable I would prescribe for you.' In September he had a hydrocele, like his contemporary John Wesley (1703–1791), which did not greatly concern him until a puncture drew blank and a diagnosis of a solid testicular growth or sarcocele was made by

Percivall Pott in consultation with William Cruikshank (1745–1800) and excision, or in Johnson's own phraseology 'amputation', recommended. Cruikshank, however, was more afraid than the patient of the operative shock, and during the delay 'the sarcocele ran off at an orifice made for mere experiment' as Johnson wrote to Reverend Dr. J. Taylor.

In the following October the edema extended to the thighs and in February 1784 a further increase after a severe attack of asthma was so extensive that Johnson commissioned Boswell to obtain the opinion of five leaders of the profession in Edinburgh: Sir Alexander Dick, Drs. Gillespie, William Cullen, John Hope and Alexander Monro *secundus*, who were at a disadvantage in giving an opinion without seeing the patient or consulting with those in attendance. They unanimously recommended squills, which Johnson took with vigor; the only other prescription given, as far as is known, was for rhubarb, then a rare and highly priced drug, from the garden of the octogenarian, Sir Alexander Dick. This, Boswell was to convey to London; but whether or not Johnson took it remains uncertain.

It was perhaps due to the seniority of the Edinburgh consultants that digitalis[2] was not recommended, for it had appeared in the Edinburgh Pharmacopoeia of 1783 after Dr. Stokes of Stourbridge in 1779 had brought before the Medical Society of Edinburgh the results obtained by Withering who, however, did not bring out his 'Account of Foxglove and its Medicinal Uses with Practical Remarks on Dropsy and Other Diseases' until 1785. Hutchison suggests that digitalis may have been the stock in trade responsible for the reputation of curing dropsy enjoyed by an irregular practitioner called Dallaway, but Johnson, though urged by a friend, declined to consult him, saying that it was too late. Irregular practitioners did not appeal to him, for he spoke of John Taylor (1703–1772), the notorious quack in eye diseases, as the most ignorant man he ever knew. He, however, had such a firm belief in squills that on one occasion he gave himself an overdose with unpleasant results, and thereafter asked Heberden's advice before dosing himself.

About 16th March, after a day of solitary prayer, humiliation and fasting, he had a urinary crisis, passing 20 pints of urine, and becoming free from the dropsy which had kept him indoors for one hundred and twenty-nine days; this he ascribed to prayer rather than treatment. For a time he was so much improved that in June he went to Oxford and travelled about, visiting Ashbourne and Lichfield; probably as the effect of these exertions on a tired and much tried heart the dropsy began to return, and, though controlled by drugs and rest until November, then progressively advanced so that he was obviously nearing his end. On 11th December the edema was so enormous that his legs were incised by 'the sweet-blooded' William Cruikshank, but Johnson thought so inadequately that on the morning of his death he got a lancet from his negro servant Francis Barber and cut more deeply so that some 10 oz. of blood came away.

NECROPSY

The question has been raised why a post-mortem examination of his body was made, and it has been suggested that it was thought advisable to obtain evidence that death was due to natural causes, because, as a result of his action in incising his legs on the morning of the day he died, rumours got about that he had committed suicide.

The necropsy was carried out by James Wilson (1725–1821) in the presence of Herberden and other notabilities. Wilson's account, the holograph of which is now at the Royal College of Physicians, has been published on several occasions. In the chest the examination showed abnormalities of the lungs, a heart 'exceedingly large and strong', and valves of the aorta which were beginning to ossify. In the abdomen there was a stone (about the size of a pigeon's egg) in the gallbladder, the pancreas was 'remarkably enlarged' and the right kidney was 'almost entirely destroyed' with the left kidney 'tolerably good'. The skull was not opened.

The interpretation of these morbid changes would appear to be longstanding high blood pressure with subsequent renal disease (chronic interstitial nephritis), the kidneys showing an excessive degree of cystic change. In Leslie Stephen's life of Johnson in the *Dictionary of National Biography* the kidneys are said to have been granular, a deduction which seems highly probable, and very likely may have been suggested by the late Sir Norman Moore, who was a friend of Leslie Stephen's, and was closely associated with the *Dictionary of National Biography* from its start. Apart from the commencing 'ossification' of the aortic valves, there is not any direct evidence of general arterial change which in some degree would be expected in a healthy man (and this Johnson was not) of 75. The exceedingly 'large and strong' heart without any mention of valvular disease, except of the aortic segments, points to high blood pressure and renal disease.

The condition of the peritoneum, and especially the cartilaginous feel of the spleen, probably due to chronic capsulitis, may be regarded as the result of the simple chronic peritonitis that may accompany chronic renal disease and arterial degeneration. The enlargement of the pancreas was probably due to engorgement of cardiac origin.

The description of the lungs admirably fits emphysema which would be largely explained as the result of the asthmatic attacks.

OTHER ASPECTS

TUBERCULOUS GLANDS

As already mentioned, at the age of two and one half, on the advice of Sir John Floyer (1649–1734) of Lichfield (whom he afterwards, perhaps for his own comfort, spoke of as having 'panted on to ninety' with asthma), he was touched for the King's Evil, or tuberculous glands in the neck, by Queen Anne at St. James's Palace on 30th March 1712; and together with two hundred others was among the last to go through this form of treatment, effective, if at all, by suggestion. But it was a failure in his case, perhaps because he was of too tender an age to be sufficiently impressed; for the scars of tuberculous abscesses were prominent and disfiguring, and according to Boswell 'hurt his visual nerves so much that he did not see at all with one of his eyes, though its appearance was little different from that of the other.'

IMPAIRED VISION

Like many literary men, and especially Samuel Pepys, he suffered much from impaired vision; thus Fanny Burney spoke of him as looking at books on the shelves of her father's library and 'almost touching the backs of them with his eyelashes as he read their titles.' His short sight would explain his remarkable lack of interest in pictures, sculpture and architecture, and has been said, though this seems unlikely, to render it probable that he never saw his wife's face. According to the late Sir Frederick Treves, the cause of his visual defect was leucomatous change in the corneae following tuberculous keratitis, which may be correlated with the tuberculous glands in the neck. In spite of treatment of the corneal ulceration by a seton in the neck, the sight of the left eye was entirely lost.

The question whether or not there was in addition the factor of an uncorrected error of refraction may reasonably be raised, for he was markedly myopic and did not wear spectacles (invented about the end of the 13th century). It may be mentioned that Johnson appears to have been unduly sensitive on this point, for he vigorously resented as the acme of rudeness being called shortsighted by the Reverend Dr. Thomas Percy, Bishop of Dromore, and was displeased with his friend Sir Joshua Reynolds for painting him in 1778 with his pen close to this eye and so emphasising his defect. It is noteworthy that in 1756, when 47 years old and the onset of presbyopia might in some degree have mitigated eyestrain, he declared that his eyesight had been restored to him. How far eyestrain can reasonably be held to account for some of Johnson's moods is a difficult problem and can hardly be solved. In 1756 and 1773 his right eye was inflamed, as a result, it was thought, of reading much small print. There does not appear to be any evidence that he obviously squinted (though this would not be surprising with one eye blind), except Mrs. Montagu's reference to his 'squinting look' made when she was much annoyed at the 'compassionate contempt' expressed for her friend the first Lyttelton in *The Lives of the Poets.*

DEAFNESS

Paracusis willisii is a peculiar form of deafness characterised by hearing better in a noise, and was first described by Thomas Willis (1621–1675) in a woman who could hear her husband only when a drum was beaten; it is thought that the intense vibrations may shake the fixed stapes and so render it capable of transmitting ordinary sounds, or that it is apparent only, the speaker, unconsciously raising his voice. There is some reason to think that this may have been one of Johnson's disabilities for he was known to be deaf, and Mrs. Piozzi wrote, 'He heard all that was said in a carriage when it was my turn to be deaf.' Johnson's indifference to music may have been in part due to his deafness.

TICS

Before his marriage with Mrs. Porter, his future stepdaughter Lucy Porter described Johnson as often having 'seemingly convulsive starts and odd gesticulations which tended to one's surprise and ridicule.' Hogarth on first meeting with him received a very erroneous impression. When calling on Samuel Richardson he 'perceived a person standing at a window in the room, shaking his head and rolling himself about in a strange ridiculous manner, and concluded that he was an idiot, whom his relations had put under the care of Mr. Richardson as a very good man.' In 1777 Fanny Burney, who subsequently delighted in his praise of her *Evelina*, and whom he called 'little Burney,' wrote in her diary after their first meeting: 'He is, indeed, very ill-favoured, tall and stout but stoops terribly. He is almost bent double. His mouth is almost constantly opening and shutting as if he were chewing. He has a strange method of frequently twirling his fingers and twisting his hands. His body is in constant agitation, see-sawing up and down; his feet are never a moment quiet, and, in short, his whole person is in perpetual motion.' Boswell wrote: 'Such was the heat and irritability of his blood that not only did he pare his nails to the quick, but scraped the joints of his fingers with a penknife, till they seemed quite red and raw,' and from his study of Sydenham's works, concluded that the condition was 'St. Vitus' dance', or what is often called Sydenham's chorea. Sir Joshua Reynolds expressed quite clearly in ordinary language what appeared to him to be the explanation, namely that it was 'a habit of accompanying his thoughts with certain untoward actions' and that he could control them; Johnson when asked by an *enfant terrible* (Elizabeth Smart), a daughter of his friend Christopher Smart, why he made such strange gestures, replied 'From bad habit. Do you, my dear, take care to guard against bad habits.' Perhaps his words were more technically accurate than he knew or actually meant; for it would now appear that he was the subject of habit spasm or a motor tic, as well as of the psychical. Of this, as Risien Russell says, no better example can be found than that of Johnson, who, as he walked along the street, used to place his hand on certain posts, and if he missed one, would turn back and perform the accustomed ceremony before proceeding on his way. The motor or convulsive and the psychical tics, which may occur in the same individual, were distinguished from the choreas by Charcot and his colleagues at the Salpêtrière in Paris in the last quarter of the last century, long after Boswell's time. Thomas Lawrence the physician also had convulsive movements of his head and shoulders which, to quote Sir John Hawkins, 'gave pain to the beholder, and drew off attention from all that he said.' Like Johnson, though there is not any known connection with tics, Lawrence had an attack of paralysis, and was deaf, at first intermittently, which of course sadly interfered with the converse of the two friends, as on the occasion in March 1782 so graphically described by Mrs. Thrale as terminating in an exchange across the table of punning notes written in Latin. Lawrence wrote his medical papers in choice Latin, and corresponded in that language with Johnson, who considered him one of the best men he had ever known.

GASTROINTESTINAL SYMPTOMS

Johnson was an erratic, not a fastidious, eater, drank 'oceans' of tea and certainly suffered from dyspepsia; in 1770 he complained of spasms of old-standing in the stomach, which for the last two years had harassed him almost to distraction. In 1772 he confided to Mrs. Thrale the statement, 'My nights are flatulent and unquiet,' and again in 1775, 'I was last night almost convulsed with flatulence.' The gallstone found after death in his gall bladder may have played some part in the production of these symptoms. This single gallstone may of course have been composed of pure cholesterol, and this form may be quite latent; but on the other hand the adhesions between the coils of the jejunum may have been caused by cholecystitis. Having suffered much, he was not inclined, though himself a hypochondriac and highly introspective, to suffer gladly the complaints of others unless they appeared to be well founded, and then he could be monstrous kind. His reproof to the Reverend Dr. Delap, 'Do not be like the spider, man, and spin conversation incessantly out of thine own bowels,' has, like Macaulay's famous if brutal criticism of Robert Montgomery's poems, perhaps saved the victim from complete oblivion; perhaps after all in Johnson's own words 'it is better a man should be abused than forgotten.'

GOUT

Gout is stated to have first attacked him in 1773, but in 1770 and 1771 he had complained to Mrs. Thrale of 'rheumatism'; in 1776 an acute gouty seizure kept him quiet, and after his hemiplegia it recurred, but this he bore with perhaps rather credulous philosophy, for he wrote to Dr. John Mudge (1721–1793) of Plymouth, 'By representing the gout as an antagonist to the palsy, you have said enough to make it welcome.'

SYPHILIS

The suggestion has been made that Johnson had syphilis, either congenital or acquired; but there does not appear to be any real clinical or pathological proof in favour of this. The opacities of the corneae, which so seriously interfered with vision, might, it is true, have been due to the interstitial keratitis of congenital syphilis which may also cause general arrest of development or infantilism, a condition quite unlike that of Johnson; further, as mentioned elsewhere, he undoubtedly had tuberculous adenitis, and tuberculous keratitis seems therefore to be far more probable. That he exposed himself to the risk of acquired lues there is not any evidence, unless Boswell's remark that when associated with the dissipated Richard Savage, the reputed son of Earl Rivers, in wandering about London by night during his late twenties he 'was imperceptibly led into some indulgences which occasioned much distress to his virtuous mind' be accepted as such. Like W. E. Gladstone at a later date, he talked and behaved charitably to women of the town with the object of reclaiming them. Lastly the post-mortem examination does not record any morbid change pointing to syphilis.

ENDOCRINE ANOMALY

The question of some form of endocrine disorder naturally arises in connection with Johnson's bulky form and massive facial appearance, and perhaps more particularly of some degree of over-activity of the anterior lobe of the pituitary, and not enough to produce definite acromegaly, for the portraits showing his hands, if they always are his, do not suggest undue enlargement. While it would be a gross exaggeration to say that he had acromegaly, it is difficult absolutely to rule out moderate hyperpituitarism combined with some hypothyroidism.

BIBLIOGRAPHY

Burr, C. W.: *Some Medical Words in Johnson's Dictionary*, Ann. Med Hist., 1927, 9, 183.
Dumont: *Union méd.*, Paris, 1857, 11, 296–297, 521–523.
Hawkins, J.: *Life of Samuel Johnson*, 1787.
Hay, J. J.: *His Characteristics and Aphorisms*, London, Ed. 2, 1884, p. xcvi.

Hollins, C.: *Dr. Johnson,* London, 1928, p. 198.

Hutchison, R.: *Edinburgh M. J.,* n.s., 1925, 32, 389–406.

Montagu, Mrs.: *Queen of the Blues,* Her Letters and Friendships from 1762 to 1800. Edited by Reginald Blunt, 2, 157, Lond., 1923.

Osler, W.: *Canad. M.A.J.,* 1, 1919, 1911.

Packard, F. R.: *Medical history of Samuel Johnson,*N.Y.M.J., 1902, 75, 441–445.

Rogers, B. M. H.: *The medical aspects of Boswell's 'life of Johnson' with some account of the medical men mentioned in that book,* Bristol Med.-Chir. J., 1911, 29, 125–148.

Rogers, B. M. H.: The Medical aspects of Boswell's *Life of Johnson* with some account of the medical men mentioned in that book. Bristol Med.-Chir. J., 1911, 29: 125–148.

Roscoe, E. S.: *Aspects of Dr. Johnson,* 1928.

Russell, J. S. R.: *System of Medicine* (Allbutt and Rolleston), 8, 628, 1910.

Squibb, S. J.: London J. Med., 1849, 1, 615–623.

Treves, F.: Cassell's Mag., pp. 38–44, Feb., 1924.

Vieillard, P. A. et Dumont: Etude de psychologie médicale de l'idée fixe. A la mémoire de Samuel Johnson. Paris, Baillière, 1854.

Warbasse, J. P.: *Doctors of Samuel Johnson and his court,* Med. Libr. & Hist. J., 1907, 5, 65, 194, 260.

The 'insanity' of King George III: a classic case of porphyria

Ida Macalpine and Richard Hunter

EDITORIAL NOTE

To Shelley in 1819, George III was
    'An old, mad, blind, despised and dying King'
and his sons were
    'Princes, the dregs of their dull race, who flow
    Through public scorn—mud from a muddy spring.'

The Whig historians of the last century said very much the same thing with less felicity but with more circumstantial evidence to the effect that George III conducted the affairs of the State not only arrogantly and autocratically but also stupidly and with deliberate bribery and corruption, and that he was directly responsible for the loss of the American colonies. American historians have added their quota of denigration of 'America's last King'; to them he was a Stuart in wolf's clothing who had forced rebellion on his loyal American subjects.

For over a century there were few apologists for the longest reign in English history (1751–1820)—a reign which spanned not only over constitutional crises and the American War of Independence, but also over the burgeoning Industrial Revolution in England and the tempest of the French Revolution and its aftermath in Europe.

The detailed analysis of English politics and of the structure of the House of Commons in the 1760s that Lewis Namier undertook at the end of the First World War, though it made little immediate impact, had, by the end of the Second World War, compelled a drastic reassessment. George III became a 'much maligned King', no longer burdened with the more venial of his alleged shortcomings—such as plotting by bribery and corruption to restore the lost powers of the Crown. To some he even became a far-sighted statesman who strove for a constitutional monarchy as a necessity of the new age. At this point the historical debate now rests.

The medical history of George III has centred on his insanity, of which he had several attacks and which became permanent by

1811. His mental derangement has been invoked by some as an explanation of his behaviour and by others in exoneration. Only the broad outline of his disabilities were known, so that the hitherto unrecorded manuscript information brought forward by Dr. Ida Macalpine and Dr. Richard Hunter in 1966 is a substantial contribution biographically and possibly also politically.

As is seen from their essay they discovered a wealth of recorded physical signs during the king's illnesses, and they interpreted these as evidence that both the physical and mental disturbances were caused by porphyria—a rare, hereditary metabolic disease. In the observations on this essay, Dr. John Brooke of the Historical Manuscripts Commission, accepting the diagnosis of porphyria and the dismissal of insanity, maintained that as the King had suffered 'from a bodily and not a mental illness,' there is 'now no longer any need to search for outbreaks of insanity or mental stress, likely to be responsible for breakdowns or weaknesses in his character . . . With the diagnosis of porphyria all the superstructure erected on the assumption of a mentally unstable and basically weak personality will have to be revised.'

An ailing King rather than an insane king fits much better with the assessment that Namier gave of George III than that given by the Whig historians. But there are substantial difficulties in accepting the conclusions that porphyria was present and that the presumed porphyrial mental attacks are in effect different from the classical forms of insanity.

Porphyria as the explanation of the king's illnesses—physical and mental—has not gained unquestioned acceptance. Dr. Geoffrey Dean, probably the most experienced authority on porphyria, finds the evidence inadequate. [Dean, G., *The Porphyrias*, 2nd ed. (London: Pitman, 1971).] The clinical picture as now recorded by Macalpine and Hunter he considers as atypical and some of the genealogical evidence as rather bizarre. That George III sometimes passed red urine is consistent with the fact that he had kidney stones, but not quite consistent with hereditary porphyria in which the urine is clear when passed and the reddish or brownish colour develops on standing. Furthermore, porphyria is not a common cause of insanity, and finally, the genetic evidence that George III suffered from a dominant hereditary affection is slender.

Equally pertinent is the question of whether mental disturbances due to porphyria rather than to unknown causes (as most mental disturbances are) really helps to assess the King's political decisions. Much more would have to be known concerning differences in behaviour in porphyrial mental anomalies compared with the more classical varieties, and such knowledge we do not have at present.

So for the moment nothing is proven: the debate continues—medically and historically.

INTRODUCTION

'The attacks of George the Third are invested with peculiar interest,' wrote Ray (1855). 'Five times' was the king 'struck down by mental disease . . . and twice the recurrence of his disorder gave rise to a degree of political feeling that has seldom been equalled, and to political discussions that settled for ever a vital principle in the British constitution.' No illness had such profound effects on the nation and its institutions as the 'madness' of George III, and indeed no other has received so much attention from commentators, biographers, and historians. The royal malady also influenced the history of psychiatry, not least by dragging the 'mad-business' into the limelight (Hunter and Macalpine, 1963).

Strangely only two clinical studies have been devoted to it, both by psychiatrists and both American: Ray in the mid-nineteenth century and Guttmacher in the mid-twentieth. From the latter historians have adopted as fact that 'His insanity was a form of manic-depression [*sic*]' (Namier, 1955) or, as in a recent narrative of the regency crisis 1788–89, that 'the king's disorder was undoubtedly psychotic, of a manic-depressive type . . . caused by an underlying conflict . . . exacerbated by violent frustrations, annoyances and emotions' (Trench, 1964). This diagnosis is challengingly unsatisfactory not only because it leaves many mental symptoms unaccounted for, but because it ignores the physical symptoms which were a major part of the king's sufferings.

NEW MEDICAL EVIDENCE

The discovery of new medical evidence in the journals and correspondence of the king's physicians made it possible to fit together all pieces of the enigma—200 years after what is generally assumed to have been the first attack in 1765. Four primary sources are drawn on for the first time in a clinical study: 47 volumes of Willis manuscripts at the British Museum (B.M. Add. MSS. 41690–41736, first catalogued 1959); 8 volumes and 10 boxes of Queen's Council Papers at Lambeth Palace Library; Sir Henry Halford's daily record of the illness, October 1811–January 1812, in the Royal Archives at Windsor; and Sir George Baker's diary in the possession of Sir Randle Baker Wilbraham. The royal malady now assumes an unsuspected significance which gives it a unique place in the annals of medicine. The new diagnosis may also necessitate revision of historical judgments and notions concerning the character and conduct of this 'much maligned monarch' (Namier, 1955).

1. THE CONTEMPORARY SCENE

SOME DIFFICULTIES

For many reasons the illness is difficult to study, foremost paradoxically because of the abundance and diversity of sources, printed and manuscript, spread over almost the sixty years of the reign which span the recurrences of the illness. It was a period teeming with great men and great events, and never had there been so many diarists, correspondents, and chroniclers who may have noted pertinent facts not recorded elsewhere.

PHYSICIANS' DAILY BULLETINS

The public bulletins were made colourless out of respect for the royal family and designed to allay alarm rather than record medical facts. They were intended to reveal no more than was 'sufficient for every good or loyal purpose' (Nisbet, 1817), as, for instance, 'His Majesty has had a restless night, and is this morning, much indisposed' (14th December 1788). Nor were the physicians explicit when they meant to be informative, as in a report to Prime Minister Spencer Perceval: 'He is under a great degree of irritation, and the whole frame is so much disturbed, as to make us consider Him in some danger' (24th December 1810). 'The report of the physicians,' complained Lord Grenville on 8th October 1811, 'is worded as foolishly as ever' (Jesse, 1867). What they did contain was not always reliable, since many were a compromise between dissenting medical opinions, as parliamentary committees criticised. When party strife centred on a regency, the physicians found themselves arbiters of government, and everything hung on their answers to whether they thought 'the State of His Majesty's Health does, or does not . . . render His Majesty incapable, either of coming to Parliament, or of attending to Public Business' (Report 1789). Not surprisingly they were also suspected of party political bias.

EIGHTEENTH CENTURY PRACTICE

Another difficulty is that observations were made and couched in the theory and language of a bygone age. Organ pathology could make little headway against the old humoral pathology in the absence of a science of physical signs. Little was known of neurology short of involvement of higher centres by injury, infection, strokes, and fits. The physicians had no stethoscope, no knee-jerk hammer, not even a clinical thermometer. Laboratory medicine did not exist but excretions were inspected. Diagnosis was made on what Dr. George Fordyce (1794) called 'an estimate of symptoms and appearances'; the doctor listened to the patient's complaints, inquired into his 'animal functions' and general health, felt the pulse, and looked at the tongue.

Even within this limited range of fact-finding the royal physicians were peculiarly handicapped. They were expected to observe protocol however ill or delirious the king was: if they were not addressed first they could ask no questions. Whole visits were spent in fruitless silence, as they reported to the Queen's Council on 8th January 1812: 'His Majesty appears to be very quiet this morning, but not having been addressed we know nothing more of His Majesty's condition of mind or body than what is obvious in his external appearances.'

MENTAL SYMPTOMS

The highpoint of the great drama of human, psychiatric, and national history was reached in 1788, when the 50-year-old king went 'mad'. Naturally the mental symptoms at once moved to the centre of the public stage in what became an intricate complex of medical and political controversy in which confusion extended far beyond the patient's mind, and so gave the illness its lasting stigma. They were the loudest, the most dreaded, and of greatest concern to government and country alike, since it was the king's mental state which determined whether he was competent to rule. And they gained added prominence because whoever came in contact with the king could, and did, form his own opinion of them.

The physical symptoms in contrast, though at times so severe that his life was in danger, did not enter the political or social arena. They receded into the background less in fact than emphasis and came to be regarded as incidental or the result of the mental illness, if not actually manufactured to hide the true facts. The seal was set on this historic bias when in December 1788 'Persons who have made this Branch of Medicine their particular study,' as 'mad-doctors' were referred to in parliament, were called to take charge of the king's management. While the balance was thus weighted against the physical side of the illness, the door was closed to the real diagnosis.

THE PROBLEM

The problematic nature of the illness emerges clearly from the sequence of events in the 1788–89 attack. It started in June with severe abdominal pain, diagnosed as 'biliary Concretions in the Gall Duct.' In July and August the king was excitable. Colic returned in October, followed by aches and pains, muscular weakness, and stiffness, diagnosed as 'rheumatism,' and as 'gout' when the legs were badly affected. His condition deteriorated with more colic and constipation, racing pulse, sweating attacks, cramp, lameness, and hoarseness, attributed to 'fever'. Intractable insomnia, incessant talking, excitement, confusion, and fits supervened, diagnosed as 'delirium' or—since the physicians could not agree whether there was fever—as 'mental derangement' caused by some severe bodily disease. By November he was 'under an intire alienation of mind' and considered 'mad.' Parliamentary committees interrogated the physicians about his competency to continue as head of State and the prognosis. In January 1789 a regency for which the party of the Prince of Wales had been agitating was accepted as unavoidable. The Bill had passed the Commons and was in progress through the Lords when the king unexpectedly began to recover. On 12th February 'a progressive state of amendment' was announced, and on 26th February 'the cessation' of the illness. Thanksgiving prayers were offered, and, though 'emaciated and enfeebled,' the king 'resumed personal exercise of His Royal Authority' on 10th March. On 23rd April services were held for 'delivering our most Gracious Sovereign from the severe illness with which He hath been afflicted' and the painful chapter closed. Twelve years elapsed before the next major attack.

ORIGINAL AND CONSEQUENTIAL MADNESS

Was the 'aberration' part of a physical disease or purely mental? The physicians thought in terms laid down by Dr. William Battie, one time president of the Royal College of Physicians, in his *Treatise on madness*, published in 1758—that is, within living memory. He taught 'that Madness with respect to its cause is distinguishable into two species . . . *viz. Original* and *Consequential* . . . The first is solely owing to an internal disorder of the nervous substance: the second . . . owing to the same . . . being disordered *ab extra*.' In modern terms he differentiated the functional psychoses from the organic mental states due to brain disease. The best known among the latter was febrile delirium and 'mental derangement', which was milder— to-day called toxic confusional states. Harper for instance wrote in 1789 under the impact of the king's disorder: 'morbid matter, or . . . acrimonious, stimulating particles settling on the brain, has likewise been accounted capable of producing Insanity' by 'translation of morbid cause'.

MANIA OR DELIRIUM?

Dr. Robert Darling Willis summed up the problem for the parliamentary committee in December 1810: 'I consider the King's derangement more nearly allied to delirium. . . . In delirium, the mind is actively employed upon past impressions . . . which rapidly pass in succession. . . . There is also a considerable disturbance in the general constitution; great restlessness, great want of sleep, and total unconsciousness of surrounding objects. In insanity, there may be little or no disturbance, apparently, in the general constitution; the mind is occupied upon some fixed assumed idea . . . and the individual is acting, always, upon that false impression . . . also, the mind is awake to objects which are present. Taking insanity, therefore, and delirium, as two points, I would place derangement of mind somewhere between them. His Majesty's illness, uniformly, partakes more of the delirium than of insanity.'

PROGNOSIS

The physicians grappled with the diagnosis not as an academic exercise nor as a guide to treatment but as the clue to prognosis. 'Original Madness', mania, or insanity was considered not amenable to art and spontaneous recovery uncommon, whereas 'Consequential Madness', delirium, and derangement were expected to subside with the underlying condition, rarely leaving a defect state called 'fatuity' or dementia. Insanity and delirium represented opposite poles of hopefulness and despair. The *Morning Chronicle* of 28th November

1788 reassured its readers: 'Although the disorder has deranged the head, it is not, as was once dreaded, a mental incapacity called Insanity, for that calamity will not admit of a sudden and effectual cure.' While the king's 'agitation', 'hurry of spirits', and changeability from confusion with excitement to insight and composure pointed to delirium, doubt arose when the condition persisted. This looked like insanity with its chronic course, and disheartened the most sanguine supporters of the fever/delirium theory. At this juncture all medical and political parties were confounded by the king's swift and complete return to clarity and reason as if it had been delirium all along.

PHYSICIANS' DILEMMA

In this quandary it is not surprising that the physicians remained evasive though hard pressed by government and parliament. Only two took a definite stand and both had sufficient political motive for their views. Dr. Richard Warren, Whig sympathiser, and physician also to the Prince of Wales, confided in a letter: '*Rex noster insanit; nulla adsunt febris signa; nulla mortis venturae indicia*'—our king is mad; there are no signs of fever; no danger to life (8th November 1788). The Reverend Dr. Francis Willis, Tory 'mad-doctor' brought down from Lincolnshire with his sons by Pitt, told the parliamentary committee in December 1788 that he had 'great Hopes of His Majesty's recovery' because in his practice he cured 'Nine out of Ten . . . Persons . . . afflicted with the Disorder', implying, as his grandson Dr. Francis Willis explained 35 years later, that he diagnosed '*delirium and derangement cum febre*'. Dr. Anthony Addington, who had looked after Earl Chatham, was hopeful that it was not mania 'from this Circumstance—that it had not for its Forerunner that Melancholy which usually precedes a tedious Illness of this Sort' (Report 1788).

WHAT OTHER CONTEMPORARY DOCTORS THOUGHT

John Hunter, surgeon extraordinary to the king, who though not consulted kept himself fully informed, thought it a systemic affection which 'would probably come to some sort of crisis, by which it would appear whether there was strength enough in the constitution to prevail over the disease,' and estimated 'that the chances were nine to one in his [the king's] favour' (Grenville, 1788).

Other medical men joined in the controversy in print. Jones (1789) diagnosed 'nervous fever' and proposed methods of treatment and prevention. Rowley (1790) concluded that the king suffered from what he had described in 1788 as 'a new species of temporary madness', a 'derangement' without fever caused by 'some prevailing irritating acrimony', to-day called toxins. Pargeter (1792) argued that 'this case could not have been *maniacal*', since undoubtedly fever had been present and by ancient usage insanity was 'delirium without fever'. In the king's last illness Sutleffe (1824) proposed a trial of his 'herbaceous tranquilliser', because of its success with 'maniacal patients'.

DIAGNOSIS IN LAST ILLNESS: A SINGULAR CASE

The physicians in attendance from 1810 were equally nonplussed. They thought his mental state more characteristic of delirium— but symptomatic of what? R. D. Willis had 'never seen a person . . . labouring under a similar complaint' but found the 'symptoms of bodily indisposition sufficient to account for all the derangement of mind.' Henry Revell Reynolds, who had seen all attacks from 1788, considered it insanity but had never known 'exactly a case parallel to the king.' William Heberden junior thought it 'a derangement attended with more or less fever, and liable to accessions and re-missions' due to 'a peculiarity of constitution, of which I can give no distinct account.' In October 1811, he replied to the Queen's Council's quarterly questionary: 'For want of terms more accurately defined respecting disorders of the human mind, His Majesty's present state might be called Insanity but . . . appears . . . to differ materially from ordinary cases . . . by that perplexity and confusion of ideas, which belong more properly to delirium.' In January 1812 he admitted that it 'is different from any other case that has occurred to my own observation.' And Sir Henry Halford told the Council: 'The King's case appears to have no exact precedent in the records of insanity.'

Their guarded answers were wiser than they could have known. But by then the need for a diagnosis had lost its immediacy. The regency had been established in February 1811 and the 72-year-old blind monarch had begun to show signs of 'fatuity'. Dr. Baillie reported in January 1812: 'I cannot state that His Majesty's recovery

George III. C. Turner (The Mansell Collection).

is altogether without hope, but I think it . . . extremely improbable . . .
His memory seems to be impaired.'

2. LATER STUDIES

In the eighteenth century physicians dealt with both physical and
mental illness alike unless a patient became unmanageable, as Dr.
Reynolds explained: 'If no Restraint is necessary . . . every Physician
of Experience will, I have no Doubt, think himself competent to
conduct . . . such a Case' (Report 1789). This changed with the
establishment of mental hospitals. Two orders of disease were then
created and psychiatry became estranged from medicine—a development reflected in later studies of the royal malady.

ACUTE MANIA

The first asylum doctor who studied George III's illness was Isaac
Ray (1855). In a paper to the Association of Medical Superintendents
of American Institutions for the Insane he gave an account of all
attacks from printed sources then available. Concerned with the
phenomena of mental illness, he considered diagnosis—'the form of
disease'—only in connexion with the royal physicians' dilemma
between delirium and insanity: 'They sought no doubt to give the
impression that it was simply a case of delirious wandering produced
by bodily disturbance, which would readily pass away with the
condition on which it depended. It is impossible to see any ground
for this opinion. This attack [1810] closely resembled the others.
It was manifested by hurry, restlessness, caprices, indiscretions,
violence, and delusions. In one word, it presented all the characters
of ordinary acute mania.' But he added a significant caveat: 'Few
men would have seemed less likely to be visited by insanity. His
general health had always been good; his powers were impaired by
none of those indulgences almost inseparable from the kingly
station; he was remarkably abstemious at the table; and took much
exercise in the open air. Insanity had never appeared in his family,
and he was quite free from those eccentricities and peculiarities
which indicate an ill-balanced mind.'

MANIC-DEPRESSIVE PSYCHOSIS

By the 1930s psychiatric emphasis had shifted from description to classification, and Jelliffe (1931), applying the Kraepelinian criteria of excitement and recurrence, diagnosed 'manic-depressive psychosis' with the manic element paramount.

Guttmacher (1941) built his full-scale medico-historical study on this diagnosis—'a disturbance of mood, rather than of mentation'—and proceeded to explain the onset of the attacks in psychopathological terms: 'Self-blame, indecision, and frustration destroyed the sanity of George III . . . Had "farmer George" . . . been a country squire, he would, in all probability, not have been psychotic.' The somatic symptoms are dismissed as subterfuges to hide the embarrassing nature of the illness. Of the 1765 attack Guttmacher wrote, 'In all probability, the disorder was purely mental and the clinical reports were falsified'; of the 1788–89, 'Physical symptoms were invented or, at least, exaggerated further to fool the public.' Only when the press mentioned mental symptoms 'did the court cease manufacturing reports of various baffling physical symptoms.' He even believed that the king 'abetted by the false interpretations of those about him . . . was trying to delude himself into viewing his illness as primarily physical.' Tachycardia, sweating, colic, hoarseness, are rated accompaniments of manic states; pain, paresis, stupor, fits as 'hysterical'.

The wheel had turned full circle from the royal physicians puzzling what physical illness had caused the mental disturbance to twentieth-century psychiatrists explaining the physical disturbance as the guise or somatic expression of mental illness.

NEUROTIC PERSONALITY AND HEREDITY

To support his thesis, and in contrast to Ray, Guttmacher held that the king was predisposed by a neurotic personality and a hereditary taint: 'This unstable man . . . this vulnerable individual' whose 'neuroticism' made him take the 'job of kingship too seriously' so that he 'broke under the strain', was 'a victim of neuropathic tainting . . . the list [of affected members] is . . . frightening.' This he modified in 1964 to 'The family history is not very impressive psychiatrically.'

No medical study as since been made. Historians had therefore to rely on the diagnosis of manic-depressive insanity or psychosis with all it implies.

3. THE PRESENT STUDY

THE EVIDENCE

THE ATTACKS

It is usually stated that there were five attacks: January–July 1765, age 26/27; October 1788–February 1789, age 50; February–March 1801, age 62; January–March 1804, age 66; and from October 1810 to his death on 29th January 1820 in his 82nd year. This was also punctuated by 'accessions' and 'remissions', which in the first year or two gave rise to hopes of full recovery.

In addition, minor attacks can be established in: May–June 1762, age 24; January–February 1766; in the summer of 1790; in December 1795; and there were probably others. These can be checked by his absences from Privy Council meetings and references in his own letters. Furthermore, during convalescence from major attacks he had 'occasional paroxysms of his disorder, though short and slight' and 'periods of flurry' (Report 1810').

All attacks were 'of the same general character' (Report 1810) and most started in winter. They left him 'wasted', 'weak', and 'aged'.

Attacks were ushered in by cold, cough, and malaise, quickly followed in the first attack by anginoid pains ('stitches in the breast') and in all others by abdominal colic with constipation ('very acute pain in the pit of the stomach shooting to the back and sides'); tachycardia up to 144 beats a minute; hoarseness (his voice 'croaking,' 'rasping', 'hardly audible'); painful weakness and stiffness making him unable to walk and even stand unaided or hold a cup or pen; tormenting 'cramps'; paraesthesiae ('complained of heat and burning'); hyperaesthesia (could not bear the touch of clothes or bedding, wig or tie); hypalgesia ('scarce sensible of the Blisters applied to His legs').

There were episodes of generalised 'tremor'; localised pain in head, face, and neck; dysphagia ('foaming at the mouth', 'tasted his food but could not eat'); visual disturbances ('could not read'); and in his last illness nystagmus ('eyes exhibit rapid vibrations'); he was also 'dizzy', 'speechless', and incontinent.

Vasomotor disturbances were marked with profuse sweating and suffusion of the face ('he changed countenance and flushed so much that water stood in his eyes from the excessive heat.') At times he had oliguria, polyuria, polydipsia, pale stools, swelling of legs and feet, and once 'great weals on his arms'.

Simultaneously signs and symptoms of encephalopathy appeared: agitation, talking 'with uncommon rapidity and vehemence', sensitivity to light and sound, emotional lability, uninhibited behaviour and nocturnal confusion. Total insomnia supervened; at one time he had no sleep for 72 hours, at another he rambled incessantly for 26, and to his death his physicians reported his sleep in quarters of an hour. 'Great irritability of frame and temper' was accompanied by 'turbulence' and frank delirium: 'he baffled all attempts to fix his attention', showed 'gross error of judgment', was aimlessly 'occupied adjusting his bedclothes' or 'sorting his papers'.

Illusions, delusions and hallucinations followed: 'impressed by false images', 'continually addressed people dead or alive as if they were present', lived 'in a world of his own', 'delirious all day', 'engrossed in visionary scenery', 'his conversation . . . like the details of a dream in its extravagant confusion', 'total alienation'.

'Extraordinary excitement and irritation' led to 'stupor', 'insensibility', incontinence and convulsions, so that his physicians feared 'a paralytic stroke' or 'imminent dissolution'.

As age and illness took their toll he became more 'tranquil', 'cheerful and good-humoured' or 'trifling and silly', 'tears and laughter in quick succession'. Two delusions, fleetingly expressed in 1788, came to the fore, one connected with Lady Pembroke, the other with Hanover: 'His Majesty's adherence to certain erroneous notions with some degree of consistence partakes of the true character of Insanity', noted Heberden in 1811.

Blindness attributed to cataract became complete about 1812 and later he also went deaf. Long periods of being 'silent and weak on his legs' were interrupted by paroxysms of abdominal and limb pains of which 'he complained loudly,' hoarseness, tachycardia, and insomnia accompanied by 'great perturbation in his system'. In his last attack, one month before he died, he spent 58 hours without sleep and gave other 'remarkable proof of the extraordinary energies of his constitution.' Thereafter he sank and quietly 'expired without pain'.

'Throughout this long and severe illness the suddenness of opposite changes has been frequent and most remarkable,' wrote Greville. One morning in November 1788 he was 'composed, conversed with very little inconsistence', and in the afternoon 'more agitated than ever, pulse very quick, determined frenzy.' In July 1811 he deteriorated so rapidly that his physicians at Windsor, in their 'very great anxiety, found it absolutely necessary to give some written account of the King at the door of the Castle' without waiting for sanction from Whitehall.

On his recovery in 1765 he requested parliament to make provision for a regency in case 'it should please God to put a Period to my Life, whilest my successor is of tender Years.' After severe attacks he realised that he had 'lost track of time and events,' as he told his friend George Rose. At the beginning of the 1801 attack he confided to the Reverend Thomas Willis: 'I do feel myself very ill, I am much weaker than I was, and I have prayed to God all night that I might die, or that He would spare my reason . . . should it be otherwise, for God's sake keep from me your father [Dr. Frances Willis].' And on recovery he wrote to his friend Richard Hurd, Bishop of Worcester, that he had 'after a most tedious and severe illness . . . most wonderfully escaped the jaws of death . . . though I cannot boast of the same strength and spirits I enjoyed before.'

TREATMENT AND RESTRAINT

No account of the illness can disregard the king's treatments and how far the 'turbulence' he displayed were provoked by the repressive, coercive, and punitive methods by which he was ruled. In 1788 the senior Willis boasted to the king's equerry that 'he broke in [patients], as horses in a menage.' For any non-compliance, as refusing food, not going to bed, or throwing off his bedclothes, he was clapped in a 'winding sheet,' or a restraint chair which he bitterly dubbed 'his coronation chair,' or mostly in a straitwaistcoat with his legs tied to the bed. 'His Majesty quarrelled with His tea and dinner and was confined;' 'He threw off His wig and tie and resisted them being replaced and was restrained,' read typical entries in the log of the Willises.

Besides mechanical restraint he was subjected to a medicinal regimen to bring down his 'fever' and 'turbulent spirits'. He had to submit, often only after 'a formidable struggle', to vomits, purges, bleeding, blistering, cupping, the application of leeches, and so on. In the last illness Drs. Baillie, Heberden, and Halford repeatedly protested to the Archbishop of Canterbury, as head of the Queen's Council, against 'the unvaried tediousness of His silent and solitary confinement' enforced by Dr. Willis's sons, Robert Darling and John, to 'minimise excitement'. They pleaded for 'a milder and more liberal system of management', and that the king should at least be permitted to 'converse'. 'He has been kept in unedifying confinement and seclusion', wrote Heberden in September 1811, which had itself 'become a source of irritation' and excited 'a fresh accession of His disorder'. That harsh treatment and enforced inactivity make violent and mischievous patients was only learnt later in the nineteenth century—in the king's time his obstreperous behaviour was taken as the ebullition of furious mania and his violent dislike of the Willises as delusional.

DIAGNOSIS

ACUTE INTERMITTENT PORPHYRIA

The clinical picture revealed by the physicians' daily record makes the diagnosis of manic-depressive psychosis untenable. Evidently his excitement lacked the cardinal feature of exaltation (Kraepelin, 1921), and his physical sufferings were an integral part of the illness.

By the triad alone of abdominal symptoms, polyneuritis, and mental disturbance the condition is at once recognisable as acute intermittent porphyria. Reviewed in this light the symptomatology and course of the royal malady reads like the description of a textbook case: colic and constipation; painful paresis of arm and legs; vocal paresis, visual disturbances and other signs of bulbar involvement, radicular pain; autonomic disturbances with marked tachycardia and sweating attacks; and encephalopathy ranging from insomnia to excitement, raging delirium, stupor, and fits. The only feature not recorded is hypertension, because blood-pressure was not measured, but the repeated crises threatening 'a stroke' may have been hypertensive.

In keeping with acute intermittent porphyria are also: age of onset; attacks precipitated by mild infections; rapid fluctuations; protracted convalescence; excess of symptoms, and hence complaints, over signs which make patients appear demanding, irascible, and difficult to manage.

The commonest misdiagnoses to-day were also considered in the king's case: biliary colic for abdominal pain; rheumatism for neuropathy; psychosis for encephalopathy. Of Goldberg and Rimington's

(1962) 50 patients 29 had mental symptoms; 14 were 'depressed, nervous, hysterical, lacrymose, peculiar'; 9 'confused, hallucinated, disorientated'; 6 'legally certified'. According to Saint (1963) patients 'show any of the stigmata of acute toxic confusion psychosis, displaying agitation, sleeplessness and hostility towards the medical attendant, and suffering visual or auditory hallucinations.' Five of his 16 patients had been admitted to mental hospitals with diagnoses of 'depression, schizophrenia, delirium tremens, and acute anxiety state.' Holt's (1963) description of a patient in an attack as 'ill, paralysed, delirious, and in agonising pain' exactly fits George III.

URINALYSIS

To-day the diagnosis would be clinched by finding abnormal metabolites in the urine or observing its characteristic blue, blood-red, purple, or 'dark' colour. Though one could hardly hope that such an observation, even if made, would have been recorded, we succeeded in locating four references to discoloured urine: 18th October 1788, Sir George Baker: 'urine bilious' (Diary); 6th January 1811, Sir Henry Halford: 'The water is of a deeper colour—and leaves a pale blue ring upon the glass near the upper surface' (Willis MSS.), and 14th January 1812, 'Bluish 8 and 9 [ounces]' (Royal Archives); 26th August 1819, report of Drs. Baillie and John Willis: 'His Majesty has passed . . . bloody water . . . during the last 16 hours,' of which 'no tinge' remained the following day (Queen's Council Papers; Willis MSS.). All these observations were made during paroxysms when the excretion of porphyrins and porphobilin-like chromogens is known to be greatest.

GENETIC CONSIDERATIONS

Acute itermittent porphyria is usually transmitted as a Mendelian dominant, and in a patient so severely ill as George III one would expect other members of the family to be affected (Waldenström, 1937). To review the medical history of the House of Hanover is, however, a major task if only because of the number of probands (George III's father was one of eight children, George III one of nine, and himself the father of 15), many of whom lived abroad. But one outstanding case was his youngest sister, Caroline Matilda (1751–75), the hapless, banished queen of Denmark and Norway.[1] The mysterious illness to which she succumbed within one week

Part of a page from the Willis Papers in the British Museum. The entry, in the hand of Sir Henry Halford, records the colour of the King's urine.

in her twenty-fourth year started with malaise, followed rapidly by paralysis of legs, arms, and bulbar centres, so that in her last hours she lay motionless, and though conscious was able to communicate only by moving her eyes. There was no fever but tachycardia of 133 before the pulse became uncountable. She had had two similar, milder yet 'dangerous' attacks before. Her puzzled physicians thought she had died of a malignant throat infection which impeded articulation, swallowing, and breathing. But since there was no other case, it was rumoured that she had been paralysed by poison. To scotch this depositions were taken from eye-witnesses, and these allow the diagnosis to be made to-day (N. W. Wraxall, 1799; C. F. L. Wraxall, 1864).

The picture of acute ascending paralysis is not uncommon in fulminating porphyria. Interestingly she manifested the disease at the same age as her brother, whom she also resembled in features and in 'a degree of quickness' of speech.

HISTORICAL IMPLICATIONS

This study allows the certain conclusion that George III's malady was not 'mental' in the accepted sense, in whatever old or modern terms it may be couched. His long and sorrowful illness in which he suffered severely from his affliction, pitifully from his treatments, and miserably from his management, takes on a new importance in the annals of medical history as the first description of a rare metabolic disorder not even to-day fully understood. Moreover, the royal malady is unique for the continuity of its documentation over 58 years—indeed, in the last illness four of the physicians who had attended the king in earlier attacks had been replaced by their sons.

The assumption that the king was 'neurotic' will also have to be revised, since porphyria may render its victim restless, hurried, agitated, and impulsive, especially in minor attacks which go unrecognised. Finally, by implication this diagnosis clears the House of Hanover of an hereditary taint of madness imputed to it by the long-sustained but erroneous interpretation of George III's illness.

Full references are given in:
Macalpine I., and Hunter, R.:
    George III and the Mad-Business (London: Allan Lane, The Penguin Press, 1969).
    Porphyria: A Royal Malady (London: British Medical Association, 1968).

CHAPTER 10

Historical Implications of Porphyria

John Brooke

GEORGE III

No one has suffered more than George III from posthumous attempts to define his recurrent illnesses. It was perhaps inevitable, once it had been put about that he suffered from mental illness, that historians avidly searched for its possible cause in the patient's mind. Deductions were even made which could be carried over from his personal life to his conduct of public affairs. All this was without any basis in fact, even contrary to what George III's own physicians thought. There is no more glaring example of an unwarranted statement, void of evidence other than that it has been generally accepted, than the story that George III was insane in 1765.

Historians failed to heed the warning given them by one master of their craft: 'The unqualified practitioner must not be let loose, not even on the dead.' Psychoanalysis imperfectly comprehended and a fashion in biography to impute all disturbances of mind to sexual tensions seemed the key to an understanding of George III's life and reign. Frustration—it was contended—led to manic-depressive insanity and accounted for such traits in his personality as obstinacy, conservatism, even the decorum and morality of his court. Nineteenth century historians saw George III in moral terms—as a good or a bad King according to their political point of view. Twentieth century historians have tended to see him as a neurotic, a man—they maintained—aware of his unfitness for his high position who took refuge from his responsibilities in insanity.

SIGNIFICANCE OF DIAGNOSIS

What difference does it make whether George III suffered from manic-depressive psychosis or porphyria? First of all it serves to establish historical fact, the prime duty of the historian. Secondly, we have seen how much this diagnosis has coloured, even dictated, the historian's picture of George III's make-up and what sort of person he was. Now with the diagnosis of porphyria all the super-structure erected on the assumption of a mentally unstable and basically weak personality will have to be revised.

Does this change of diagnosis make any difference on the broad canvas of history? Would not Great Britain have still lost her American colonies had George III never fallen ill? Would not the Industrial Revolution still have transformed her into the workshop of the world? Would not the French Revolution and Napoleon still have brought new ideas into European politics, affecting even the enemies of France as well as France herself? All these statements are true and the reader who is looking for a sensational outcome from the discovery that George III suffered from a bodily and not a mental illness will be disappointed.

Yet this new diagnosis is all-important for the historian. He is concerned not only with the broad content of history but with the understanding of particular ages. The historian of the eighteenth century cannot neglect the mass movements which led to the up-heavals in America and France. Nor can he neglect the personality of the King who reigned in Great Britain during the age of the American and French Revolutions. History aims above all at understanding the past. We must try to put ourselves in the position of the men and women of a bygone age, recreate it with the aid of the information we may discover and a true historical imagination, and see the past from the point of view of those to whom it was the present.

When there seemed to be no alternative but to believe that George III had a mental breakdown in 1788 and fell into complete and permanent insanity in 1810 (when he was 73 years old), every action of his life was judged as that of a man who eventually died insane. To begin with it seemed logical to discover some premonitions of the disease. Two earlier illnesses were known, in 1762 and 1765; and it was assumed by historians and biographers and woven into the tapestry of historical tradition that at least the illness of 1765 was the same as in 1788. Dr. Macalpine and Dr. Hunter have else-where convincingly demonstrated that there is no contemporary evidence that George III exhibited any symptoms of mental derange-ment during the illness of 1765, the existence of which had already been questioned before they published their research.

The King's conduct of political affairs was also evaluated according to the theory that he had attacks of insanity. His firmness during the American war in adhering to a policy which was unwise and ultimately disastrous, but was undoubtedly supported by Parliament and public opinion, was regarded as the result of an inability to face reality—a defect in his personality which ultimately drove him insane. His moral qualities during these years, which in more fortunate circumstances might have been deemed virtues, were degraded into vices. His perseverance in supporting what he (and the majority of the nation) believed to be the right of Parliament was pathological obstinacy; his courage, a refusal to face facts; his loyalty to his ministers, a wish to govern by corruption. So long as it was believed that he suffered from insanity every aspect of his life and character was seen as in a distorting mirror. Even his fidelity to his marriage vow was turned against him, and he was reproached for sexual timidity, presumably because he did not have mistresses. No doubt had he been as loose in his morals as his father and grandfather, this would also have been taken as pointing to mental instability.

PERSONAL QUALITIES

There is now no longer any need to search for outbreaks of insanity or mental stresses likely to be responsible for breakdowns, or weaknesses in his character which made him a prey to them. For the first time it is possible to make a fair assessment free from psychopathological speculation. He was not a man of outstanding mental ability, but he was honest, hardworking, honourable, and conscientious, and aware of his responsibilities—all qualities most desirable in a monarch. He had very decided religious opinions and believed strongly and quite correctly that his family had been called to the throne of Great Britain in order to preserve the Protestant establishment. His court was decent and his personal life above reproach. To speculate, as some historians have done, that he was sexually frustrated is now seen to be irrelevant. The fact is that he remained faithful to one woman and had fifteen children by her. He had a quick temper, which required considerable pains to curtail, and he did not easily forgive those who had offended him. The high standards of morality he set for himself induced him to bear hard on those who did not maintain similar standards. He was firm, often to the point of obstinacy, and did not yield graciously; and as he grew older he became, as most people, more rigid and less amenable to change. He found great pleasure in family life and intellectual enjoyments. He was fond of, and a liberal patron to, music, art, and literature, and took an active and intelligent part in all branches of science. The man who encouraged Herschel—the greatest observational astronomer of all time—and who amassed the magnificent collection of books now on display in the King's Library at the British Museum did not lack intellectual curiosity.

Strangely the diagnosis of porphyria which exonerates George III from so much speculative psychologising brings him nearer to us as a human being. For the first time we can appreciate facets of his life which were previously obscured and which must have exerted a great influence on him: firstly that he suffered physically and was for long periods in extreme pain; and secondly that he was fully aware that when attacks were severe his mind was affected. It must rouse our sympathy to read that after the illness of 1788–89 he said he could never again show his face in this country and would retire to Hanover. His determination to resume his royal duties reveals a remarkable degree of moral strength and courage.

Nearly forty years ago Sir Lewis Namier showed that there was no basis for the story that George III attempted to restore the lost powers of the Crown by building up a personal following in the House of Commons. The war against the American colonies, the great disaster of his reign, resulted from a challenge to the authority of Parliament not to the authority of the Crown. Dr. Macalpine and Dr. Hunter have done for George III's personal life what Namier did for his political. 'The great historian,' Namier wrote, 'is like the great artist or doctor: after he has done his work, others should not be able to practise within its sphere in the terms of the preceding era.' No one can now write the political history of George III's reign in pre-Namier terms. Henceforth no one will be able to write George III's biography without taking into account the diagnosis that he did not suffer from insanity but from porphyria. Historians and biographers will now be in a position to do justice to the man whom Namier described as 'a much maligned ruler.'

GEORGE IV

Important too is the suggestion that four of George III's sons also suffered from the same disorder. Moreover, it solves the mystery of that great national disaster, the tragic death in childbirth of Princess Charlotte, George III's grandchild, which at one blow robbed the country of the two heirs to the throne in 1817—two years before the birth of Victoria.

The traditional image of George IV will need revision almost as much as that of George III. He has had a bad press from historians, and there are certain incidents in his life which it is hard to defend. His early extravagance, his love affair with Mrs. Fitzherbert (leading to a 'marriage' which was illegal under the Royal Marriage Act), his equivocal conduct towards his political friends suggest a frivolous, irresponsible, and explosive character to say the least. His unfortunate marriage and the hatred he displayed against his wife does not present him in an endearing light. Those who held office under him when he was Regent and King thought little of his personal qualities. In his reign the power of the Crown was weakened, though ministers could never be certain that they might not be overthrown by an intrigue at Court. The conduct of George IV and his brothers brought the Crown and Royal Family into disrepute and dishonour. 'By God!', said the Duke of Wellington, 'They are the damnedest millstones about the necks of any Government that can be imagined.' It is probable that at no time since the Civil War has there been so much sympathy with republicanism in Great Britain as there was during the Regency and the reign of George IV.

Let us now look at George IV in the light of the diagnosis of porphyria. The symptoms of the disease can be traced back to the age of 20—that is, about 1782. Long before the age of 30 he had been bled a hundred times. It seems possible that George IV realised that his symptoms were similar to those of his father, and after 1789 he could hardly have failed to dread that his illness might culminate as that of his father had done. This may incline us to take a more charitable view of his behaviour. His apparent irresponsibility, his vanity and childishness, appear in a new light when his sufferings are seen to have been real and severe. We can better understand why he made Sir William Knighton, one of his physicians, his private secretary and keeper of his privy purse. We also have an explanation for his endeavour to conceal his sufferings and for the hallucinations of his last years. Perhaps also his dependence on women was due less to passion than to a need for sympathy.

The decline in the effective power of the Crown is a notable feature of British political history during the reigns of George III and George IV. In less than a hundred years the centre of power shifted from the Court to the Cabinet. In the main this was due to the increasingly complex nature of government under the stress of war and its aftermath. The work of government during the Napoleonic wars was far more elaborate than it had been fifty years earlier during the Seven Years' War, and called for a higher degree of skill and expert knowledge on the part of ministers and officials. It was during these years that the civil service as we know it came into being. But in addition to the political factor which was working to reduce the power of the Crown there was also the personal one, and the knowledge that two successive British sovereigns suffered from a disease which impaired their powers. Where they used to be considered blameworthy we must now allow for the fact that periodically they laboured under considerable handicaps, if they were not completely incapacitated.

A ROYAL MALADY

Medically it may be of the greatest interest that George III has been shown to have suffered from a rare disease. For the historian it has far wider implications and ramifications than a mere change of diagnosis. This applies equally to Mary Queen of Scots, to whom the disorder has been traced back. Historically she is also an enigmatic character in whose life mysterious illnesses played a large part. Because these were not understood she has been regarded as 'hysterical'. Her behaviour may well repay re-examination in the light of this study.

Porphyria may cause rapid death, which being unexplained led in a number of celebrated instances to rumours of foul play. Henry, Prince of Wales, was rumoured to have been poisoned by his father, James I; Henrietta Anne, Duchess of Orleans, by agents of her jealous husband; Caroline Matilda, Queen of Denmark, at the instigation of her mother-in-law. In all of these cases suspicion fell on close relatives, and this naturally tarnished their historical image. In this way the mysterious manifestations of the disease may implicate also those around the sufferer. Another striking example is that of James I and the Duke of Buckingham. Curiously Buckingham may have owed something of his rise to the position of all-powerful favourite to the fact that the King was frequently incapacitated from attending to state business and so more likely to yield to the influence of a minister who could relieve him of the burden. When James I died unexpectedly Buckingham was suspected of having poisoned him. Although today no reputable historian will give credit to this suspicion, he still has to take into account that contemporaries thought Buckingham capable of the deed. There is therefore a tendency to scrutinise every aspect of his career more severely than it perhaps deserves and even to admit too readily evidence which tells against him.

Most of the royal houses of Europe of the eighteenth and nineteenth centuries trace descent from James I: the House of Hanover; the exiled family of the Stuarts; the House of Brandenburg Prussia, who in the nineteenth century became Emperors of Germany; the House of Orleans; the House of Savoy who became Kings of Italy; the House of Orange who became Kings of Holland; and besides any number of minor German princely families as Brunswick-Wolfenbüttel, Hesse-Cassel, Mecklenburg-Schwerin, etc. It does not follow that each of these families must have inherited porphyria—as the authors point out there is no evidence that Queen Victoria suffered from it or transmitted it to her descendants. But it has been diagnosed in a Queen of Scotland in the sixteenth century, a King and Queen of England and Scotland in the seventeenth, a King of Great Britain and a King of Prussia in the eighteenth, and a King of Great Britain in the nineteenth. The claim that porphyria may be called a royal malady seems justified. And whatever concerns the medical history of the royal houses of Europe concerns the history of Europe.

Full references are given in:
Brooke, J.: *King George III* (London: Constable, 1972).

CHAPTER 11

Jane Austen's Last Illness

Zachary Cope

Jane Austen died at 4.30 a.m. on 18th July 1817 at the age of 41 from an ailment the nature of which has never been ascertained, or so far as I am aware, seriously discussed. No information was furnished by the doctors who attended her, and her relatives were reticent about her illness, so that we are compelled to rely chiefly on the few comments made by the patient herself in the letters that have survived.[1] Fortunately Jane Austen was an accurate observer, and though she made light of her troubles until near the end one can rely on her definite statements.

THE EVIDENCE

The onset of her illness was insidious, but we know that she began to have a feeling of weakness or tiredness round about July 1816, and within a few weeks she experienced severe pain in the back, for in a letter dated 8th September she wrote to her sister saying:

> 'Thank you, my back has given me scarcely any pain for many days. I have an idea that agitation does it as much harm as fatigue, and that I was ill at the time of your going away from the very circumstance of your going.'

That comment is noteworthy. Three months later (16th December) she refused an invitation to dinner, giving as a reason:

> 'I was forced to decline it, the walk is beyond my strength (though I am otherwise very well).'

A month later, though she told her niece Caroline that she felt stronger, yet in a letter to her friend Alethea Bigg she for the first time confesses that her illness is serious:

> 'I have certainly gained strength through the winter and am not far from being well; and I think I understand my own case now

so much better than I did, as to be able by care to keep off any serious return of illness. I am more and more convinced that *bile* is at the bottom of all I have suffered which makes it easy to know how to treat myself.'

'Serious return' and 'all I have suffered' are significant words. The self-diagnosis of 'bile' must indicate some gastro-intestinal irritation, probably nausea or vomiting or both. Up to that time she appears to have been treating herself.

Little information is available for the month of February 1817, though we learn that there was pain in one knee, which was therefore wrapped in flannel, but in a letter dated 23rd March and written to her favourite niece Fanny we find important evidence:

'I certainly have not been well for many weeks, and about a week ago I was very poorly, I have had a good deal of fever at times and indifferent nights, but am considerably better now and recovering my looks a little, which have been bad enough, black and white and every wrong colour. I must not depend upon ever being blooming again. Sickness is a dangerous indulgence at my time of life.'

She was evidently distressed by her changing facial appearance.
Two weeks later, on 6th April, a letter written to her brother Charles tells of severer attacks:

'I have been really too unwell the last fortnight to write anything that was not absolutely necessary, I have been suffering from a bilious attack attended with a good deal of fever. . . . I was so ill on Friday and thought myself so likely to be worse that I could not but press for Cassandra's return with Frank.'

Obviously the attacks or crises were becoming more serious and she was now apprehensive. The last two available letters were written in May and show a rapid deterioration. On 22nd May she wrote to her dear friend Anne Sharp a despairing letter which, however, contains several important clues.

'In spite of my hopes and promises when I wrote to you I have since been very ill indeed. An attack of my sad complaint seized me within a few days afterwards—the most severe I ever had and coming upon me after weeks of indisposition, it reduced me very low. . . . My head was always clear, and I had scarcely any pain; my chief sufferings were from feverish nights, weakness and langour.'

Jane Austen by an unknown artist (The Mansell Collection).

In the same letter she tells her friend that she had arranged to go to Winchester so as to be under the care of a well-known surgeon there, Mr. Lyford. The other letter was to her nephew Edward and mentions that the appearance of her face was still distressing:

'I will not boast of my handwriting; neither that nor my face have yet recovered their proper beauty, but in other respects I am gaining strength very fast.'

In this letter she also mentions that she was eating her meals in a rational way and was employing herself, though lying on the sofa most of the day.

Two other witnesses must now be called. First, just before the move to Winchester her niece Caroline paid her a visit and later she was able to remember that her Aunt Jane was sitting down, dressed in a dressing-gown, looking very pale, and speaking in a weak and low voice. This testifies to her anaemia, for when in health Jane Austen had a rich colour. The last and very important piece of evidence is to be obtained from the letter in which Cassandra Austen describes the last few hours of her sister's life in such moving words. The letter was written to Fanny Knight on 20th July 1817. The important passage is the following:

'On Thursday I went into the town to do an errand your dear Aunt was anxious about. I returned about a quarter before six and found her recovering from faintness and oppression, she got so well as to be able to give me a minute account of her seisure and when the clock struck 6 she was talking quietly to me. I cannot say how soon afterwards she was seized again with the same faintness, which was followed by sufferings she could not describe, but Mr. Lyford had been sent for, had applied something to give her ease and she was in a state of quiet insensibility by seven at the latest. From that time till half past four, when she ceased to breathe, she scarcely moved a limb.'

One further fact must be mentioned. Henry Austen, Jane's favourite brother, whom she had nursed through a serious illness in 1815, who greatly encouraged her writing and helped to get her novels published, and who seemed to be very prosperous, went bankrupt in March 1816. This was a terrible mental shock to Jane, and might well have precipitated any disease susceptible of being influenced by mental shock.

DISCUSSION

Here then we have the story of an illness coming on soon after a severe mental shock, beginning with an insidious languor and a pain in the back, progressing steadily yet with definite periods of intermission, and attended by critical attacks of faintness and gastro-intestinal disturbance, yet unaccompanied by any noticeable pain anywhere, whether in abdomen, chest, or head. During the intermissions, the intelligence was acute and the appetite good. The end came in one of the crises in which faintness was a very noticeable feature.

No doubt many of the above symptoms might be accounted for by a number of conditions, but there are very few diseases which could account for them all. There is no symptom indicative of intracranial or intrathoracic disease, unless we regard the attacks of faintness as of cardiac origin. Nor, apart from bilious attacks, is there any symptom that incriminates the abdominal viscera, and bilious attacks are common accompaniments of various diseases.

The increasing lassitude and weakness might make us suspect myasthenia gravis, but in this disease we should expect some interference with speech or with chewing of food or even swallowing, and we should not expect the gastro-intestinal disturbances. Another disease that begins insidiously and has intermissions is subacute bacterial endocarditis, but in this disease gastro-intestinal attacks are uncommon and severe fainting crises rare or unknown.

There are indeed some abdominal diseases that give no signs and yet may progress and cause no other symptoms than great weakness and anaemia. Tabes mesenterica and some other forms of tuberculosis should also be considered, but such conditions are not attended by acute painless crises. Latent cancer of the stomach might cause severe anaemia and weakness before it became obvious, but should not give rise to prolonged fainting attacks, and with cancer the course is progressively downhill. Yet after reading all the evidence many times I had almost come to the conclusion that cancer of the stomach would most readily account for most of the symptoms when I bethought myself of two pathological conditions, either of which would account for most of them—Addison's disease or pernicious anaemia, and Addison's disease of the suprarenal capsules.[2] Neither of these diseases had at that time been recognised, and when Thomas Addison made his investigations he at first found difficulty in discriminating the one from the other. Both give rise to an insidiously developing weakness and languor, to anaemia, and to severe gastro-intestinal disturbances. Both are liable to intermissions during which the patient feels much better and is hopeful of recovery. Yet, in the absence of all laboratory assistance, Addison found one symptom that, in the majority of cases, enabled him to distinguish between the two conditions, and that was the appearance of the skin. In the disease which he found constantly associated with a pathological condition (usually tuberculosis) of the suprarenal bodies he noted that the skin in certain parts changed to a darker colour, usually brown but sometimes almost black, and the face was nearly always affected. He summarised the main distinguishing features as follows:

'The leading and characteristic features of the morbid state to which I would draw attention are: anaemia, general languor and debility, remarkable feebleness of the heart's action, irritability of the stomach and a peculiar change of colour in the skin.'

In some cases the dark patches of the skin are mingled with areas showing a lack of pigment—a true black and white appearance.

Though I had read the letter of 23rd March 1817 many times, it was long before I realised the true significance of that symptom which is almost pathognomonic of Addison's disease in Jane Austen's pathetic lament:

'Recovering my looks a little, which have been bad enough, black and white and every wrong colour.'

Again, when she wrote to her nephew two months later she was distressed that her face had not recovered its beauty. There is no disease other than Addison's disease that could present a face that was 'black and white' and at the same time give rise to the other symptoms described in her letters.

Addison's disease is usually—Wilks said always—due to tuberculosis of the suprarenal capsules, and it is likely that it was so in Jane Austen's case. The disease ran its course rapidly, indicating an active pathological process that might well account for any fever. Pain in the back has been noted in Addison's disease by several observers.

If our surmise be correct, Jane Austen did something more than write excellent novels—she also described the first recorded case of Addison's disease of the adrenal bodies.

CHAPTER 12

Beethoven's Deafness

Maurice Sorsby

The deafness of Beethoven has all the elements of Greek tragedy. The titanic forces in opposition are there, and the inevitable and relentless chaining of Prometheus. The world's supreme moulder of mighty harmonies is struggling against imprisonment in a world devoid of all sound. The struggle is long and bitter: it stretches over a period of more than twenty years. It wrings moving cries of despair from one whose genius was the spirit and interpreter of revolt. For the enchained Prometheus suffers and hopes; even till hope creates out of its wreck the thing it contemplates. When at length Beethoven walked in eternal silence, there came to him the mightiest of all cataracts of sound; it could hardly have mattered to him that he missed the noise of the street and the clamour of the market, for had not the gods given him to hear and to hand down the Ninth Symphony?

More than a century has passed since Beethoven died, but his inner life is so well-known and so well-documented, that it is today possible to diagnose his illnesses with more certainty than could his own medical advisers. The sources of information are mainly those autobiographical notes contained in his letters, and also the evidence from the post-mortem examinations carried out two days after his death.

THE EVOLUTION OF BEETHOVEN'S DEAFNESS

The age at which Beethoven first felt his oncoming deafness is not definitely known; nor is it definitely established that he became totally deaf, though there is no doubt that the deafness was complete for all practical purposes. At the age of 31, in 1801, Beethoven could still successfully hide his deafness from people, but by 1814 his hardness of hearing had advanced to such a degree that conversation became impossible; contemporary records say that he was 'stone-deaf' in 1819, eight years before his death, yet there is some evidence that in 1825 or 1826 Beethoven did hear a loud cry.

The first reference to his deafness is contained in a letter, dated 29th June 1801, written to his friend Wegeler. Beethoven speaks of failing hearing for the past three years, and though treatment has improved his general condition, the noises in the ears (*'sausen und brausen'*) are ever present.

'I may say that I lead a miserable life. For two years now I avoid all society for I cannot say to people "I am deaf". In another calling such a course might be possible, but in mine it creates a terrible situation . . . That you might have some idea of this strange deafness, I must tell you that at the theatre I must sit quite near the orchestra in order to follow the actors . . . It is surprising that in conversation there are people who have not noticed it [the deafness].'

In a letter written at about the same time to the Pastor Amenda, similar information is to be found. '. . . my hearing has become much weaker. Already at the time when you were with me, I felt the symptoms coming on and I kept them secret; since then it has become much worse.' That the symptoms of deafness, more manifest in 1801, had been developing for some years is also supported by the Fischhoff manuscript quoted in Thayer's classic *Life of Beethoven*; according to this document Beethoven's deafness began during the convalescence which followed on a 'severe illness' contracted in 1796 as the result of a chill. There is no evidence of any hardness of hearing before the age of 26 or 28 and, apparently, it did not become marked to any extent till about the age of 31. Another letter to Wegeler, written five months after the one already quoted (16th November 1801), shows Beethoven's pre-occupation with his ear trouble. A certain surgeon, Vering, had been treating him by blistering his arms; the noises in the ears had diminished, but hearing had not improved. 'I dare not think whether it has become worse.'

He is inclined to try Schmidt.

'Marvels are being told of galvanism: what do you think of it? A physician has told me that he saw a deaf-mute child recover its hearing, and a man, deaf for seven years, also cured. You can hardly imagine what a sad and solitary life I have been leading these last two years. My infirmity is always before me, like a spectre, and I flee from men. I must appear a misanthrope, the very thing I am not.'

Things must have been going from bad to worse in those years, 1800–02. Frantic hope and despair alternate and at the height of a fit of despair, whilst undergoing treatment at Heiligenstadt, he writes a will 'to be read and executed after my death'. It is a document written in red-hot rage against his fate. He had ceased to hope. 'It is a cry of revolt and of heart-rendering pain; one cannot hear it but be shaken with pity. He is ready to end his life; only his moral recititude keeps him back.' (Romain Rolland)

Apparently, his deafness must have been progressing but it could not have been very severe even at this stage. It was to this year, 1802, that the observation of Ries refers to. Ries relates that when walking with Beethoven he drew the master's attention to the playing of a flute by a shepherd. Beethoven could not hear it, and became very gloomy. It is probably this event that Beethoven speaks of in his will. 'But what a humiliation it is, when having some one near me who hears a flute in the distance, and I hear nothing; or that he should hear the shepherd sing, and I hear nothing.'

This period of depression passed into one of apparent tranquillity. No reference is found to the state of his ears during the subsequent years, until 1810, when he writes again to Wegeler: 'I would be happy, perhaps the happiest of men, if the demon had not pitched his tent in my ears.' To this same year belongs a letter (addressed to Bettina Brentano), according to which it would appear that Beethoven had to resort to having remarks addressed to him written down; but this letter is in all probability a forgery, all the evidence pointing that it was not till 1814 that Beethoven's hearing had deteriorated to such a degree. By 1814 his deafness must have been quite severe; this can be gathered from the remarks made by his contemporary Spohr, on Beethoven's public performance on the piano. 'It was no pleasure. To begin with, the piano was badly tuned, which hardly troubled Beethoven for he could not hear it anyhow, and secondly, as a result of his deafness there was but little left of his skill that was once so greatly admired. At *forte* the poor man was so heavy, that the chords rattled, and at *piano* he played so softly, that whole groups of notes were left out.' It was from 1814 that he depended on those writing books of which a great many exist, and no less than 138 are to be found in the National

Museum of Berlin. He always carried one about with him. But though his deafness was now so severe he still persisted in conducting. He conducted as late as 1822, but with ever-decreasing success. His friends were in fear that sooner or later it would end in a painful fiasco, such as in fact did occur in the latter year. Shindler's account of it is moving in its simplicity.

> Beethoven insisted on conducting the rehearsal [of Fidelio] . . . From the duetto of the first Act, it was evident that he heard nothing of what was passing on the stage. He slowed the movement considerably, and whilst the orchestra followed his baton, the singers kept to their proper time. A general confusion resulted. . . . Umflauf proposed an interval, without giving any reason; then after a few words with the singers, the performance went on. But the same chaos came about again. Another pause was necessary. The impossibility of continuing under Beethoven's guidance became evident; but how could one convey that to him? No one had the heart to say to him: 'Withdraw, you poor man, you cannot conduct.'
>
> Beethoven, uneasy and agitated, was looking around trying to read in the faces of people the cause of the obstacle; there was silence everywhere. Then he called me over brusquely, and giving me his writing-pad he made me write. I wrote: 'I beg you not to continue; I'll explain why at home.' In one movement he jumped down calling to me to follow him. He ran in one breath to his house: entering, he threw himself on the sofa, covering his face with his hands, remaining in this attitude till dinner. At the table it was impossible to get a word out of him: he had an expression of collapse and of the deepest sorrow. After dinner, when I wanted to leave him, he kept me back begging me not to leave him alone.
>
> 'When I was about to leave him, he asked me to accompany him to his doctor, who had a great reputation for his treatment of ear conditions . . . In all my future dealings with Beethoven, I have never known a day that could be compared to this fatal day of November. . . . He was stricken to the root of his being, and until the very end, he lived under the shadow of this terrible event.'

In between 1814 and 1822 his hearing seems to have been progressively deteriorating. There is the evidence of Czerny that in 1816 Beethoven could still carry on a conversation by the aid of the speaking-tubes made for him by Maelzar, but that a year later he could no longer hear music. It was in this year that Maelzar made a special apparatus for him to help him to continue his activities as a conductor. By 1818, according to Shindler, conversation, even with the help of speaking-tubes, had become impossible. In 1819, he is spoken of as totally deaf, by Zeltzer, who writes to that effect to Goethe, and by Atterbohm. ('He is now what is called stone-deaf.')

This is borne out by the scene at the first public performance of the Ninth Symphony in 1824. At the conclusion of the performance the audience broke out in a tumultuous applause. But Beethoven, whose back was turned to the cheering crowd, was unaware of it till one of the singers made him turn round. There is also the evidence of Gerhard von Breuning that in 1825 or 1826 Beethoven did not hear him enter his room and produce noises by striking musical instruments; he was certainly deaf for all practical purposes, though doubt as to total deafness is thrown by the following remark of von Breuning.

'At the table one of my sisters once uttered a loud and shrill scream ('*einen gellenden hohen Schrei.*') Beethoven apparently heard it, and this made him so happy that he laughed whole-heartedly, so disclosing two rows of his blinding white teeth.'

Total or subtotal deafness was therefore the condition of Beethoven towards the end of his life. Apart from the chronology of his developing deafness the following points of subjective interest are also worth noting.

(1) In the incipient stages of his deafness, Beethoven lost his hearing for high notes. He records this in his letter to Wegeler, dated 29th June 1801: 'If I am some little distance away, I cannot hear the high notes of voices and of instruments.'

(2) Earlier in life Beethoven claims to have had more perfect hearing than almost any other musician (Heiligenstadt will, 1802).

(3) In 1809, the French shelled Vienna. Ries reports that Beethoven went to his cellar and covered his head with pillows in order not to hear the shelling. According to Wegeler, these noises were painful to Beethoven's ears (Wegeler and Ries).

(4) The one mention of pain by Beethoven occurs in 1822, when he writes in February: 'Last night I was again attacked by earache from which I generally suffer at this season of the year.'

BEETHOVEN'S GENERAL CONDITION

It is necessary to review briefly such data as are available concerning Beethoven's general condition, for the light they may throw on the origin and course of his deafness.

Beethoven, though possessed of great vitality, had chronic ill-

Beethoven (Camera Press).

health. There is evidence that in his childhood he had an attack of smallpox; most of his biographers say that his face had marks bearing permanent witness to this affection. Of more doubtful value is the evidence of Dr. Weisenbach, who wrote in 1814 that Beethoven had at one time 'typhus', and that his deafness dates from that time, his nervous system having broken down. ('*Verfall seines Nerven-system.*') The earliest evidence to be gathered from Beethoven's letters is that to be found in a letter addressed to Schade (1787), in which he relates how he had hastened back to his mother who was dying from phthisis. He speaks of his own troubles with 'asthma', and of the fear that it might develop into phthisis. He is also worried by his depression of spirits 'which is to me as great an evil as my illness'. The evidence becomes more plentiful from 1800. In the letters to Amenda and Wegeler he speaks of intestinal trouble as something not new. He links up his deafness with the intestinal affection, and writes to Amenda that though the alimentary con-dition has improved by treatment, his deafness has remained un-influenced. To Wegeler he writes of his 'long-standing intestinal weakness', with its terrible colics, constant diarrhoea, leading to great prostration. In his subsequent letters complaints of diarrhoea and colicky pains keep on recurring. It would appear that he was hardly ever free from these troubles, though sometimes, and in 1812, he had particularly severe exacerbations.

Headaches of a severe type are first mentioned in a letter to Gleichenstein in 1807. They were apparently sufficiently severe and of sufficiently long duration to affect his work seriously. In 1811 he writes to the Archduke Rudolph: 'For two weeks now I have again been afflicted with headaches. I have hoped till now they would become better, but in vain; my physician still gives me hope that they will improve with time.' The letters of later years bear evidence that his physicians were wrong.

In a letter to Franz Brentano, in 1821, he relates that 'since last year till now, I have continually been ill; this summer, I had jaundice, which had persisted till the end of August. . . . Now things are better, and it seems to me that I shall again be able to live for my work . . . which has not been the case for the past two years.' But things did not go better for long. In 1823 some trouble with his eyes, probably conjunctivitis, was added to his many distractions. He spent most of his time in Baden; 1824–1825 seem to have been particularly bad years. In a letter, written in 1825 to his medical adviser (Branhoffer), he relates of spitting up blood and of blood flowing from his nose, 'a frequent occurrence in winter'.

The jaundice of 1821 and the epistaxis of 1824–25 seem to have been the prelude to the terminal illness which overtook him at the end of 1826. Starting acutely, with some pulmonary disturbance, according to Professor Wawruch who attended on him, he became better only to develop jaundice, associated with diarrhoea and vomiting, so severe that in themselves they had threatened to kill the patient. The legs, which up till then had been only mildly swollen, become more swollen and ascites became established. Between the 9th December 1826 and the 27th February 1827, Beethoven was tapped four times for his ascites. Improvement was only temporary and the condition became progressively worse. On the 26th March 1827 he died whilst a storm was shaking Vienna.

He had received the sacraments on the 24th; when the priest had gone, Beethoven addressed himself to his friends standing at the bedside: '*Plaudite amici, comoedia finita est.*'

POST-MORTEM EXAMINATION AND EXHUMATIONS

POST-MORTEM FINDINGS

Johan Wagner and his assistant Rokitansky carried out the post-mortem examination two days after Beethoven's death. They also removed the petrous portions of both temporal bones and placed them in the Anatomical Museum in Vienna. But when later on it was desired to study these bones in detail, the specimens had disappeared.

The findings given in the post-mortem report are of considerable significance, the essential features being shrunken auditory nerves and a liver reduced in size to half the normal, leathery in consistency and its cut surface was full of knotted masses.

EXHUMATIONS

Beethoven's body was exhumed twice, once in 1863, and a second time in 1888. On both occasions the remains of the skeleton were carefully investigated. It was found on the first occasion that the skull had crumbled into nine pieces. To Gerhard von Beuning it was a labour of love to piece these fragments together, and to attempt some reconstruction of these bones. The fragments, as pieced together, were photographed by Rottmayer, and a copy of this photograph is at the Beethoven Museum in Bonn. The sculptor, Alois Wittman, was charged with modelling a reconstruction of the skull. This reconstruction rests in the Anatomical Museum in Vienna. A cast of the base of the skull was also taken at the time. At the second exhumation in 1888 Dr. Choulant made drawings of the skull reconstructed once more. These drawings, showing front, back and side views, are also to be found in the Beethoven Museum at Bonn.

A good deal of controversy has raged around the photograph taken by Rottmayer. This shows a distinct bulge over the right parietal bone. No such bulge is shown in the masks of Beethoven taken during life, and on his death. The post-mortem report speaks of the uniform thickness of the vault of the skull. The careful description of the fragments disinterred in 1888, when they were in very much the same condition as in 1863, makes no mention of any irregularity in the bones, and Choulant's drawings do not show it. The bulge in the Rottmayer photograph—and enlargements based on it—is, therefore, regarded as an artifact, probably a piece of clay attached to the bones. The evidence for regarding the bulge as genuine is mainly an unpublished sketch spoken of by Jacobsohn, which is supposed to be a drawing of the fresh skull, and which is said to show this swelling of the right parietal bone.

THE TYPE AND NATURE OF BEETHOVEN'S DEAFNESS

THE TYPE OF DEAFNESS

At the age of 31 Beethoven first speaks of his deafness, and refers to it having troubled him for some three years. We have his own evidence that it could hardly have been very severe at that time, and even a year later when he felt his position so keenly as to write his Heiligenstadt will, his deafness was essentially only a reduction of the auditory field, for his complaint is that he failed to hear a shepherd in the distance playing a flute. Beethoven also relates that before the onset of his deafness, he had exceptionally keen hearing. All this taken together with the reference in the Fischhoff manuscript, which dates the beginning of his trouble to his twenty-sixth year of life, lead to the strong probability that the auditory disturbances did indeed first become apparent when Beethoven was 26, as he himself states in the Heiligenstadt will. The very fact that Beethoven's psychological reaction in 1802 was so very violent, may perhaps be taken as some indication of the fact that his deafness had not been developing insidiously since childhood but was of a fairly recent origin. We are, therefore, dealing with a type of deafness that beginning between 20 and 30 is relentlessly progressive, leading to practically total deafness by the age of 45 (at 44, in 1814, Beethoven took to his 'conversation books'.)

It is unlikely that the deafness was of the middle-ear type. There is no history of any discharge or any complaints later on of acute exacerbations, such as one is likely to get during the course of a progressive and active chronic middle-ear disease. Moreover, a middle-ear condition of such severity is not infrequently associated with vestibular symptoms, such as giddiness. Of this there is no evidence in Beethoven's history. Beethoven speaks of loss of notes of high pitch in the early stage of his deafness; this is unlike middle-ear disease, in which both high and low pitch are lost, the most preserved being the middle-scale. Moreover, both the negative and positive findings in the postmortem examination exclude the possibility of middle-ear disease; no reference is made to any perforation in the drum; if this were present it could hardly have been overlooked in the painstaking examination conducted by Wagner and Rokitansky. The postmortem findings on the Eustachian tubes exclude any severe lesion in that region. The presence in the mastoid process of 'conspicuous air-cells lined by a highly vascular mucosa', is final and conclusive evidence against the chronic suppurative variety of middle-ear diseases, though it does not exclude the possibility of the chronic adhesive type. The only support for the diagnosis of middle-ear deafness is the observation reported by Rattel in Gelineau's book *Hygiene de l'oreille et des sourds*, and quoted by Klotz-Forest to the effect that when Beethoven became completely deaf, he used the wooden drum-stick (*baguette de bois*) to hear the piano when he was composing—'one extremity he applied to the frame of the piano and the other he held between his teeth.' This is important evidence, if true, and it is rather curious that such an unusual mode of listening to the piano should have escaped notice by the many contemporary biographers of Beethoven. The original report of Rattel's observations has unfortunately been inaccessible to the present writer, and it is therefore difficult to assess its value, or to know whether it is a first-hand observation, or hearsay evidence. The absence of any history of pain in the course of the development of his deafness is further evidence against middle-ear disease, though the reference in February 1822 to earache 'from which I generally suffer at this season of the year', is rather puzzling.

Rather more evidence can be brought forward for otosclerosis. The course of the deafness suggests this affection, though of course progressive deafness may be associated with the other varieties. Beethoven's complaints of noises in the ears have been advanced by some as evidence in support of otosclerosis, but again this distressing symptom may be present with any other variety of deafness. Against otosclerosis it may be urged that in the post-mortem examination the cochlea was inspected; to have done so the region of stapes must have been looked at and bony fixation of the stapes could hardly have escaped observation. The absence of vestibular symptoms, so commonly present in oto-sclerosis, is also noteworthy. Further evidence against otosclerosis is the fact that apparently Beethoven's deafness was not of a familiar type; his brother and cousins seem to have been normal; it must, however, be admitted that very little is known of his mother and her relatives.

Nerve-deafness first manifests itself by loss of high-pitched tones, and this is what appears to have happened in Beethoven's case. But the diagnosis of nerve-deafness, strongly supported by the post-mortem findings as to the nerves being 'shrunken and without pith', has to overcome the difficulty that this type of deafness is not usually progressive; whatever damage is done is permanent, neither diminishing nor increasing with time. It is of course true that the original exciting cause of the nerve affection may persist and produce a chronic progressive lesion; and this may possibly have been the case with Beethoven, who all his life suffered from gastro-intestinal disturbances, with periodic attacks of diarrhoea.

If it was indeed nerve-deafness from which Beethoven was suffering, it is worth while noting that it was not the particular clear-cut type seen with syphilitic lesions. There was certainly no sudden onset, as is commonly seen in syphilis; nor the quickly total deafness or sudden total deafness as not infrequently occurs. There is nothing in the history to suggest acute exacerbations with complete loss of hearing during the attacks; nor is there any history of giddiness, vomiting or nystagmus, all of which occur in this variety of lesion. Moreover, syphilitic nerve-deafness has a characteristic feature all of its own, in the loss early on not only of notes of high-pitch, but also those of low-pitch (Siebenmann).

It is not at all unlikely that Beethoven's deafness was of that indeterminate type so commonly seen in practice, a type that does not lend itself to any definite diagnosis, being a composite lesion of all possible affections leading to deafness. It is only necessary to point out the extreme difficulty that so many cases present in diagnosis, and that different reputable diagnosticians will regard one and the same case as being example of otosclerosis, chronic adhesive middle-ear catarrh, or nerve-deafness. Making a retrospective diagnosis on an incomplete history, on evidence collected at a time when otology in the modern sense was hardly existent, and the pathology of the ear barely perceived, it is, of course, impossible to come to any final conclusion. It can only be said, looking backward across the gulf of a century, that Beethoven's deafness presented no features that would put it in any specially clear-cut class such as familial deafness or the dramatic nerve-deafness of syphilis.

THE CAUSE OF DEAFNESS

It is no more possible to establish the cause of Beethoven's deafness than it is in the case of the majority of patients seen at the present day. Our knowledge of the pathology of deafness is still too obscure, and certainly insufficient to recover a secret from under the dust of a century. Only speculations are possible.

Beethoven and his contemporaries seemed to have been satisfied that they knew the cause of the deafness. Beethoven himself (according to the story of Charles Neate) attributed the onset of his affliction to a fall. 'I fell on my hands. On getting up I found I was deaf, and have so remained since. The doctor said that there was an injury to a nerve.' But this story of injury, implying a severe cranial lesion, finds no support in what is known of Beethoven's life. Besides, this cause advanced by Beethoven in 1815 is not at all what he considered to be the cause in 1801, when in his letter to Wegeler, to whom he writes about his failing hearing, he states that this must have been caused by 'my long-standing intestinal weakness, which had become worse.' As already noted, Weisenbach, writing in 1814, relates that Beethoven at one time (no definite date given) had typhus, and that the deafness dated from the convalescence of this illness. The Fischhoff document, already quoted, ascribed the deafness to an illness contracted as a result of a chill in 1796.

The post-mortem examination reveals no definite cause for the deafness, but many have attempted to link up the findings which show a marked cirrhosis of the liver, with the loss of hearing. The common cause is supposed to be syphilis.

The evidence for such a far-reaching suggestion is very feeble.

Theodor von Frimmel and Leo Jacobsohn are the chief protagonists for this view. They base their decision on the following arguments:

(1) Beethoven's deafness was of the otosclerotic type. This is commonly syphilitic in origin.

(2) Beethoven had cirrhosis. This, too, is not infrequently syphilitic.

(3) The association of both these conditions makes syphilis even more probable.

(4) Von Frimmel claims that it was common knowledge in Beethoven's time that the master had venereal disease. This claim is based on a personal communication (unpublished) said to be addressed by Thayer, Beethoven's biographer, to von Frimmel. Thayer in turn obtained his information not from documents but from conversation with people who knew Beethoven.

(5) Jacobsohn had access to a private collection (which cannot be published) in which there is a document in Beethoven's own writing, which shows 'with a great probability that Beethoven was suffering from a certain disease.' No further details of this document are given.

(6) Friederich Schultze speaks of prescriptions also only to be found in a private collection, and which cannot be published, which make the diagnosis of syphilis 'undoubted'. These prescriptions seem to have had a chequered career.

(7) A deformity in Beethoven's skull is the last link of this chain. The belief in the genuineness of the deformity is based on the doubtful evidence of an unpublished sketch for which Jacobsohn vouches. But swellings of the skull are not necessarily syphilitic, and are by no means frequently due to acquired syphilis.

The circumstantial evidence is therefore hardly deserving of any serious attention and, even if it were proved that Beethoven had syphilis, there is nothing to prove that this was the cause of his deafness and of his cirrhosis.

There remains to consider whether the association of these two affections could indeed be ascribed to syphilis in Beethoven's case. It has already been shown that whatever else the deafness might have been due to, it was not a syphilitic nerve-deafness. Even the view that the deafness was otosclerotic in type gives no support for syphilis, for Jacobsohn is advancing an exploded fallacy in regarding syphilis as a very common cause of otosclerosis. Moreover, if syphilis caused the deafness somewhere at about 25, it followed a most unusual course in killing by cirrhosis of the liver at 57. Further-more, cirrhosis of the liver of syphilitic origin is as questionable an entity as otosclerosis of syphilitic origin. There are quite enough causes in Beethoven's life for cirrhosis without having to call in a problematic syphilitic infection. We know that all his life he suffered from severe gastro-intestinal disturbances. That in itself is generally recognised today as being the precursor of cirrhosis; syphilis is certainly not a factor of primary importance in cirrhosis of the liver in adults, and alcoholism has lost the great significance that was once attached to it. To the modern clinician, Beethoven's gastro-intestinal disturbances would be enough to account for the cirrhosis coming on late in life, and, if an additional factor were necessary, the widespread habit of the age to indulge in beverages—a habit that Beethoven shared with his contemporaries—would supply it. Beethoven was certainly no drunkard—in spite of his very unfor-tunate family history—but there is evidence that in the last five years of life he indulged rather freely in spirituous drinks, and this may well have contributed to cirrhosis, which could have developed as a result of the many years of gastro-intestinal affliction. The association of deafness with cirrhosis does not lend the support to syphilis that Jacobsohn sees in this association; two distinct lesions, not due to the common exciting cause of syphilis, have been known before.

SELECTED REFERENCES

Postmortem findings:
von Seyfried: *L. van Beethoven Studien*, 1832, p. 49.
Findings at exhumations:
Schaafhausen: *Corrspondenzblatt der deutsche Gesellscaft für Anthro-pologie, Ethnology und Uhrgeschichte*, October 1885, p. 147.
Langer von Edenberg, C.: 'Die Cranien dreier musikalischer koryphaen,' *Mittheilungen der Anthropolog. Gesellsch. in Wein*, 1887, Sitzungs-berichte, vol. xvii, p. 33.
Weisbach, A., Tolde, C., and Meynert, Th.: 'Bericht an den Gebeinern L. van Beethoven ... 1888,' *ibid.*, 1888, Sitzungsberichte, vol. xviii, p. 73.
Tandler, J.: 'Uber den Schadel Haydns,' *ibid.*, 1909, Sitzungsberichte, vol. xxxix, p. 260.
Biographical data and medical discussions:
A substantial number of studies are listed in the original essay.

CHAPTER 13

The Illness and Death of Napoleon

Arnold Chaplin

EDITORIAL NOTE

Three reports on the autopsy findings on Napoleon are available. The post-mortem examination was carried out by Antommarchi, his personal physician, in the presence of seven surgeons from the British Army and Navy services. The reports agree on the essential finding of a perforated gastric ulcer, sealed off by adhesions to the liver and on extensive hardening of much of the stomach, regarded as cancer. One of the reports was signed by the British surgeons, a second was an extended version by one of its signatories and the third was by Antommarchi, who on the advice of Count Bertrand (one of Napoleon's counsellors) had refused to sign the joint report and produced one of his own two years later in his memoir on Napoleon. Antommarchi's report is technically much the most competent and differs from the others in containing an unconvincing account of changes in the liver: one sentence recorded the liver as hardened devoid of 'any remarkable alterations in structure,' but the following sentence carries the bald remark that the liver was 'affected with chronic hepatitis'. This was a direct contradiction of the findings in the other reports which recorded 'no unhealthy appearances'.

This hesitant difference on the pathological findings reflected the virulent disputes on Napoleon's health at St. Helena. That he was ill was obvious to himself, his household, at least two of the British surgeons and to Antommarchi, all of whom appeared to have held that Napoleon was suffering from hepatitis induced by the climate, but Sir Hudson Lowe and the rest of the British establishment would have it that Napoleon was a hypochondriac or—as was hinted—he was merely malingering.

The essay by Arnold Chaplin is an outstanding document based largely on the unpublished Lowe papers in the British Museum. The violent partisan passions are discounted and the reconstruction of the day to day events at St. Helena during October 1815 to May 1821 show an insensitive and wooden-headed bureaucracy in conflict with a broken man clinging to a bygone tinsel glory. Chaplin accepts the diagnosis of cancer of the stomach and holds this to have developed as a complication of a gastric ulcer. That an ulcer of the stomach was present and had perforated is beyond doubt, and in the absence of present-day abdominal surgery, a lethal outcome—immediate or delayed—was inevitable. On these grounds Napoleon's captivity can be absolved from any responsibility for his death, but the incrimination of cancer is open to question.

The criteria for the diagnosis of cancer were distinctly less exacting in 1821 than those of today. Microscopy of tissues was still to come; there is thus no confirmatory evidence of the diagnosis. Cancer of the stomach gives marked emaciation and secondary deposits in the liver. Both these were lacking. Furthermore cancer as a complication of gastric ulcer is distinctly uncommon. The marked hardening of much of the stomach is indeed suggestive of cancer, but the use of calomel and possibly also other irritants in treatment cannot be overlooked as a possible explanation. In fact the treatment by calomel freely used by Stockoe and O'Meara appears to have been incriminated as the cause of death by Robert Gooch in a proposed review of Antommarchi's memoirs found by Chaplin in the Lowe papers. Other irritants might possibly also have been used. If the climate of St. Helena can be absolved from any responsibility for Napoleon's death, his medical attendants cannot be absolved as readily from being unintentional accessories.

The distinctly incompetent treatment inflicted on Napoleon has had some further faint echoes. When the body was exhumed in 1840 for reburial at Paris, Dr. Guillard, the physician who supervised the arrangements reported that the corpse was in good preservation—the appearances were of one recently interred— and the features so little changed that the face was instantly recognised by those who had known Napoleon in life. If this is taken as true, preservation for twenty years after death raises the question whether arsenic was one of the irritants used. This would of course persist in the hair and would be recoverable after very many years; a claim to that effect has in fact been made (*Nature*, 1961; 1, 103 and 1962; 194, 725).

THE EVIDENCE

There is abundant material from which to glean details as to the course taken by Napoleon's last illness, yet the pall of unveracity which hangs like a cloud over the whole period of the captivity has penetrated even to the sick-room of the stricken Emperor.

From the date of the landing in St. Helena to his death in 1821, every day is accounted for, and all those physicians who played a part in the drama have left behind them either complete accounts or fragmentary depositions. O'Meara, Stockoe, Antommarchi, and Arnott have written down their narratives of the respective periods of the last illness during which they were in attendance, but on these statements implicit reliance cannot be placed, for they were published *after* the death of Napoleon, and after the cause of his death was evident to the world. For the real opinions of these doctors, and the errors they committed, search must be made in that mine of information concerning St. Helena, the 'Lowe Papers' in the British Museum. These volumes contain the daily reports of the physicians responsible for the treatment of the patient, and in many respects they are completely at variance with the published statements.

Political considerations were responsible also for much of the misconception which arose as to the nature of the malady. On the one hand were the British Government and its instruments, ever anxious to proclaim to the world that Napoleon was in good health, and was enjoying, as far as was compatible with his position, the 'bracing airs and salubrious climate' of St. Helena. On the other was the entourage of the Emperor, ever insistent to prove the fact that the climate of St. Helena was slowly but surely sapping his strength, and that, as a result of residence on the Island, chronic hepatitis had laid its hold on him and had numbered his days. Two hostile camps were thus established, and any diagnosis which included the word 'liver' was rejected and ridiculed by the one and applauded by the other. But in pursuing this policy both parties seem to forget that, within two years after the arrival of Napoleon in St. Helena, symptoms made their appearance which, although not fitting in with the diagnosis of either party, should at least have given rise to serious apprehensions as to the grave nature of the disease. Mainly owing to this attitude the case was completely misunderstood and reflected little credit on those entrusted with the treatment.

ANTECEDENT MEDICAL HISTORY

Up to the time of his detention in St. Helena, Napoleon enjoyed the most uniform robust health. There are, however, some facts of medical interest connected with Napoleon's health which, although they do not amount to actual disease, have, nevertheless, been thrust into undue prominence by historians. One peculiar characteristic of his temperament was an habitual slow pulse. Some observers, such

Napoleon. H. Vernet. (The Mansell Collection)

as Corvisart, have stated that it rarely beat above 50 per minute, and Napoleon himself said that he had never been conscious of the beating of his heart and doubted if it did. O'Meara on the other hand, says that he found the pulse to be generally from 54 to 60 per minute, but as Napoleon was rarely well during O'Meara's stay, the former average may be accepted as correct. Records exist also of occasional attacks of vomiting followed by a state of lethargy and stupor, amounting almost to unconsciousness. These attacks occurred generally after prolonged physical exertion and mental strain, and outbursts of temper preceded them on more than one occasion. A particularly bad one is mentioned after the fatigue and disappointment incident at the battle of Aspern. Now these attacks, observed for the most part by untrained witnesses, have given rise to the statement that Napoleon was the subject of epilepsy, and it is to be regretted that some text-books of medicine when describing that disease boldly assert on such slender and doubtful data that Napoleon was epileptic. It cannot be pressed too strongly that no evidence worthy of the name exists in support of such a contention. Gusts of passion and severe vomiting followed by lethargy are poor facts on which to brand a man with the stigma of epilepsy. But in recent days the exponents of the new cardiac pathology have regarded the slow pulse and the attacks of stupor verging on unconsciousness as indications that Napoleon suffered from partial or complete 'heart block'. It may be so, but in the absence of graphic records and any reliable evidence of the state of the heart and pulse at the time of the attacks, this view must remain a supposition only.

Segur, in his classic monograph, when describing the battle of Borodino, gives an account of the health of the Emperor. He states that in addition to fever he suffered from rheumatism and an aggravation of his habitual complaint, dysuria, and that the condition became so bad that riding caused considerable pain. Since Antommarchi found at the post-mortem small calculi in the bladder and the coats of that organ diseased, it is possible that cystitis was responsible for the discomfort at that time. Difficulty of micturition was a condition from which Napoleon suffered all his life. He told Antommarchi that he had always experienced this trouble, and that after an attempt lasting some minutes only a small quantity of urine was voided, and sometimes attended with pain. He also attributed his short periods of sleep to this weakness, saying that the irritability of his bladder would not permit him to sleep for more than a few hours at a time. To complete the previous history of the case of Napoleon it remains to be said that he was always subject to constipation, and had an invincible objection to taking medicine of any kind.

It may be accepted, therefore, that the medical history of the Emperor antecedent to his deportation to St. Helena was remarkably free from any indication of the commencement of grave disease. Not a day had been lost on account of illness, and the stomachic and other ailments from which he suffered had always subsided without special treatment.

MEDICAL HISTORY AT ST. HELENA

The account of the health of Napoleon at St. Helena, for the purposes of convenience, may be divided into three periods. The first dates from October 1815 to July 1818, and occupies the time during which O'Meara acted as physician. The second extends from July 1818 to September 1819, and accounts for the time in which, with the exception of the five visits paid by Stockoe, Napoleon was not seen by any medical man; and the third, dating from September 1819 to 5th May 1821, includes the period of Antommarchi's attendance, during the last thirty-five days of which Arnott was associated with him in the treatment.

(i) OCTOBER 1815–JULY 1818 (O'MEARA IN ATTENDANCE)

Napoleon set foot on St. Helena on 17th October 1815, accompanied by Barry Edward O'Meara, the late surgeon of the 'Bellerophon', as his physician. Of O'Meara's medical record little is known beyond the fact that he had been in the Navy for some years. No unsatisfactory medical reports concerning him are in existence, and it may be assumed that he was not below the standard of medical intelligence in the Navy of his day. Of his ability as a writer there can be no doubt, for he wielded a facile pen, and his 'Voice from St. Helena' is written with more than ordinary skill in literary composition, whatever may be thought of its veracity.

Napoleon enjoyed fairly good health in St. Helena until June 1817. He was able to go out and take exercise, either riding, driving, or walking. His former precise habits of activity, however, soon gave place to those of indolence and lethargy. Still there was nothing to suggest failing health and strength, and much of his laziness and peevishness was due, no doubt, to his refusal to take exercise, so long as the restrictions of limits so repugnant to him were in force. For twenty years he had lived mostly on horse-back, and the sudden cessation of this exercise brought in its train corpulence, slackness, and indifference.

As early as October 1816, O'Meara, in his reports to Sir Hudson Lowe, describes Napoleon as being far from well. Two or three carious teeth were giving trouble, slight oedema of the feet made its appearance, and some enlarged glands in the right groin were detected. But these conditions soon subsided and nothing worthy of record took place until May and June 1817, when the patient suffered from headaches, and in July, he was laid up with a slight attack of bronchial catarrh. On 25th September, the oedema of the feet recurred, and gingivitis was troublesome, the gums being described as spongy and bleeding at the slightest touch. A tendency to nausea was also remarked.

O'Meara experienced the greatest difficulty in treating his patient, for Napoleon obstinately refused to take medicine, and demanded a satisfactory reason for every symptom and every step in the treatment. The inexact science of medicine was quite unacceptable to his mathematical mind, and he delighted in railing at the physicians who, he asserted, killed as many men as generals. For surgeons, however, he showed a decided preference since they did not work in the dark.

On 30th September 1817, the first symptoms pointing to the situation of the malady are recorded. On that day Napoleon complained for the first time of a dull pain, a heaviness, a sensation of heat in the right hypochondrium, and numbness and pain in the right scapular region. On 3rd October, O'Meara made a systematic examination of his patient and stated that the right hypochondrium felt firm to the touch, and that the tumefaction in that region was evident to the sight. On being questioned, Napoleon said he had himself observed the tumefaction two months ago, but had attributed it to corpulence. From these appearances O'Meara feared hepatitis and prescribed frictions, calomel, antiscorbutics, and sea-water baths.

From 30th September 1817 to the end, Napoleon was never completely free from the symptoms just described, and, as will be shown, with the exception of a short period of remission from October 1819 to June 1820, his health slowly but steadily deteriorated. Early in October 1817, Sir Hudson Lowe objected to the title of

'Emperor' being employed in O'Meara's official reports, and as Napoleon would not permit his physician to use any other form of address, and forbade any official report concerning his health to be made to Lowe, the services of O'Meara were dispensed with for several days. But on 19th October, Lowe agreed to accept reports from Dr. Alexander Baxter, the Deputy Inspector of Hospitals, on the understanding that they were founded on verbal statements communicated by O'Meara. By this arrangement Napoleon allowed his physician to continue his visits, and at the interview told him that he was never free from a dull pain in the right side, attended with nausea, want of sleep, and depression of spirits.

A slight amelioration of the symptoms took place at the end of March 1818, but no complete cessation, and on several occasions vomiting of undigested material was recorded. Palpitation and dyspnoea were also present at this time. But the difficulties between Sir Hudson Lowe and O'Meara had now become so acute that the latter was removed from the island at the end of July 1818, and on the 25th of that month he paid his last visit to Napoleon and reported that he found him in much the same condition.

In the preceding account of O'Meara's connection with Napoleon nothing has been taken from 'The Voice from St. Helena,' unless it agrees with the written reports to be found among the 'Lowe Papers'. For O'Meara's evidence is not trustworthy in the absence of some form of collateral testimony. Furthermore, he was an enemy of the British Government, an adherent of the chronic hepatitis theory, and at times it looks as if a link or two in the chain of symptoms had been strengthened. In any case it is evident that any other diagnosis than that of chronic hepatitis had never crossed his mind. The tumefaction over the liver, which he claimed to have noticed, was never mentioned by any other observer, and it seems probable that stress was laid on that sign to support the theory of enlarged liver as the result of chronic hepatitis.

Baxter's reports to Lowe, founded on the verbal communications of O'Meara, certainly gave the impression of an attempt to discredit the belief that Napoleon was suffering from pronounced ill-health. This was the policy of the British authorities, and Baxter was, before all, Lowe's man. He was on terms of intimacy with him, and singular in addressing him sometimes as 'Dear General' instead of the official 'Sir' adopted by all others.

(ii) JULY 1817–SEPTEMBER 1819
  (VERLING AND STOCKOE IN ATTENDANCE)

After the departure of O'Meara, the arrangements for the medical care of the Emperor became chaotic and at times verged on comedy. Lowe appointed Mr. Verling of the Royal Artillery to the post of British physician at Longwood, and presumably with the chief duty of reporting on the health of Napoleon. But the prisoner steadfastly refused to see anyone appointed by the Governor, and from July 1817 to September 1820, Verling was in charge, lived in the same house, but never even saw the patient, except by ruse and subterfuge.

During this period but little is known of the health of the Emperor. Montholon, it is true, states that he was far from well and that he spent the greater part of the day indolently, with frequent recourse to hot baths in which he remained for hours at a time. But there is no report by a medical man. One gleam of light did, however, break through the obscurity. On 17th January 1819, Napoleon had a serious attack of vertigo followed by fainting which appeared so grave that measures were taken to summon medical aid at once. On representations being made to Sir Hudson Lowe, Dr. John Stockoe, the surgeon of the 'Conqueror,' was permitted to visit him. Verling was in attendance at Longwood but, for the reasons given above, his services were not requisitioned. Stockoe found Napoleon complaining of the same old pain in the right hypochondrium and shooting pains in the right shoulder. In the night he had been seized with an attack of vertigo and faintness lasting fifteen minutes, but a warm bath had brought relief with abundant sweating. The next day the headache and giddiness still continued and the heat of the skin was reported to be considerable. No action of the bowels having taken place for twenty-four hours, Stockoe recommended a slight bleeding and a purgative and, after some difficulty, the patient agreed to be bled, and to take a dose of 'Cheltenham salt', (a then popular medication consisting of common salt and the sulphates of sodium and magnesium).

Stockoe examined the region of the liver and 'detected a degree of hardness'. But during his visits to Napoleon he had seriously compromised himself with the authorities. He had broken the regulations laid down, absurd as they were, for the guidance of any British doctor who might be called in to render medical assistance to the Emperor, and he had agreed to conditions made by Napoleon which were at variance with those demanded by the Governor. In addition he had committed the two unpardonable faults of thinking his patient really ill and, following O'Meara, had diagnosed the case as hepatitis. This could not be endured and, without regard to the preferences of the patient, his visits were ordered to cease.

(iii) SEPTEMBER 1819 TILL DEATH ON MAY 5TH 1821
   (ANTOMMARCHI AND ARNOTT)

(i) *Antommarchi*

While these events were taking place in St. Helena, representations had been made to the British Government to permit a physician chosen by the family of Napoleon to proceed to the island. The permission was granted, and the choice fell upon a young Corsican, Francesco Antommarchi, who was reputed to be a good anatomist. Accordingly he proceeded to Rome, and received there the reports of O'Meara and later those of Stockoe, both of whom insisted that the Emperor was suffering from hepatitis. Antommarchi was only 30 years old and had but little experience in medicine, whatever may have been his skill in anatomy. He accepted without question the statements of O'Meara and Stockoe and, before he left London, had diagnosed Napoleon's illness as hepatitis. In London at his interview at the Colonial Office, he states that he was told, in effect, that there was no occasion to hurry, that O'Meara and Stockoe were unworthy of credence, and that he might take it as true that Napoleon was very well. Whether true or not, this was at any rate in accordance with the official view, and it is not pleasant to observe the way in which the British authorities clung obstinately, throughout the whole course of the illness, to the opinion that nothing serious was taking place, in spite of the fact that definite statements to the contrary were being made by those in personal attendance. Baxter and Verling must have known that Napoleon's health was far from good, but they had their cue, and took frequent opportunities to disparage any account which mentioned illness.

Antommarchi arrived in St. Helena on 20th September 1819, and remained in more or less constant attendance on Napoleon to the end. He published, in 1823, a book entitled *Les Derniers Moments de Napoleon*, in which he described more fully than any other writer the symptoms and progress of the malady. This information would be of immense value to the medical student of the last illness, did it not come from such a thoroughly untrustworthy source for, unforfortunately, Antommarchi's book is highly tinctured with romance and without corroboration is of very little value. The book takes the form of a journal, and at the beginning of the record of the day's events, a short paragraph is given of the medical condition of the patient. It is known, however, that Napoleon early conceived a dislike for Antommarchi, which went to the length of ordering a letter to be written to him in which it was stated, that the Emperor had lost all confidence in him, and that his daily visits might be dispensed with. The 'Lowe Papers' also contain an excellent criticism of the errors, to give them no worse name, in Antommarchi's book. But his account of the progress of Napoleon's malady contains nothing improbable in it, and it is almost inconceivable that Antommarchi's description of the case was specially 'cooked' from day to day. Indeed his story of the illness, where it can be corroborated, has not been found to err to any considerable extent.

Antommarchi made his first examination of the patient on 23rd September 1819, and found him with a pulse of 60, and a tongue coated with fur. Napoleon complained of constant pain or uneasiness in the right hypochondrium, in the right shoulder, and in the right breast. A dry cough was present, and from time to time nausea and vomiting had supervened. On examination of the affected parts, Antommarchi states that he found the region over the left lobe of the liver hard and painful to the touch. For these conditions he prescribed exercise, a calming potion, hot baths, and a liniment composed of opium and ammonia.

On 19th December, Napoleon had a sharp attack of colicky pains which soon subsided, and it may be inferred that he was in fair health from this date to 18th July 1820, for there is a hiatus in Antommarchi's diary covering that period. Indeed Napoleon had so far recovered his health that in May 1820, he resumed exercise on horse-back, and this was rendered more easy by the relaxation of the limits assigned to him which took place on 31st December1819.

But a change for the worse manifested itself in July 1820, and for the greater part of this month Napoleon suffered severely from the old pain, occasional vomiting of bitter bilious matters, a slight dry cough, sweatings, and constipation. The treatment appears to have consisted of enemas and frictions with liniments of various kinds.

During August, and up to the middle of September, a remission of all the symptoms took place, but on the 15th, he was again attacked with increased abdominal pain, nausea, vomiting, and fever. Fresh signs of serious import soon made their appearance. Fatigue after the slightest exertion became pronounced, the pulse was 80 and sometimes irregular, the extremities were often of icy coldness, and frequent fits of lethargy were noticed. But the more acute symptoms of this attack did not persist for long for, on the 18th, the Emperor rode round the limits, and returned in two and a half hours somewhat exhausted. On 4th October, he took his last ride in public, proceeding across the island to the residence of Sir William Doveton, where he had breakfast, but on his way home he was so tired that he was compelled to complete the journey in his carriage.

Napoleon tried to 'ride off' the ever-increasing weakness, but soon carriage exercise and short walks were all that could be attempted, and even these taxed his strength severely. A new sign of the progress of the disease was constipation alternating with diarrhoea, the motions consisting of mucus and undigested material, and to this was added flatulent distention of the abdomen. After 15th September, although the symptoms abated from time to time, there was no real improvement, and from thence onward to the end of the history of the case is but a plain tale of gradually failing health. The increasing infirmity and an accentuation of the symptoms continued all through the end of 1820 and the beginning of 1821, and on 18th March, Napoleon went out in his carriage for the last time. It was now a melancholy picture, the greatest genius, and the most powerful energy of modern times, at the age of 51, a prisoner, with strength exhausted, and body wracked with pain, slowly creeping about Longwood, leaning for support on the arm of an attendant.

The chief symptoms of the illness previous to its final stage may be recapitulated here with advantage. They were: (1) Persistent pain situated in the right hypochondrium. (2) Pain, either dull or lancinating in character, fixed in the right scapular region and in the right breast. (3) Nausea and vomiting. (4) Constipation at times alternating with diarrhoea. (5) Flatulent distention of the abdomen. (6) Fever attended with profuse sweatings. (7) A more or less constant dry cough. (8) Increased pulse rate. (9) Coldness of the extremities. (10) Loss of appetite. (11) Marked and increasing prostration.

At no time was there any evidence of jaundice, and the motions always appeared normally coloured. It is true the complexion had a sallow appearance, but that had always been a marked characteristic of the Emperor.

Now many of the symptoms given above pointed strongly to definite disease in some part of the alimentary tract, presumably the stomach, but this idea appears to have hardly crossed Antommarchi's mind for, as late as 17th March 1821, he wrote to his friend Colonna re-affirming his belief that endemic chronic hepatitis was the correct diagnosis, and that as a result the digestive functions had become impaired. Dramatically he called all the world to witness that the malady of Napoleon was due to climatic influences and that, unless removal from St. Helena took place, death would soon close the scene.

In the main, Antommarchi appears to have prescribed suitable remedies for the relief of the symptoms, with one important exception. On 22nd, 23rd, and 24th March, he administered a quarter of a grain of tartar emetic and says the vomiting was abundant. No doubt it was, with the stomach in a state of severe ulceration. But what must have been the agony of the patient who was made to submit to such treatment? No wonder Napoleon stigmatised his physician as 'assassin', and consigned him and his drugs to the devil.

During the last half of March 1821, Antommarchi frequently reports exacerbations of fever, followed by profuse sweatings and extreme coldness of the limbs. These were of course rigors; but his view seems to have been that they were manifestations of the activity of the hepatitis which was supposed to be killing his patient. Constipation of a particularly obstinate type became prominent at this time, and the vomiting was more frequent and severe. The pain which before had remained localised now extended over the greater part of the abdomen, and the whole of that region became very tender on manipulation. Much of this tenderness was due to the excessive amount of gaseous distention which was partially relieved by frictions and hot fomentations. The appetite was very poor and capricious, and Madame Bertrand told Assistant Surgeon Rutledge that for some weeks Napoleon had contented himself, while the others were at dinner, with chewing small pieces of underdone meat, which he rejected after having extracted the juice.

(ii) *Arnott*

On 25th March 1821, the condition was so serious that Antommarchi deemed it necessary to consult with Dr. Archibald Arnott, the surgeon of the 20th Regiment, and, for the time being, the senior medical man on the island. Arnott did not see Napoleon on that occasion, but was told by Antommarchi that the patient was labouring under great functional derangement of the stomach, with gastrodynia, vomiting, costiveness, and wasting, and that, on 17th March, he had been seized with a febrile attack. On hearing this description Arnott advised purgatives, a blister to the stomach, and saline draughts. But these methods were repugnant to Napoleon's desires, and they were not adopted. On 30th March, Antommarchi administered six grains of extract of rhubarb which produced abundant vomiting. On the two succeeding days the Emperor was much worse, and became somnolent and lethargic. Antommarchi now lost no time but insisted on the British physician being called in, and on 1st April, Arnott saw Napoleon for the first time.

Before dealing with Arnott's treatment of the case it will be necessary to comment upon the documents in existence which disclose the attitude he took throughout the time he was in attendance. In 1822, Arnott published a little book, now very rare, in which he describes his treatment of the Emperor. The book is a series of daily reports in which are recorded the chief symptoms, and the measures adopted for their relief. As a diary of a case, the book is concise, accurate, and in every way admirable, and from a perusal, one would suppose that the physician, who wrote it understood perfectly the serious-nature of the case he was called upon to treat. But the book was written *after* the death of the patient, and after the cause of death was known to the world. The 'Lowe Papers' are rarely silent regarding any incident connected with the captivity, and in volumes 20,157, and 20,214, in the British Museum, any one can read Arnott's reports made from day to day, also his verbal reports given to Lowe and Sir Thomas Reade, and carefully written down by that most accurate of military secretaries, Major Gorrequer. There, can be read as plainly as if they were written and spoken yesterday, the views of Dr. Archibald Arnott concerning the illness of his patient Napoleon. After a survey of these reports, a feeling akin to consternation is left, that any physician attending a man so obviously in a dying condition could misread the signs so completely, that on 22nd April 1821, that is eight days before Napoleon became moribund, he was able to assure the British authorities that there was no danger, that the disease was merely hypochondriasis, and that the cure would be tedious owing to the fact that the patient could not be given the thing he most desired, liberty. On 17th April, Arnott had already told Sir Thomas Reade that the disease was hypochondriasis, and that if a 74-gun frigate appeared in the bay to set him at liberty, Napoleon would be up and on his legs directly!

Now Arnott was the medical representative of the British Government at Longwood, and he was perhaps influenced by the official view that Napoleon was well or, at all events, that the reports of his ill-health were over-stated. It was in a sense his business to contest the view held at Longwood, that 'liver' and climate had anything to do with the Emperor's illness, if illness there was, and it may be accepted as certain, that had he countenanced either the one or the other, his reign at Longwood would have been cut short promptly, and all hope of preferment in the future sacrificed. In minimising the illness of his patient he followed only in the footsteps of his predecessors Baxter and Verling. But there was a difference; they had never attended Napoleon professionally while Arnott was in constant attendance for thirty-five days. According to all accounts Arnott deservedly held a high reputation for integrity which was shared equally by the Frenchmen at Longwood and the authorities at Plantation House. But, with the disasters which had befallen O'Meara and Stockoe ever in his mind, it is conceivable that he shrank from taking upon himself the responsibility of proclaiming the unpalatable truth, until it was patent to everybody, that Napoleon was a dying man. The only other view that provides any explanation of his attitude is equally unfortunate, for it convicts him of medical incapacity. Still if a choice must be made, it is hoped for the credit of Arnott that his mistaken diagnosis was made honestly, and not with a desire to accommodate himself to the official view. Well might Forsyth the apologist of Sir Hudson Lowe, with Arnott's reports before him, desire to draw a veil over the official accounts of the closing scenes of the illness, on the ground that decency and good taste would be violated. He refers very little to the reports, and contents himself with saying that Arnott did not at first understand the serious nature of the illness.

The first visit of Arnott to Napoleon took place on 1st April 1821, in the evening. The room was so darkened that he was unable to distinguish the features of the Emperor. As a result of the examination he could discover no tension or hardness of the abdomen, the pulse was tranquil, and the heat moderate. In his official report he is careful to say, 'the room was dark, so that I could not see General Bonaparte, but I felt him, or some one else.' However, on the following day Arnott saw his patient again, in broad daylight, and could no longer support the implied doubt as to his identity. He found the room and the bed-linen in a dirty state, for Napoleon had been allowed to expectorate anywhere at will. The pulse of the patient was 72, the tongue loaded with fur, and complaint was made of an incessant gnawing pain in the stomach with more or less constant nausea and vomiting. The bowels never acted without assistance, and the treatment was, therefore, directed towards overcoming this condition, and allaying the pain and vomiting. Various purgatives were prescribed, but Napoleon could only with difficulty be prevailed upon to take them, and use was made of enemas. It was soon found that the vomiting and pain was always relieved after free evacuation, and the attainment of this result constituted the main principle of Arnott's treatment. The febrile attacks of which Antommarchi had spoken were frequent, and Arnott rightly viewed these exacerbations as true rigors. After several examinations of the patient, the physician was able to report to Sir Thomas Reade that the condition was 'mainly mental,' that there was no wasting of the body, and that, although Napoleon constantly said 'le foie', and winced when the right hypochondrium was palpated, no induration or swelling could be detected. Montholon had asserted that Napoleon was as thin as he was in 1800, but Arnott would not admit any wasting, and said that his patient's wrist was as round as his. He was, however, much struck with the pastiness and the cadaverousness of the Emperor's countenance. On 11th April, Arnott made a more extended examination, and had to admit that the legs were much fallen away, or as Napoleon preferred to put it, 'the devil had eaten his legs', and on 16th April, he stated that the wasting was considerable.

On several occasions Arnott told Lowe that he could discover no organic affection and that the disease was hypochondriasis. When Lowe appeared incredulous and instanced the pain, the vomiting, and the feeling of heat over the liver as hardly compatible with such a diagnosis, Arnott assured him they were all symptoms of hypochondriasis. But at the time he was making these airy statements he notes in his book, vomiting, pain in the stomach, rigors and the pulse 84. When asked by Napoleon where he thought the disease was situated, he replied that 'he conceived it to be in the digestive organs.'

(iii) *The end*

In the meantime Napoleon's condition was becoming daily more serious. The vomiting was incessant, on one occasion lasting from 9 p.m. to 5 a.m.; the pain and distention of the abdomen were severe, and the rigors of daily occurrence. The pulse was often irregular, and generally from 30 to 35 beats above the normal. After 16th April, he was comatose several times, and the progressive weakness made rapid strides. The mental condition showed considerable deterioration, and towards the end of the month he recollected everything of previous days, but made frequent mistakes with respect to present events. On 17th April, when Arnott made his customary visit he found the patient whistling and, on seeing the doctor, he stopped abruptly with his mouth wide open, staring vacantly. He also mistook Arnott for Stockoe, or O'Meara. On 14th and 15th April, taking advantage of a slight remission of the symptoms, Napoleon summoned Montholon and Marchand, shut himself up in his room with them, and dictated in clear terms his last will and testament.

But little advantage will be gained by detailing the symptoms of the illness from day to day during the month of April, for beyond the fact that they all became more and more accentuated there is little else to tell. The treatment of the patient by means of drugs appears to have been appropriate. Various prescriptions containing stomachic sedatives, such as bicarbonate of potash, cinnamon, and gentian, were tried, and use was also made of the bitter infusions. But very few of the prescriptions were taken, and enemas, and occasional purgatives by the mouth were the only regular methods of medical treatment. When it is remembered that vomiting of a persistent and distressing kind was the main symptom, it may perhaps be wondered why no attempt was made to use bismuth, and opium [sedatives then available]. On two or three occasions opium in the form of tincture was administered but was not persevered with. It is however, possible that some of the pain and discomfort produced by the incessant vomiting might have been alleviated had the patient been placed under the influence of these drugs. But no medicines could do more than palliate such a grave condition and, on 25th April, two days after Arnott had asserted that there was no danger, symptoms made their appearance which could not be disregarded. The prostration became extreme, the vomiting incessant, and the material thrown off the stomach for the first time was of a grumous nature, which changed on the 27th to distinct 'coffee ground' vomit. The stools were also tarry in consistence and colour. The Emperor was now generally somnolent, or actually comatose, and on 28th April, he talked incoherently and became delirious. The pulse rose in frequency, varying from 100 to 108, and became perceptibly weaker. On 1st May, singultus made its appearance, and at 3 a.m. on the next day Napoleon was insensible. Arnott, who had become seriously alarmed when the saw the 'coffee ground' vomit on 27th April, had some slight hope for his patient on 4th May but on what grounds it is difficult to say, seeing that Napoleon had been comatose or delirious for three days previously. On 4th May, the pulse rose to 110, the patient was unconscious, the motions were passed involuntarily, *risus sardonicus* was present, and the eyes were fixed. Napoleon remained in this condition until eleven minutes to six on the evening of 5th May 1821, when he expired.

DISCUSSION

In the light of present-day knowledge of disorders of the digestive tract it is fairly easy to reconstruct the case of Napoleon, and to advance a theory which will account for the symptoms and progress of his disease. From an investigation of its symptoms and course, and remembering the appearances of the stomach as disclosed by the post-mortem examination, it would seem to be most probable that Napoleon suffered in the first instance from a chronic ulcer of the stomach, from the edges of which a cancer developed about seven or eight months before his death.

There are several reasons which render it improbable that Napoleon was suffering from cancer of the stomach during the whole period he was in indifferent health. It has been stated already that the first symptoms pointing to definite disease made their appearance on 30th September 1817. The illness lasted, therefore, three years and seven months, and that is an unusual time for malignant disease of the stomach to continue. On the other hand, this length of time is not incompatible with the form of slow growing cancer at the pylorus, and that which produces the small thick-walled 'leather bottle' variety of stomach, conditions which were not found in Napoleon's case. The clinical history is also against the probability of cancer having been present throughout the illness. Up to October 1820, indifferent health would have been a correct description of the condition of Napoleon; but at that time a sudden declension took place, and from then on to the end he was dangerously ill. Something had happened which rapidly sapped the strength and produced symptoms of gastric disorder far more acute than those which had been endured for three years. Napoleon began to lose strength rapidly emaciation supervened, vomiting became more persistent, and the pain increased in severity. Was not this grave change due to the development of a rapid growing cancer in the lips of the chronic ulcer?

The absence of secondary growths elsewhere may also be urged against the theory of cancer during the whole period of the illness. All three accounts of the post-mortem examination assert the healthiness of the other organs, but from the appearances post-mortem and the clinical history, it is highly probable that the cancer was of rapid growth. At any rate, ulceration of the growth must have taken place rapidly towards the end, for it will be remembered that no vomiting of 'coffee ground' material occurred until within eight days of death. Finally, there is the all-important post-mortem evidence of the chronic ulcer of the stomach, from the lips of which were sprouting fungous scirrhous masses which were invading successive portions of the gastric mucous membrane.

Chronic ulcer of the stomach during the first three years of the illness is then a most likely solution of the symptoms, and several clinical facts may be adduced in support of this opinion.

The character and situation of the pain have an important bearing on the diagnosis between cancer and chronic ulcer. For the first three years the pain was never severe, but was unalterably fixed in the right hypochondrium and in the region of the right shoulder. Now the right hypochondrium is not the common situation for the pain produced by chronic ulcer; but such an acute observer as Brinton has laid great stress on the region of the pain as a guide to the situation of the ulcer and has stated that, when the ulcer is in the neighbourhood of the pylorus, the pain is felt in the right hypochondrium. Fenwick also remarks on the fact that the pain in the right shoulder, so often complained of in chronic ulcer, is sometimes associated with adhesions formed between the stomach and the liver, and this also expresses the condition in the case under review.

The onset of exacerbations of fever attended with profuse perspirations, which became such a constant symptom during the closing months of Napoleon's life, is of much interest, for Van Valzah and Nesbit remark that cancer of the stomach is as a rule a disease without fever, but that when perigastritis is present, an irregular febrile type often manifests itself which closely resembles malaria, and is attended with abundant perspiration.

Carious teeth and gingivitis were considerable sources of trouble to Napoleon for the first year and a half of his stay on the island and, on 15th October 1817, a tooth was extracted which Baxter claimed to be the first surgical operation to which the Emperor had been subjected. There can be no doubt that 'oral sepsis' was present in a marked degree, and it has been suggested that this condition may have played a part in the production of gastric ulcer by infecting the stomach.

Therefore, from a consideration of the evidence adduced, it may be stated, that although no proofs exist to make certain the diagnosis of chronic ulcer developing later into a cancer, yet the presumption of such being the case is warranted and highly probable.

A few more matters in connection with the illness remain to be considered. The position of the disease rendered it most unlikely that a tumour could have been seen or felt. The emaciation as the result of the disease was trivial when the duration is taken into account, and is an additional reason for refusing to regard the case as one of cancer from its inception.

There is no pathological evidence to support the view that Napoleon suffered from, or that his life was shortened by, attacks of hepatitis produced by climatic influences, for the parenchyma of the liver was sound and free from defect. It is true that perihepatitis affecting the capsule of the liver was found, but that was clearly secondary to the disease of the stomach. The clinical evidence against the hepatitis theory is, however, not nearly so strong. On the first appearance of the symptoms it was not unreasonable of O'Meara to suspect interference with the proper functions of the liver, but when, after a long period, no amelioration of the condition of his patient was shown, he should have seen reason to reconsider his diagnosis.

Napoleon, then, died of cancer of the stomach which most likely originated in a chronic ulcer, and remained undiagnosed until the post-mortem examination was made. Of the medical acumen displayed by those who attended him, enough has been said to show that not one of the doctors had any correct idea of the true nature of the disease. Political bias of necessity divided them into two opposite camps and obscured the issues. On the one hand, were those who were interested to represent the Emperor as being slowly done to death by the rigours of harsh confinement, in an unhealthy climate where tropical influences would have a baneful effect; on the other, those who were chiefly concerned to show that captivity in St. Helena was as healthy and almost as blissful as residence in the Garden of Eden, and to assert, in spite of malicious reports to the contrary, that Napoleon was either very well, or, at all events, that the reports of his ill-health were much exaggerated. Engaged in this unworthy wrangling, the physicians lost all sense of proper perspective, and the great patient himself became of little more account than a pawn in the game. Arnott is undoubtedly the worst offender in this respect, and if the opinions he expressed in his reports were governed by politics his conduct is most blameworthy. But he bore a high reputation for honour and honesty, and it is possible that, swayed by the official desire to minimise the alarming reports of the Emperor's health emanating from Longwood, he completely misjudged the case and honestly thought that the illness was one of hypochondriasis. But even on that supposition he stands convicted of culpable ignorance.

No reasonable doubt can exist that Napoleon was in ill-health for the greater part of his period of detention, but his indisposition was due to the slow but steady march of a mortal disease, in which climatic influences and diplomatic illnesses played no part. The doctors were all men of limited professional attainments and, in some cases, of mediocre intelligence. Through force of circumstances, over which they had no control, they were called upon for a brief span to play a part in the closing scenes of the greatest of political dramas, and were thrust into undue prominence on the stage. When the curtain fell, they passed from the light, and were heard of no more.

CHAPTER 14

Darwin's Health in Relation to His Voyage to South America

A. W. Woodruff

The nature of Darwin's illness presents a fascinating problem bearing on general and tropical medicine, and on the understanding of the minds of men of genius. There can be no doubt that Darwin was a genius and also that he was an intensely kind, sensitive, and gentle person. Throughout all his letters and writings his warm humanity is abundantly apparent, and this sensitivity, perceptiveness, and brilliance may have rendered him more susceptible than most people to anxiety when under stress.

His voyage to South America is relevant to his illness principally because it was there that he may have been exposed to infection with South American trypanosomiasis or Chagas's disease, and also there that he made observations from which he came to conclusions about the origin of species. He delayed publication of those conclusions for nearly thirty years, a delay which may well have a bearing on the diagnosis.

Darwin was $22\frac{1}{2}$ years old when he embarked on HMS *Beagle* for a voyage round the world, and he was 5 years older when he returned to Britain to lead a life of chronic semi-invalidism for which Adler (1959) made the brilliant suggestion that South American trypanosomiasis was responsible. It was at Luxan, in the province of Mendoza, Argentina, that, while on a trek, he 'experienced an attack (for it deserves no less a name) of the Benchuca, a species of Reduvius, the great black bug of the Pampas,' and he stated, 'it is most disgusting to feel soft wingless insects, about an inch long, crawling over one's body' (Darwin, C., 1906). These bugs were almost certainly *Triatama infestans*, the principle vector of Chagas's disease, or South American trypanosomiasis. This disease can cause myocardial damage and heart failure, and may also damage autonomic

215

plexuses in the oesophagus and colon, causing dilation of these organs which becomes gross in some cases. It may be associated with dysphagia, regurgitation of food, vomiting, or constipation. In many persons, however, the infection is symptomless, and surveys latterly carried out in South America have shown considerable proportions of the healthy population to have a positive complement-fixation test for the disease, the position in this respect being somewhat similar to that caused by primary tuberculosis with its effect on the tuberculin test.[1]

CLINICAL CONSIDERATIONS

CLINICAL PICTURE

In examining the cause of Darwin's illness the first question to consider is what the symptoms were. In his autobiography (Barlow, 1958, p. 79) one finds one of the first references to it in the account of the period just before the *Beagle* set sail for South America. He wrote: 'These two months at Plymouth were the most miserable which I ever spent, though I exerted myself in various ways. I was out of spirits at the thought of leaving all my family and friends for so long a time, and the weather seemed to me inexpressibly gloomy. I was also troubled with palpitation and pain about the heart, and like many a young ignorant man, especially one with a smattering of medical knowledge, was convinced that I had heart disease. I did not consult any doctor, as I fully expected to hear the verdict that I was not fit for the voyage, and I was resolved to go at all hazards.'

Chronic undue fatigability was a feature of the illness, but this too he had before leaving for South America, and he wrote to his sister and to Professor Henslow in September 1831 about it (Darwin, F., 1958, pp. 125–6). The fatigue mentioned in these two letters may have been no more than normal, for he had been travelling at the time; but, even so, for a young man of 22 to emphasise his fatigue in multiple letters indicates his concern about it. A more important reference to it, however, is in a letter to Professor Henslow (*ibid.*, p. 123) written at a time when he was uncertain, as a result of his father's objections, whether he would go on the voyage. He wrote: 'Even if I was to go, my father disliking would take away all energy, and I should want a good stock of that.' From this it seems that, at this early age, he appreciated that, in him, lack of energy could arise from the stress of mental conflict and opposition to the views of those whom he respected, stress to which his later work subjected him greatly.

In the same month, September 1831, he also wrote about his hands, and from later references to the same complaint it appears that this consisted of trembling of the fingers and possibly some degree of dermatitis. He wrote: 'Ask my father if he thinks there would be any objection to my taking arsenic for a little time, as my hands are not quite well, and I have always observed that if I once get them well, and change my manner of living about the same time, they will generally remain well. What is the dose?' (*ibid.*, p. 127). The quotation shows that this affection of the hands, like the fatigability and heart symptoms, had been present for some time before he embarked.

He returned home from his voyage in October 1836, and in 1838 was offered, and hesitatingly accepted, the post of secretary to the Geological Society, London. The reason for this hesitation is described in the volume of reminiscences and selected letters edited by his son (*ibid.*, p. 153). Darwin's doctors had urged him, so he wrote, 'to give up entirely all writing and even correcting press for some weeks. Of late anything which flurries me completely knocks me up afterwards, and brings on a violent palpitation of the heart.'

In September 1842 Darwin and his family moved from London to Down, and of this period he wrote in his autobiography (Barlow, 1958, p. 115): 'We went a little into society, and received a few friends here; but my health almost invariably suffered from the excitement, violent shivering and vomiting attacks being thus brought on. I have therefore been compelled for many years to give up all dinner-parties; and this has been somewhat of a deprivation to me, as such parties always put me into high spirits. From the same cause I have been able to invite here very few scientific acquaintances.'

Adler (1959) suggested that Darwin's exhaustion after physical effort could be explained on the basis of myocardial involvement with *Trypanosoma cruzi*, the causative organism for South American trypanosomiasis. There is, however, good documentary evidence from his letters, some of which I have quoted, that the complaint of exhaustion existed before his exposure to infection with Chagas's disease. A second very important point is that these symptoms were

Charles Darwin (The Mansell Collection).

brought on by emotionally charged situations, not by physical efforts as they would have been were they caused by myocarditis.

Thus within a few weeks of his severe ill-health in 1838 he went on a geological expedition to Glen Roy, in Scotland, and wrote in a letter to Lyell (Darwin, E., 1958, p. 155): 'I wandered over the mountains in all directions, and examined that most extraordinary district.' He mentioned studying an erratic block on a peak 2,200 feet above sea-level. Clearly the palpitations at this time, three years after the biting by the benchuca bugs, were not associated with impairment in exercise tolerance but were similar to those which he had before sailing.

In 1848, just after his father's death, he wrote to his friend Hooker (*ibid.*, p. 169): 'All this winter I have been bad enough . . . and my nervous system began to be affected, so that my hands trembled, and my head was often swimming.' Again it seems that he was suffering from a continuation of the trouble with his hands, of which he wrote to his sister while waiting for the *Beagle* to sail. In 1852 he wrote to Mr. W. D. Fox (*ibid.*, p. 171): 'My nights are *always* bad, and that stops my becoming vigorous. . . . My dread is hereditary ill-health.' In 1858 he wrote to his friend Hooker (*ibid.*, p. 214) concerning the proofs of the *Origin of Species*: 'Murray proposes to publish the first week in November. Oh, good heavens, what a relief to my body to banish the whole subject from my mind!' In 1860 again to Hooker he wrote (*ibid.*, p. 255): 'I have been very poorly, with almost continuous bad headache for 48 hours and I was low enough, and thinking what a useless burden I was to myself and all others, when your letter came, and it has so cheered me.' In 1871 he wrote to Professor Lankester (*ibid.*, p. 304) concerning vivisection, 'it is a subject which makes me sick with horror so I will not say another word about it, else I shall not sleep tonight.' In his son's reminiscences of him it is stated (*ibid.*, p. 85) that 'in 1871 he went to the little church for the wedding of his elder daughter, but could hardly bear the fatigue of being present through the service.' The same was true of other occasions when he was present at such ceremonies, and it is also recorded that this symptom prevented him from attending his father's funeral.

The causative relationship between mental stress and fatigue is noteworthy, particularly when it is recalled that he had earlier recognised that to go against his father's wishes would deprive him of energy. A special emotional relationship with his father appears to be indicated and is referred to later.

The clinical picture, then, is of palpitations, lassitude but not true weakness, headaches, shivering, tremulousness, sleeplessness, and, we now know from his health diary, flatulence. These symptoms were brought on or aggravated not by exercise but by meeting people, facing public gatherings, the anxiety of correcting proofs against time (editors and publishers please note), and emotionally charged meetings, including attendance at church.

SUGGESTION OF CHAGAS'S DISEASE

In seeking the truth about the nature of his illness, of which it is certain Darwin himself would have approved no matter what the findings were, the question that can most usefully be tackled probably is whether this clinical picture could have been caused by Chagas's disease. Adler, in making this thought-provoking suggestion, states that 'a purely psychological aetiology for Darwin's illness cannot be accepted as conclusive until all other factors have been eliminated.' This, of course, is arguable. Diagnosis is best made not by a negative process of exclusion but by positive recognition of symptoms and signs. In that respect we are fortunate in this case; Darwin in his letters and writings gives us a better history than one can obtain from most patients, and he was examined by the best observers of the day, who assure us there were no abnormal physical signs. But can we eliminate Chagas's disease? I believe we can. Regarding the suggestion that Darwin's exhaustion after little effort could be explained on the basis of an infection with *Trypanosoma cruzi* there is good documentary evidence from his letters, some of which I have quoted, that symptoms of exhaustion existed before his exposure to infection with Chagas's disease.

A second very important point is that these symptoms were brought on by emotionally charged situations rather than by physical effort, as they would be were they caused by myocarditis. The record of going off to Scotland in 1838 and undertaking strenuous mountain walking just after being severely ill is important. There is no evidence here of myocardial failure. Writing in 1876 at the age of 67, he recollects that it was in 1842 that he was for the last time strong enough to climb mountains or take long walks for geological work (Barlow, 1958, p. 99), but there is nothing to suggest that true physical incapacity rather than lassitude of functional origin was the cause of this lack of strength. Moreover, in 1842 he was becoming increasingly preoccupied with non-geological work and with his family and residence at Down. If in 1842 myocardial failure had been the cause of his giving up high mountain walking, is it conceivable that he could live till 1882 withnot developing overt physical signs of such failure? I have discussed this point with several eminent cardiologists and physicians, and they all consider such a course inconceivable. This point, even were it the only one to be taken into consideration, virtually excludes an organic basis for his illness.

EXERCISE TOLERANCE

I have gone further into his exercise tolerance because it is fundamental to a consideration of this diagnostic problem and have done some little research into exercise known to have been carried out by Darwin throughout his long life. In his son's reminiscences of his father (Darwin, F., 1959, p. 75) one finds that he 'took a short turn before breakfast, a habit which began when he went for the first time to Down and which was preserved to almost the end of his life.' After breakfast he worked, read his letters, had others read to him, and at midday took a walk whether it was wet or fine—a point to note, for a sick man seldom ventures out in bad weather if he can avoid it. This exercise usually consisted of several turns round the sand-walk. This he did almost to the end of his life at the age of 73. I visited Down and asked the way to the sand-walk to see for myself what a round of it entailed. I was surprised to be told by the janitor, 'It will take you a full 20 minutes to go round.' I had imagined it to be a much less arduous piece of exercise. It consists of a circuit, and a very pleasant one, through trees, many planted by Darwin. Pacing it out showed that the nearest part of the circuit was 475 yards from the house and that a single circuit of the sand-walk itself measured 580 yards, so that to walk to the sand-walk, take a single turn round it, and return to the house is almost one mile. We know that he took several turns round the sand-walk, and, according to his son's reminiscences (*ibid.*, p. 75), 'used to count them by means of a heap of flints, one of which he kicked out of the path each time he passed.'

His exercise tolerance was very well maintained until the end, for his son writes: 'It is curious to think now, with regard to the sand-walk in connection with my father, my earliest recollections coincide with my latest; it shows the unvarying character of his habits.' A further point concerns his gait. Again his son wrote (*ibid.*, p. 71): 'He walked with a swinging gait using a stick heavily shod with iron, which he struck loudly against the ground, producing as he went round the sand-walk at Down, a rhythmical click which is with us all a very distinct remembrance. . . . When interested in his work he moved about quickly and easily enough, and often in the midst of dictating he went eagerly into the hall to get a pinch of snuff, leaving the study door open, and calling out the last words of his sentence as he left the room.' In order to limit his use of snuff he kept the snuffbox on the hall table; thus he had to get up from the sitting-room or study and walk out into the hall in order to get a pinch of it.

Much new information has come from the recent publication of the correspondence between Darwin and the vicar of Down, the Reverend Brodie Innes (Stecher, 1961, p. 256). From this we learn that for six months Darwin kept his snuffbox in the cellar and the key to it in the garret of his house. Surely this habit in itself is one which indicates strongly that there could be no significant degree of cardiac insufficiency. A person with symptoms due to such a cause soon learns to use habits which avoid exertion and would not resort to one like this, requiring effort. The exercise tolerance, the swinging gait, the heavy striking of the stick, and the deliberately contrived, effort-requiring impediment to the obtaining snuff all combine to exclude symptoms due to significant myocardial damage. It was not exercise but anxiety and meeting people which caused his complaints.

NAUSEA AND FLATULENCE

The nausea and flatulence would, it has been suggested, fit in with Chagas's disease. Again, however, the evidence is against this. First, it is very doubtful whether alimentary symptoms occur in Chagas's disease in the absence of myocardial damage, and of this, as had been indicated, there was no good evidence. Second, it is a common psychosomatic symptom; a large proportion of those with psychosomatic disease are air swallowers and have just these complaints. Thirdly, of these alimentary symptoms also there is evidence that they existed before he could have been infected. Before sailing in the *Beagle* he wrote to Professor Henslow from Devonport (Darwin, F., 1958, p. 128): 'I have only now to pray for the sickness to moderate its fierceness, and I shall do very well.' It has been suggested that the sickness here referred to was sea-sickness. The letter was written on 15th November 1831 and the *Beagle* did not attempt to leave harbour till 10th December 1831 so that the sickness he then complained of, if sea-sickness, must have been due to motion of the ship while at anchor in harbour. Such a set of circumstances would in itself indicate that Darwin was unusually susceptible to nausea, but it is doubtful if he was living aboard the *Beagle* at that time, for in the same letter of 15th November he wrote: 'My chief employment is to go on board the *Beagle*, and try to look as much like a sailor as I can.' In a letter of 3rd December (*ibid.*, p. 129) he wrote, 'tonight I am going to sleep on board,' and it seems that this was the first time he had done so.

PHYSICAL SIGNS

Darwin was intermittently ill for about fifty years, from shortly before he sailed in the *Beagle* in December 1831 until his death in 1882. He was looked after by many doctors, some of them among the most distinguished of his day, including Sir Andrew Clark and Dr. Bence Jones, an astute clinical observer whose discovery of the proteinuria which bears his name is a lasting tribute to that ability. Yet none of these found any sign of organic disease. Such signs would not have been difficult to find had his symptoms for all these years been due to organic disease such as Chagas's disease. If palpitations, weakness, and prostration had been due to myocardial damage, oedema or some other sign of cardiac insufficiency would certainly have been present at some stage; but instead we find that no physician could detect any organic source of his trouble and that Dr. Bence Jones, from whose treatment his son states he derived much benefit, prescribed for it not rest but horse-riding, and 'he enjoyed these rides extremely' (*ibid.*, p. 77). It is possible for persons to die and for evidence of unsuspected, asymptomatic Chagas's disease to be found at necropsy, but it is beyond credibility that Chagas's disease could produce symptoms of cardiac insufficiency for between 40 and 50 years and not produce some physical signs.

EPIDEMIOLOGICAL EVIDENCE

It has been stated (Adler) as evidence for Darwin's illness being Chagas's disease that in the Argentinian province of Mendoza, where Darwin was bitten, as many as 60 per cent of the population give a positive complement-fixation test for the disease and as many as 70 per cent of *Triatoma infestans* are infected with causative trypanosomes. 'Darwin was therefore definitely exposed to infection.' The validity of these figures for some surveys is not disputed, but the deduction that Darwin was definitely exposed to infection cannot be allowed to stand. There is no certainty that the bugs which bit him were infected.

Precise figures for Mendoza are not available, but Professor Rodrigues da Silva, Director of the Department of Tropical and Infectious Disease, University of Brazil, Rio de Janeiro, has kindly provided me with figures collected by Neghme and Schenone (1962) indicating that in the epidemiologically continuous Chilean regions bordering on Mendoza *Triatoma* infection rates are not as high as 70 per cent. Thus of 2,332 people examined by the complement-fixation test in the Provinces of Santiago, Valparaiso, and Aconcagua between 1949 and 1958, only 346, or 14·8 per cent were positive. These were people of all ages, so that they had had many years of opportunity to become infected, whereas Darwin was exposed for only a quite brief period. In the Province of Aconcagua 147, or 24·2 per cent of 607 *Triatoma infestans* captured between 1939 and 1959 were infected, and in Santiago Province the comparable figure was 31·8 per cent of 12,791 bugs. Professor A. Neghme, Director of the Department of Tropical Medicine and Parasitology, University of Chile, Santiago, has also provided me with figures collected by Mazza *et al.* (1941) and Coll (1940) in Mendoza itself giving the age-groups of those presenting with acute manifestations of Chagas's disease. These indicate primary infection, and it is notable that the peak incidence of them occurs in the group aged 10–15 years (fig. 1). In other words, the majority of persons who develop such infection have been exposed, we can say with certainty, not just for a few weeks but for several years.

A point to be remembered is that it is not the bite of these insects which causes infection but contamination of wounds with their excreta, which they produce at the time of biting. To be bitten even by several infected insects would not therefore of necessity produce infection.

Several members of the crew of HMS *Beagle* went with Darwin on his excursions inland, and in his *Journal* he also records the way in which an officer permitted a *Triatoma* bug which he had caught to feed upon him. I therefore sought evidence of illness which might have been Chagas's disease among the crew of the *Beagle* when Darwin was with the ship. The Admiralty records on this matter are remarkably complete, and through the kindness of Mr. J. S. Stevenson, of the Admiralty Records Department, I was able to consult the statistical reports of the health of the Navy. They paid particular attention to superficial inflammations and swellings and, of course, to fevers. From the records of the ships on the South American station during the years 1832–36 Mr. Stevenson has abstracted all entries relative to the crew of the *Beagle*, and found that no fevers

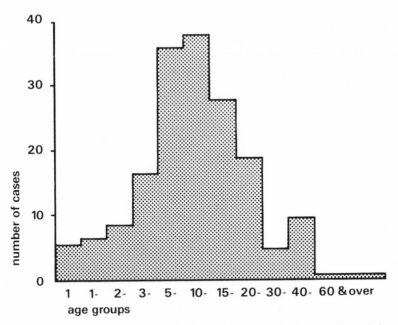

Fig. 1. Ages of patients with acute Chaga's disease confirmed in Menduza, Argentina where Darwin was bitten by *Triatoma* bugs.

other than those associated with disease of the lungs, bowels, rheumatism, whitlows, boils (then biles), and respiratory infections were reported, nor were there any unusual swellings. It would be unwise to place much reliance on clinical records approximately 130 years old, but the evidence has some small value and its existence is in itself of considerable interest. The epidemiological evidence therefore indicates that although there was the possibility of exposure to infection there is no strong probability that he was infected.

FAMILY HISTORY AND COURSE

FAMILIAL NATURE OF THE ILLNESS

The Darwin–Innes (Stecher, 1961, p. 201) letters have made generally available, for the first time, details of the illness of Darwin's fourth child, Henrietta, who became well known in the Darwin literature as Aunt Etty. In 1860, when Etty was 7 years old, Darwin wrote to Innes (*ibid.*, p. 205): 'I have been a good deal knocked up of late and had to resort to the water cure; but our anxiety with Etty for twelve weeks has been enough to knock us up,' and in September of the same year 'the doctors are convinced there is no organic mischief.' Etty appears to have been a problem child from a very early age, for her mother wrote to her aunt when Etty was 3 years old (Litchfield, 1915): 'Charlotte writes to me for a receipt for a punishment for Edmund. If she will send me ditto for Etty I will engage to furnish her, but I am quite as much non-plussed as she can be. Since she has been unwell the whims in her little head are wonderful. Now she will never have her night shift on, and it has to be put on after she is asleep. I must come to a downright quarrel I am afraid, but I am always in hopes these fancies will blow over.' Later in 1860 Darwin wrote to Innes (Stecher, 1961, p. 207), 'on account of Etty we lead a more retired life than ever, though this seems hardly possible.' Etty's illness was evidently being brought in to reinforce his wish for seclusion.

It is perhaps significant that the year 1860 was, for Darwin, one of considerable stress, for his *Origin of Species* had been published in 1859 and it was in 1860 that Bishop Samuel Wilberforce attacked Darwin bitterly both verbally and in writing.

> Gwen Raverat, one of Darwin's grandchildren, has written a charming account of life at Down. I hesitate to quote from it, for in reading it I have the impression of having access to a very personal diary or being allowed to participate, confidentially, in highly personal family matters. She writes of Aunt Etty (Raverat, 1960, p. 122) that when '13 the doctor recommended, after she had had a "low fever" that she should have breakfast in bed for a time. She never got up for breakfast again in all her life' and in spite of all this illness she lived until she was 86 years old. We also read (*ibid.*, p. 123) that 'ill health became her profession and absorbing interest,' and further she writes (*ibid.*, p. 122): 'but of one thing I am quite certain; that the attitude of the whole Darwin family to sickness was most unwholesome. At Down ill-health was considered normal.' Her husband came under the same influence, and 'if the window had to be opened to air a room in cold weather Aunt Etty covered him up entirely with a dust sheet for fear of draughts; and he sat there as patient as a statue until he could be unveiled.' (*ibid.*, p. 125).

From the Darwin–Innes letters we learn that other members of the family were similarly affected. Darwin wrote to Innes (Stecher, 1961, p. 212): 'but now we have Horace failing badly with intermittent weak pulse, like four of our other children previously. It is a curious form of inheritance of my poor constitution, though I never failed in exactly that way.' We also learn (*ibid.*, p. 206) that Etty, on being taken to the seaside to recover, 'progressed very well here for four weeks, but I am sure you will sympathise with us to hear that she had a terrible attack of sickness.' Again symptoms similar to her father's.

There is evidence, therefore, that a condition very similar to that which affected Darwin—that is, weak and irregular pulse, with sickness, lassitude and headache—affected also four other members of the family—none of whom had been to South America. This surely is a further strong indication that the condition which caused his trouble was not South American trypanosomiasis.

COURSE OF THE ILLNESS

The course that the illness took gives us a further clue to its nature. Among his bad years was 1831, when he was going against his father's wishes and making up his mind to sail in the *Beagle* rather than become a parson; 1837, when he had just returned from his five-year voyage and was adjusting himself to his fresh life in London; the few years that followed 1837, including the period of his marriage in 1838 and his decision to move to Down; the time around his father's death in November 1847 and the year or two just after the publication of the *Origin of Species* in 1859.

His son in his reminiscences of his father (Darwin, F., 1958, p. 345) wrote: 'During the last ten years of his life the state of his health was a cause of satisfaction and hope to the family. His condition showed signs of amendment in several particulars. He suffered less distress and discomfort, and was able to work more steadily. Scattered through his letters are one or two references to pain or uneasiness felt in the region of the heart. How far these indicate that the heart was affected early in life I cannot pretend to say; in any case it is certain that he had no serious or permanent trouble of this nature until shortly before his death.' It was not until December 1881 that he was seized by serious precordial pain, and after several such incidents during the next four months he died in April 1882 in his 74th year. If Darwin's weakness and other symptoms were to be explained by organic damage brought about by Chagas's disease it would have had to cause a very curious form of myocardial degeneration to prostrate him in his 30's and at intervals during his middle age and then to have become materially better during his last decade.

The course of the illness is surely much more compatible with a psychological or psychosomatic disorder which, like so many of its kind, becomes a 'pestilence which wasteth the noon day' of life but which eventually as the emotional fires die down allows some 'peace at eventide'.

DIAGNOSIS

If Chagas's disease did not cause Darwin's symptoms what did? My personal diagnosis would be an anxiety state with obsessive features and psychosomatic manifestations. Anxiety clearly precipitated much of his physical trouble, and regarding the obsessive component there are several important points. In this respect he would not be unusual among men of genius (Brain, 1949).

Darwin exhibited the obsessional's trait of having everything 'just so'; he kept meticulous records of his health and symptoms like many obsessional hypochondriacs. Everything had to be in its place; he even had a special drawer for the sponge which he used in bathing; this is perhaps a minor point, but it is only by close attention to such detail that an accurate diagnosis can be made. The obsessive nature of his make-up comes out more clearly in his son's reminiscences (*ibid.*, p. 84): 'each week he used to read nearly the whole of *Nature*, though so much of it deals with mathematics and physics. I have often heard him say that he got a kind of satisfaction in reading articles which (according to himself) he could not understand.' Surely the obsessive, compulsive driving force which made him do this must have been one of very considerable intensity. Then there is the health diary he kept. Days and nights were given a score according to how good they were; the score was added up at the end of each week, and there is evidence of frequent changing of mind in deciding whether a night was very good or just good.

Finally, there is the question of why he 'sat on the fence' for over 25 years in delaying publication of his *Origin of Species*. From my earlier reference it is clear that he had the main idea in 1832. Greenacre (1963) has pointed out that in 1844 he made a draft of his ideas, confiding them to only a few intimate friends: his sense of patricide in entertaining this idea was so great, however, that he wrote to his friend Professor Hooker that in stating his views he felt as though he were confessing murder. It should be noted here that the conflicts which his ideas generated within him were such that they became 'expressed in obsessional doubts and exaggerated need for certainty which undoubtedly slowed up his work and made him quite ill.' That is the opinion of one of the world's leading psychoanalysts, an opinion which has much in common with that of Hubble (1943) and of Kempf (1921). It was only under the stimulus of fear of loss of priority when Wallace was known to be about to publish on the same subject that he finally went to press.

It may well be that many of the points which I have made, taken individually, would not exclude the diagnosis of Chagas's disease: Darwin's good exercise tolerance, the absence of Chagas's disease among the other members of the *Beagle's* crew, the fact that the illness was compatible with long life although Darwin suffered from it for more than 50 years, and the fact that his symptoms improved towards the end of his life. Each of these would cause doubts, and some of them grave doubts, about a diagnosis of Chagas's disease, but taken collectively they make a case of overwhelming strength against it. If he had been infected with it the infection could not account for the features of the illness but was similar to that, for example, with primary tuberculosis and remained quiescent and asymptomatic. But over and above all these points is the fact that the complaints that incapacitated him throughout these 50 years were complaints of which there is evidence that he suffered before he went to South America and before he could therefore have become infected.

REFERENCES

Adler, S. (1959). *Nature (Lond.)*, 184, 1102.
Barlow, N. (1958). *Autobiography of Charles Darwin 1809–1882*, edited by Norah Barlow. Collins, London.
Brain, W. R. (1949). *Brit. med. J.*, 2, 1427.
Coll, J. A. (1940). *Journal of Researches into the Geology and Nature History of the Various Countries visited during the Voyage of H.M.S. Beagle round the world*, p. 316. Everyman's Library. Dent, London.
Darwin, C. (1906). *Journal of Researches into the Geology and natural History of the Various Countries visited during the Voyage of H.M.S. Beagle round the world*, p. 316. Everyman's Library. Dent, London.
Darwin, F. (1958). *Autobiography of Charles Darwin and Selected Letters*, edited by Francis Darwin. Constable, London.
Greenacre, P. (1963). *The Quest for the Father*, p. 28. International University Press, New York.
Hubble, D. (1943). *Lancet*, 1, 129.
Kempf, E. J. (1921). *Psychopathology*, p. 208. Kimpton, London.
Litchfield, H. (1915). *Emma Darwin: A Century of Family Letters 1792–1896*, edited by Henrietta Litchfield, 2, 104. Murray, London.

Mazza, S., Miyara, S., Basso, G., and Basso, Y. R. (1941). Prime quin-
quenio de la investigacion por la MEPRA de en Enfermedae de Chagas
en la provincia de Mendoza. Imprenta Oficial, Mendoza, Argentina.

Neghme, R. A., and Schenone, F. H. (1962). *Anais de Congresso Inter-
nacional sobre a Doenca de Chagas*, 3, 1069.

Raverat, G. M. (1960). *Period Piece: A Cambridge Childhood.* Faber and
Faber Ltd., London.

Stecher, R. M. (1961). *Ann. Sci.*, Vol. 17.

CHAPTER 15

Abraham Lincoln's Marfan Syndrome

Harold Schwartz

EDITORIAL NOTE

When Marfan in 1896 described an anomaly of the skeleton characterised by tall stature and long graceful fingers and toes, he merely put on record an appearance that must have been known clinically but attracted little attention as it seemed to have no pathological significance. The designation of arachnodactyly (spider fingers) was introduced by Achard in 1902.

That these skeletal anomalies could be mild manifestations of a widespread serious disease involving the eyes, heart, blood vessels, musculature, and other organs and tissues, came to be recognised only slowly. Still more slowly came the recognition that the disorder is hereditary, the pattern of inheritance being dominant with variable penetrance in different families and marked variation in expression. In other words, transmission to less than 50 per cent of offspring was frequently seen and the affection was often little more than a skeletal anomaly, sometimes so slight as to be barely recognisable. Furthermore the associated disturbances could be severely incapacitating, slight, or entirely lacking. Incomplete manifestations of this protean disorder (*'formes frustes'*) were therefore common and not easy to recognise in an isolated individual. The affection is now generally known as the Marfan syndrome.

When the skeleton is fully affected, the individual is physically so striking that he can be recognised at a glance; he is tall, lanky, and has large hands and feet with 'spider fingers.' Abraham Lincoln clearly showed these figures. It is also known that he had eye trouble which the present study shows to be consistent with the eye troubles seen in the Marfan syndrome. Dr. Schwartz further establishes that different degrees of the Marfan syndrome have occurred in at least four generations in two collateral branches of the Lincoln family. Abraham Lincoln himself was moderately affected.

The underlying cause of this dominant disorder is not known. In 1962 Field and his associates described a closely related recessive affection[1] with mental defect and the presence of homocystinuria. This raises the possibility that the Marfan syndrome is also a metabolic disorder, but as yet there is no evidence for this.

It is a matter of some historical interest that the clinical picture presented by Abraham Lincoln—tall stature, spidery fingers and dislocated lenses—was described (though not related to Abraham Lincoln) by E. Williams, an American oculist, in 1876 in a brother and sister (*Trans. Amer. Ophthal. Society*, 2, 291). In this he anticipated not only Marfan but also the recognition by Börger in 1915 that subluxation of the lens is a part of the syndrome. As regards the naming of the syndrome after Marfan, eponymous designations of diseases bristle with difficulties. Some—like Addison's disease and Bright's disease—commemorate those who contributed substantially to the recognition and elucidation of a particular disorder. Many eponyms are however merely short-hand terms for a complex disorder which is ill-understood and not readily described by a technical name; such eponyms may record the name of a patient (as in Christmas disease) or of an observer who drew attention to a particular aspect of the affection (as Marfan did). The designation of Marfan's syndrome (a better name than arachnodactyly which is only one feature of the disorder) is thus justifiable, but it would be more correct historically to speak of the Lincoln syndrome or perhaps Lincoln–Williams syndrome.

POSTULATION

From the vast Lincoln literature a description of the sixteenth president was obtained which disclosed growth, skeletal, and eye findings consistent with a postulated diagnosis of Marfan's syndrome.

ABRAHAM LINCOLN

Many well-documented and repeated descriptions show that Abraham Lincoln was unusually tall as a child and that, beginning at 11 years of age, he experienced a period of rapid growth which brought him to his full height of 76 inches (193 cm)—at 17 years of age. His extremities were disproportionately long as compared to his overall height; his fingers were elongated and bony, and he had unusually large feet. In weight he varied from 160 to 180 lb (72·6 to 81·6 kg); his leanness and lack of subcutaneous fat accentuated his linear proportions. The skin was leathery and sallow. His head, while relatively small for his body, was thin and elongated, with large ears set at a wide angle. The midfacial and nasal structures

Fig. 1. Lincoln seated. Note attitude of fingers of left hand, due to elongation of distal segments of skelatal structure. Note height of knees in relation to plane of thighs, consistent with increased length of lower segment in Marfan syndrome. (Meserve Collection).

were similarly long, thin, and somewhat asymmetrical. The eyes were small, blue-grey; the eyelids were heavy with a tendency to droop. It was frequently noted that there was an intermittent squint of the left eye, and it has been established that he was hyperopic.

Standing, he had a slight stoop, which emphasised the narrowness of his sloping shoulders, and a chest so thin as to have been described by Herndon as a 'sunken breast.' Seated, he had been described by a contemporary as having 'spiderlike legs' (fig. 1), the very simile used years later by Marfan in his original description of this entity. When moving about he was characteristically loose-jointed in all his actions and motions.

MARFAN SYNDROME

Marfan syndrome is a hereditary disarrangement of connective tissue, affecting one or more of three systems—skeletal, visual, and cardiovascular.

(i) Excessive long-bone growth produces disproportionately elongated arms, legs, fingers, and toes [arachnodactyly] as well as dolichocephaly with long facial features, resulting in a high-arched palate. Overgrowth of the ribs may lead to various pectus deformities or to a very thin chest. Weakness and laxness of ligaments, tendons, and fasciae produce kyphoscoliosis, pes planus, loose-jointedness, herniae, and malpositioned ears. A striking sparcity of subcutaneous fat exaggerates the already linear structure.

(ii) In the visual system, dislocation of the lenses is diagnostic, whereas other cases show various abnormalities of the lens, cornea, or sclera. Strabismus may occur; severe myopia is common, and there may be high-grade hyperopia from a subluxated lens exposing an aphakic pupil.

(iii) The cardiovascular system is frequently affected with changes that produce aneurysms, usually but not invariably of the ascending aorta. These aneurysms tend to dissect or rupture, resulting in sudden death. The aortic and mitral valves of the heart may be disturbed, resulting eventually in congestive heart failure. Varicosities are common. The only histological finding is that of medionecrosis of the aorta with fragmentation and degeneration of the elastic fibres.

Relating this summary to the physical features of Abraham Lincoln, we see that in the skeletal system he manifested many of the characteristics of arachnodactyly. Likewise, he has been shown

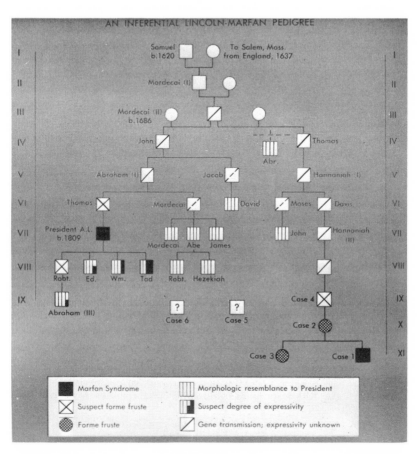

Fig. 2. Inferential Lincoln-Marfan pedigree. Only pertinent kin are shown.

to have two applicable eye findings, hyperopia and strabismus. It must be noted that cardiovascular involvement and herniae were not present to our knowledge.

OBSERVATIONS ON A COLLATERAL BRANCH

The evidence that Lincoln's unusual build could be due to the Marfan syndrome has evolved from the case of a 7-year-old boy whom I saw in 1959 and in whom the classic skeletal features and proportions of the Marfan syndrome were manifest. Some months subsequent to the initial diagnosis in the proband, his connection with the Lincoln lineage was uncovered and his genealogy traced back nine generations to Mordecai Lincoln II, born in 1686. Mordecai Lincoln was also the great-great-grandfather of Abraham Lincoln (fig. 2).

Apart from the clear-cut picture in the proband, a sister and also their mother showed abortive forms of his affection, whilst suggestive findings were also recorded in the maternal grandfather. The case reports are here summarised.

CASE REPORTS

Case 1   The proband. This boy seen at the age of 7 years and again at 11 was tall for his age. Clinically and on X-ray examination he showed the characteristic bone anomalies of achondroplasia in the hands and feet (fig. 3). He had first come under observation for a hernia and had a history of intermittent asthmatic attack. The eyes were normal. Both his parents were of moderate physical proportions.

Case 2   His mother. She had no symptoms and her overall appearance was not remarkable. There were minor orthopaedic anomalies.

Case 3   His sister. Despite several suggestive features, there were no unequivocal skeletal findings. The metacarpal index was 8·3—the extreme limit of normal.

Case 4   His maternal grandfather. Again a case history was available, and this was little more than suggestive. He had died suddenly from a cardiac infarct.

DISCUSSION

That Lincoln's features were consistent with the Marfan syndrome on descriptive grounds was also suggested by Gordon in 1962. In

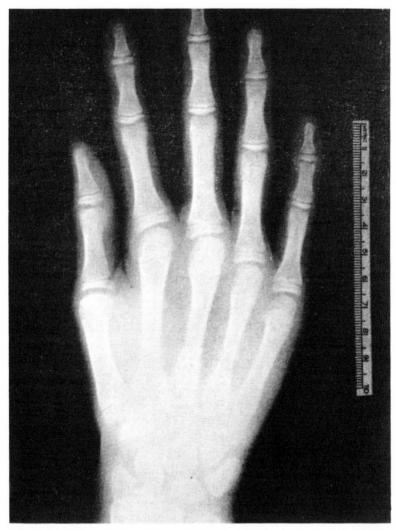

Fig. 3. Proband, Case 1. X-ray of right hand; metacarpal index (length: width) 9.0. (Note long, narrow metacarpals).

this we concur. However, he has attributed the dominant source of Lincoln's genetic make-up to the maternal line, through his mother, Nancy Hanks. This seems unlikely in view of the genealogical evidence presented here. Figure 2 summarises the available evidence on the two collateral family lines established by Mordecai Lincoln II. One line, through John Lincoln, is that of the sixteenth president; the other, via Thomas Lincoln, half-brother of John, is that of the proband. As Abraham Lincoln's unusual morphological characteristics were inherited not from the maternal Hanks lineage but from his Lincoln ancestors, this is also evidence on the paternity of Abraham Lincoln by Thomas Lincoln—a matter discussed by Barton.

GENEALOGY

Samuel Lincoln was born in England in 1620 and settled in Massachusetts Bay Colony in 1637. His son, Mordecai I (fig. 2), had a son Mordecai II, born in 1686. Mordecai II, of the third generation of Lincolns in America, is the common ancestor of both Abraham Lincoln and the subject whose case is reported here.

Mordecai II settled in New Jersey and had, among his many children, John by his first wife and Thomas by his second wife. These two half-brothers of the fourth generation were the founders of two notable collateral lines of Lincoln.

As the lineage of John migrated southward and westward, the subsequent offspring were Abraham I, grandfather of the president, and his son Thomas, of the sixth generation. Thomas married Nancy Hanks and in 1809 had a son, Abraham II (the president) of the seventh generation.

Thomas Lincoln of the fourth generation (son of Mordecai II and half-brother of John) extended his line through Hannaniah I, who was therefore a first cousin of the president's grandfather. Following in this succession were Davis and his son, Hannaniah II, of the same generation as the president. Next in this same descent was the great-grandfather of the proband. His son (case 4) was the father of the woman (case 2) of this line who gave birth to the proband, the eleventh generation male child of the Lincoln lineage here considered (case 1). The patient is eight times removed from Mordecai II, the common ancestor from whom Abraham Lincoln is four generations descended.

EVIDENCE FOR 'FORMES FRUSTES' IN THE PROBAND'S MOTHER AND SISTER

In arachnodactyly, disproportionate elongation of the skeletal structure is more important than actual height or length. In the classical adult syndrome, it has been suggested that the arm span should be three inches greater than the height, and the lower segment should exceed the upper segment by two inches. The metacarpal index has been reported as within normal up to 7·9 and definitely abnormal above 8·4. The hand-height and foot-height ratios should be greater than 11 per cent and 15 per cent respectively.

Many factors detract from the value of any one or combination of indices. Their principal value lies in detecting doubtful cases, the *formes frustes* and in making family surveys. The proband, even before his anticipated pubertal growth spurt and further disproportionate elongation, has already fulfilled several of these criteria. The mother has an increased lower-segment measurement and a metacarpal index above normal and approaching the definitely abnormal range. Her hand-height and foot-height ratios just exceed the normal range. The sibling of the proband is typically pyknic at her present age of $15\frac{1}{2}$; however, her skeletal indices are at least suggestive of a *forme fruste* manifestation of arachnodactyly. No comparative data are available for the grandfather of the proband.

DATA ON ABRAHAM LINCOLN

(i) *Measurements*

No exact measure of his arm span has been found to my knowledge. However, during the Civil War, he remarked, while observing a regiment of Maine lumbermen, 'I don't believe that there is a man in that regiment with longer arms than mine.' Reasonably valid reconstructions in several other linear dimensions are also possible. Lawrence has studied sitting and standing height relationships to lower and upper segments and found that in only 5 per cent of normal individuals did the lower segment exceed the upper by more than two inches. Herndon observed that 'in sitting down on common chairs he (Lincoln) was no taller than ordinary men from the chair to the crown of his head . . . it was only when he stood up that he loomed above other men.' Certain pictures (fig. 1) illustrate that when seated, the height of Lincoln's knees was considerably above the plane of his thighs, which sloped downwards to the pelvis, further

Abraham Lincoln in the camp at Antietam (also known as Sharpsburg). The man facing Lincoln (fourth to the left) is General McClellan, Commander-in-Chief of the Army of the Potomac. (The Mansell Collection)

indicating the excessive elongation of the lower extremities. This downward slope in relation to the knees is the specific feature which gives the arachnoid appearance to the legs in the Marfan syndrome.

Another index of arachnodactyly specifies that 'the finger, especially the middle finger, should be $1\frac{1}{2}$ times greater than the length of the (longest) metacarpal.' Bartlett, a sculptor and Lincoln student, commented in 1907 on the hands of Lincoln as studied from the casts made by Volk in the year of Lincoln's nomination: 'they are large, long hands. The first phalanx of the middle finger is nearly half an inch longer than that of an ordinary hand.' This observation indicates a measurement which comes remarkably close to the index mentioned. Bartlett went on, 'The bones are finely shaped, not unusually large, muscles thin . . . the joints are very supple . . . the action of the folded fingers on the left hand is particularly noticeable.' This accurately depicts other features of an arachnodactylic hand.

A consistent difference in the size of Lincoln's hands, agreeing with another observation of Bartlett, was found by T. D. Stewart, Curator of the Division of Physical Anthropology at the US National Museum, in his studies on the Volk casts at the Smithsonian Institute in 1952. Both observed Lincoln's left hand to be longer than his right hand. Stewart mentioned further that it is unusual for the left hand to predominate in a right-handed individual, as he presumed Lincoln to be; he felt that this asymmetry could not be attributed solely to the contrasting positions of the two hands. He also measured the length of each finger and the breadth of each hand and made comparative studies, from which he concluded that Lincoln's hands, like the rest of his body, were long and narrow. This length and breadth analysis is very similar to the metacarpal index, which is based on the proportion between length and width as calculated directly from the X-ray.

The numerous asymmetries in the Marfan syndrome would explain the discrepancy in the lengths of the two hands as well as the curious fact that the thumb of the longer hand is 10mm shorter than the thumb on the right or smaller hand and is the shortest of all ten digits.

(ii) *Eye findings*

Besides his skeletal disproportionments, Lincoln also suffered from strabismus and severe hyperopia (lenses of $+6\cdot75$ dioptres) the former occurring frequently in arachnodactyly and the latter being an occasional component of the Marfan syndrome as the result of a subluxated lens.

(iii) *Findings on his father and on his sons*

'Thomas Lincoln was blind in one eye and the other was weak,' stated an Indiana neighbour, referring to a period when the father of the president would have been about 47 years of age. Robert Lincoln, the president's son, resembled his paternal grandfather, both being relatively pyknic, even as Robert's only son resembled the president. However, like his father (and presumably like his grandfather, Thomas) the president's son had an eye problem which caused him considerable difficulty. A vertical strabismus of the left eye is apparent even in the photographs of Robert and the president. The three other children of Abraham Lincoln favoured their father. Tad suffered a speech impediment and misshapen palate present from birth. He died at 18 years of age with symptoms highly suggestive of orthopnea, and cardiovascular involvement must be suspected. Other evidence suggest that similar complications may have been present in Tad's brothers, William and Edward, as well as in Abraham 'Jack' Lincoln, the son of Robert.

SELECTED REFERENCES

Barton, W. E.: *Paternity of Abraham Lincoln*, New York: G. H. Doran C., 1920.
Gordon, A. M.: Abraham Lincoln: Medical Appraisal, *J. Kentucky Med. Ass.*, 60: 249–253 (March) 1962.
Herndon, W. H., and Weik, J. W.: *Herndon's Lincoln*, Springfield, Ill.: Herndon's Lincoln Publishing Co., 1921, vol. 1–3; vol. 2, p. 408.
Sandburg, C.: *Abraham Lincoln*, New York: Charles Scribner's Sons, 1949, vol. 1–6; vol. 2, p. 303.
Shurz, C., and Bartlett, T. H.: *Abraham Lincoln* (*Two Essays*), New York: Houghton–Mifflin & Co., 1907, p. 25.
Stewart, T. D.: An Anthropologist Looks at Lincoln, *Ann. Rep. Smithsonian Inst.*, pp. 419–436, 1952

Glossary

Achondroplasia   A variety of dwarfism, caused mainly by abnormal shortness of the legs. The arms are also very short

Acromegaly   The extreme manifestation of anterior pituitary disturbances, characterised by coarsened hands and facial features

Addison's Disease   A severe and generally rapidly fatal affection of the suprarenal glands

Adenitis   Inflammation of the lymphatic glands

Aetiology   Causation

Agraphia   Inability to write

Albinism   A hereditary metabolic affection characterised by lack of pigment normally present in the skin, hair and eyes.

Amaurosis   An obsolete term for blindness

Aneurysms   Morbid dilatations of an artery (or vein)

Angina   Sore throat ('Angina pectoris' is the pain experienced in some forms of heart disease).

Ankylosed   Fused together by new bone formation

Antiscorbutics   Medicaments against scurvy

Aphakic   With the lens absent

Aphasia   A speech defect common in *hemiplegia.*

Apoplectiform Cerebral Congestion   An obsolete term. 'Congestion of the brain' was regarded as a form of apoplexy (stroke)

Arteriosclerosis   Hardening of the arteries

Ascites   Fluid in the abdominal cavity

Astigmatism   This is generally due to abnormal curvature of the cornea. Not all the rays of light which enter the eye are focussed at the same point in the retina, giving one of the forms of blurred sight

Ataxia, Ataxy   Unsteady gait

Auricular Height   Height to the ears

Autonomic Plexuses   Autonomic nerve supply

Autonomic   Of the involuntary nervous system (as opposed to conscious and willed activity)

Axial   See *Myopia* (Axial)

Blepharitis   Inflammation of the lid margin

Bulbar   Of the bulb (root) of the brain

Calculi   Stones

Calomel   A mercury compound

Calvarium   The top part of the skull

Capsulitis   Inflammation of the capsule (of the spleen or liver)

Chagas's Disease   see *Trypanosomiasis*

Cholecystitis   Inflammation of the gall-bladder

Choroid   A layer of bloodvessels which nourish the retina

Choroido-Retinitis   Inflammation of the choroid and the overlying retina

Chronic Adhesive Type   see *Deafness*

Cicatricial   Caused by scarring

Cirrhosis   Hardening, generally of the liver

Cochlea   The spiral cavity of the inner-ear

Conjunctivitis   Inflammation of the conjunctiva (the thin membrane lining the inner surface of the lids and the visible part of the sclera)

Cortical   Arising in the cortex, the outer gray matter of the brain

Costal   Referring to the ribs

Cystitis   Inflammation of the bladder

Deafness   Deafness is classically distinguished as due to disturbances in the outer ear (ear wax being a common cause), middle ear (generally catarrhal or infective in origin), and inner ear (nerve deafness). The chronic adhesive type results from adhesions around the small bones of the middle ear. 'Otosclerosis' is a form of deafness produced by increased density of the bony structure of the ear.

Dementia Alcoholica   Alcohol induced insanity

Dementia Paralytica   G.P.I. (generalised paralysis of the insane), a characteristic late complication of syphilis

Dermatitis   Inflammation of the skin

Dioptre   Measure used in assessing the power of a lens

Disseminated Choroiditis   An inflammation of the choroid seen in congenital syphilis (see also *Choroid*)

Dolichocephaly   Longheadedness

Dropsy   Waterlogging of the body

Dysphagia   Difficulty in swallowing

Dyspnoea   Difficulty in breathing

Dysuria   Difficult or painful passing of water

Eclampsia (alcoholic)   Gait disturbance in acute alcoholism

Ecthyma   A skin disease allied to *impetigo*

Edema   see *oedema*

Emphysema   A chronic affection of the lungs which lose their elasticity

Encephalopathy   Disease of the brain

Endocarditis   A septic affection of the interior of the heart

Endocrine   Glands (like thyroid and pituitary) which produce chemical regulators of the body

Epidermis   Superficial layers of the skin

Epidemiological   Relating to the study of the incidence and distribution of disease

Epileptic Vertigo   An obsolete term suggesting dizziness arising from epilepsy

Epistaxis   Bleeding from the nose

Erythema   Reddening of the skin

Eustachian Tube   This leads from the throat to the middle ear

Exfoliation   Peeling

Extragenital   A term applied to infections, generally syphilis, contacted from sources other than sexual intercourse

Fasciae   Connective tissue

Foeie (le)   The liver

Formes Frustres   Incomplete forms

Fossa   Depression; cavity

Furunculosis   Development of pustules and boils

G.P.I. Generalised paralysis of the insane, also know as *dementia paralytica*. See also *Tabo-paralysis*

Gangrene Mortification of tissues; in symmetrical gangrene this is similarly placed on the two sides of the body

Gastrodynia An obsolete term for abdominal pain

Grumous Simulating clotted blood

Gumma, Syphilitic (pl. Gummata) A localised inflammatory mass seen in the late stages of syphilis

Gummatous Osteitis A localised syphilitic inflammation of the bone

Gutta Serena An obsolete term applied to blindness in which the pupil of the eye was 'serene', i.e. not opaque

Hemiplegia Paralysis of one side of the body, generally the result of a stroke

Hepatitis This term was used indiscriminately for any disorder of the liver

Herpes A variety of blister formation. See *Labial Herpes.*

Histology The study of cells

Homocystinuria A condition in which there is an abnormal constituent (homocystine) in the urine

Hydrocele see *Sarcocele*

Hyperchondriasis An obsolete term, poorly distinguished from hypochondriasis, itself a vague reference to imaginary illnesses

Hyperchondrium Upper part of the abdomen

Hypermetropia Long sight

Hyperoptic Longsighted

Hyperpituitarism   Excessive action of the pituitary gland. *Acromegaly* is one of the possible consequences

Hyperthyroidism   Excessive action of the thyroid gland. Exophthalmic goitre (Graves' disease) is one of the possible consequences

Iconography   Pictorial representation

Impetigo   A pustular eruption of the skin producing scabs

Inebriety   Drunkeness regarded as a disease

Infarct   An area cut off from its bloodsupply

Interstitial Keratitis   Inflammation of the middle layers of the cornea, generally due to congenital syphilis

Intracranial   Inside the skull

Intrathoracic   Inside the chest

Iritis   Inflammation of the iris

Keratitis   Inflammation of the cornea. See also *Interstitial Keratitis*

Keratitis (Tuberculous)   Scarring or inflammation in tuberculous disease of the cornea.

Jejunum   A part of the small intestine

Kraepelinian Criteria   Criteria advanced by E. Kraepelin (1856–1926) for the classification of mental disorders.

Kyphoscoliosis   An abnormal curvature of the spinal column

Labial Herpes   Blisters on the lips

Labyrinthitis   Inflammation of the labyrinth of the inner ear (sometimes syphilitic)

Lancinating   Spear-like

Lepra   Leprosy

Leucomatous   Scars or nodules, white in colour

Locomotor Ataxia (Ataxy)   A neurological complication of the late stages of syphilis.

Lues   Syphilis

Lumbar   Appertaining to the lumbar vertebrae (in the lower part of the spine)

Mastoid Process   Part of the mastoid bone (in which the middle and inner ear are placed)

Medionecrosis   Degenerative changes in the muscular coat of an artery

Medullar   Pertaining to the brain stem

Mendelian Dominant   The dominant mode of inheritance (as established by Mendel) by which an affected individual passes his disorder on to 50 per cent of his offspring.

Ménière's Disease   An affection of the labyrinth of the inner ear producing intense dizziness, deafness and episodes of vomiting

Metabolic   Relating to the synthesis and breakdown of tissues

Metabolites   Products of metabolism

Metacarpal Index   A measure used to assess the relative length of the metacarpal bone to the finger it carries

Metamorphopsia   A condition in which objects appear distorted

Micropsia   A condition in which objects appear small

Middle Ear   see *Deafness*

Myasthenia Gravis   A severe form of muscular weakness

Myocardial Damage   Damage to the heart muscle

Myopia of the axial type   In myopia (short sight) the eye is generally longer than normal (axial myopia); occasionally myopia develops late in life from increased refraction of the lens in early cataract.

Myopic   Short-sighted

Neuropathic Tainting   Nervous derangement

Neuro-Retinitis   Inflammation involving both the optic nerve and the retina

Nyctalope   Someone who sees better at night

Nystagmus   Jerkiness of eye movements, sometimes caused by troubles of the inner ear (labyrinth).

Occiput   The back of the skull

Oedema   Waterlogging

Oliguria   Diminished excretion of urine

Oral Sepsis   Sepsis from decayed teeth

Orbital Cellulitis   Inflammation of the fatty tissues of the orbit

Orthopnoea   Difficulty in breathing except in the upright position

Osteomyelitis   Inflammation of the whole thickness of the bone (hard tissues and bone marrow)

Otitis   Inflammation of the ear. Otitis media is inflammation of the middle ear.

Otology   Study of diseases of the ear

Otosclerosis   see *Deafness*

Parenchyma   The actual material of a tissue, as opposed to the supporting scaffolding

Paresis   Muscular weakness short of paralysis

Parietal Bone   Bone at the side of the skull

Pathogenic   Arising from disease

Pathognomonic   Characteristic of a particular disease and no other

Photophobia   Increased sensitivity to light

Pellagra   A skin disease with severe general manifestations known in antiquity and confused with leprosy and other affections. *Pellagra* in the modern sense is a well-defined nutritional disturbance

Perigastritis   Inflammation around the stomach

Perihepatitis   Inflammation of the capsule of the liver

Peristalsis   Movement of the intestines

Peritoneum   The lining of the cavity and organs of the abdomen

Peritonitis   Inflammation of the *peritoneum*

Pernicious Anaemia   A severe anaemia in which there are gross disturbances in the red blood corpuscles

Pes Planus   Flat foot

Petrous   Appertaining to the petrous portion of the temporal bone in which the inner ear is lodged

Phthisis   Tuberculosis of the lungs

Polydipsia   Excessive thirst

Polyneuritis   Inflammation of the nerves, generally those of the limbs

Polyuria   Excessive excretion of urine

Porphobilin-like Chromogens   see *Porphyrins*

Porphyria   A generalised disorder of which several types occur. They are characterised by purplish-coloured urine, abdominal symptoms, nervous and mental derangements.

Porphyrins   Pigments in the urine from which the name of the affection is derived.

Precordial   Around the heart

Tenements of Clay

Presbyopia 'Old sight': inability to read without glasses after middle age

Proband The individual who is the starting-point in an investigation of a pedigree

Proteinuria Protein (albumen) in the urine

Pseudo-Tabes Alcoholic peripheral neuritis with its disturbances in gait simulating locomotor ataxia

Ptosis Drooping (of the eyelids or other tissues)

Puerperal Fever Fever of childbirth, a not infrequent cause of death even in the recent past

Pyknic Thickset

Pylorus The lower end of the stomach, a common site of cancer of the stomach

Pyogenic Cocci Pus-forming microbes

Radicular Pain Pain along the branches of the nerves

Renal Of the kidneys

Rhesus-Negative Miscarriage may occur from a woman not having the same rhesus bloodgroup as her husband

Risus Sardonicus An involuntary spasmodic grin occasionally preceding death

Saccus Endolymphaticus A part of labyrinth of the inner ear

Sarcocele A fluid collection in the scrotum

Scapular Region Shoulder-blade region

Scarletina Scarlet fever, formerly a fairly common infectious fever of childhood

Scirrhous Masses Wart-like excrescences

Sclera The white coat of the eye globe

Secondary Infection Superadded infection—an infection complicating a disease, itself generally not infective in type.

Septum The cartilage that separates the two sides of the cavity of the nose. An abnormality of the septum may block the Eustachian tube.

Seton A cutting instrument (to evacuate 'disordered humours'). Obsolete.

Singultus Hiccups

Spirochaeta Pallida Causative organism of syphilis

Stapes One of the small bones in the inner ear

Staphyloccal Infection A particular form of microbial infection (due to staphylococci)

Stirp Stock (in the genealogical sense)

Strabismus Squint

Streptococcal Infection A particular form of microbial infection (due to streptococci)

Subluxation Partial displacement

Sulci Fissures

Suppuration Formation of pus

Sydenham's Chorea Under this term were included many different affections with uncontrollable jerky movements

Syphilis Insons Syphilis of non-sexual origin

Systemic Generalised

Tabes Dorsalis Locomotor ataxia: a neurological complication of the late stages of syphilis, characterised by a jerky, unsteady gait.

Tabes Mesenterica Severe involvement of the abdominal lymph glands

Tabo-Paralysis or Tabo-Paresis Locomotor ataxia and *G.P.I.*

Tachycardia Rapid action of the heart of which the patient is conscious

Tapped Fluid was removed from the body by needling

Tartar Emetic A chemical irritant no longer used, to induce vomiting

Temporal Bones Bony structures containing the middle and inner ear

Traumatic Due to injury

Trephined Treated by opening the skull; trepanned

Triatama Infestans The insects which transmit the trypanosome to man through their bites

Trypanosomiasis Infection by trypanoma, a variety of protozoa

Tumefaction Swelling

Uric Arthritis Gouty arthritis

Usquebagh An obsolete medicament

Varicellae Chicken-pox

Varicosities Abnormalities of the vein, generally localised enlargements

Variolae Small-pox

Vascular Mucosa A mucous membrane rich in bloodvessels, the membrane lining the middle ear is an example

Vasomotor (disturbances) Disturbances in the width of blood vessels induced by the nerve mechanism of such vessels

Vertigo Dizziness

Vestibular Symptoms Generally dizziness, produced by disturbances of the vestibule of the inner ear

Viscera Internal organs

Vocal Paresis Weakness of vocal chords

Vomer A small thin bone forming part of the partition between the nostrils

Zygomatic arch Bony arch in the centre of each cheek

References

CHAPTER 1 Noah

1 Genesis v, 28–29.
2 The Book of Enoch the Prophet. Translated by R. Lawrence, 3rd ed. Oxford, 1838; xii, 5; vii, 11; cv, 120.
3 Avigad, N. and Yadin, Y., *A Genesis Apocryphon* (Jerusalem: The Magnes Press of the Hebrew University, 1956), p. 40.
4 *ibid.*, p. 18.

CHAPTER 2 Job

1 Deuteronomy xxviii, 27
2 *ibid.*, xxviii, 25
3 Job ii, 7
4 Job xix, 23–24
5 *ibid.*, xxx, 18
6 Job xxxi, 9–11

CHAPTER 3 Henry VIII

1 Her health was poor, and after having married Philip II of Spain, she seems to have had a miscarriage. She had bad sight, which has been attributed to syphilitic keratitis (inflammation of the cornea) or to common short-sightedness; both are pure guesses.
2 He died when 17 years old, presumably from lung tuberculosis. A picture from his boyhood reveals him as a weakling with signs of adenoids and scrofula. He displays no signs of congenital syphilis.
3 Elizabeth died almost 70 years old; she was presumably a pseudo-hermaphrodite. She does not seem to have displayed any symptoms of congenital syphilis. Henry's paternity has been considered doubtful.
4 He died 16 years old from a lung disease. Some months before death he suffered from an ulcerous skin disease which eventually made his hair, nails, fingers and toes fall off. It may have been congenital syphilis or lepra; the diagnosis is uncertain.
5 During Henry's war in France in 1544, his 'nervous affection' is mentioned, but according to Chamberlin this must be due to the mis-understanding by a Spanish secretary of a French letter to the Queen of

Hungary and the Emperor; besides, as to the term 'nervous affection', it is doubtful what the exact meaning of it is according to modern medical terminology.

[6] 'That sprig Henry thinks he is God and can do anything.'

[7] Where this Paper was read on the 26th January, 1956.

CHAPTER 6 Milton

[1] Sonnet XIX.

[2] Sonnet XXII.

[3] Defensio Secunda Pro Populo Anglicano.

[4] *Paradise Lost*, III, 21–26.

[5] Letter to Philaras, in D. Masson's *Life of Milton*, vol. IV, p. 640.

[6] The portraits of John Milton exhibited at Christ's College Tercentenary Celebration. 1908 (Souvenir).

[7] March, J. F. On the engraved portraits of Milton, 1860.

[8] The earliest *Life of Milton*. Edited by E. S. Parsons, vol. X,Colorado College Studies, 1903.

[9] Taken in its context the reference to Milton's eyes being none of the quickest seems to imply an anatomical rather than a physiological defect. But all the evidence is against such a reading.

[10] Aubrey, J. *Life of Milton*. Available in Alfred Stern's *Milton und seine Zeit*, vol. 1, Appendix, 1887.

[11] Philips, Edward. *Life of Milton*. Available in W. Godwin's *Lives of E. and J. Philips*, 1815.

[12] Masson, D. *Life of Milton*, vol. IV, p. 427.

[13] Philips says Milton's sight 'had been decaying for about a dozen years.' That puts back the onset of the trouble to the 31st year.

[14] Lawrence, W. *Treatise on diseases of the eyes*, 1832.

[15] Mackenzie, W. *A practical treatise on the diseases of the eyes*, p. 891 1840.

[16] Stern, Alfred. *Milton und seine Zeit*, 1879, note on p. 93, vol. III.

[17] Hirschberg, J. *Geschichte der Augenheilkunde* in Graefe-Saemisch Handbuch der Augenheilkunde 2te Auflage, vol. XIV, 4 Abteil, 3 Buch, p. 146, footnote 2.

[18] American Encyclopaedia of Ophthalmology, vol. X; Article on Milton.

[19] Mutschmann, H. Milton's eyesight and the chronology of his work. (in English in Eestu Vabraugi Tartu, etc. B. 5, Dorpat, 1924).

[20] Squires, N. P. In *Modern Language Notes*. IX, p. 454, 1894.

[21] Dufour, M. A note on Milton's blindness. *The Ophthalmoscope*, 1909, vol. VII, p. 599.

[22] Saurat, D. and Cabannes, C. Milton devant la Medecine, *Journal de Medecine de Bordeaux*, 1924, p. 7 (also as appendix in Saurat, D., *Milton: Man and Thinker*, 1925.

[23] No individual is completely devoid of pigmentation. In albinism

there is congenital deficiency of colouring pigment in the skin, hair, eyes; there is intolerance to light and the sight is affected.

[24] Mutschman, H. Milton und das Licht. Beiblatt zu Anglia, XXX, 11/12, 1920 Der Andere, Milton, 1920.

[25] This is questionable.

CHAPTER 8   Johnson

[1] A lot of blood, even by the standards of that age.

[2] A then recently introduced extract of the Foxglove, still invaluable in some forms of heart disease.

CHAPTER 9   George III

[1] Two sibs overtly affected among nine (three of whom died in their teens), would in fact accord with the transmission of a dominant character.

CHAPTER 11   Jane Austen

[1] The extracts quoted below are taken from *Jane Austen's Letters*, collected and edited by R. W. Chapman, 2nd ed.

[2] This is now regarded as tuberculous in origin. It is fatal, by depriving the body of the important chemical regulators the suprarenal capsules (or glands) secrete.

CHAPTER 14   Darwin

[1] In some latent disorders, evidence of a pre-existing infection may be obtained by special blood and skin tests.

CHAPTER 15   Lincoln

[1] In hereditary recessive disorders, both parents are clinically normal, but carry an abnormal gene which becomes manifest in 25 per cent of their offspring.